D1556728

Terrace and Courtyard Gardens

Denis Wood, until lately head of one of the leading firms of garden contractors of Great Britain, and now an independent garden adviser, is in a unique position to advise on the treatment of those parts of the garden close to the house. With the modern trend pressure on space—and the increasing awareness of the benefits which accrue from integrating the garden with the house, more and more garden owners will find that the ideas and recommendations of Mr Wood are relevant to the problems they are trying to solve.

The author has directed his attention to the plants and materials which can be used successfully in the vicinity of the house—and on the house itself, where a balcony provides a setting for plants or where window boxes can be used. As Mr Wood remarks in his introduction, he has written this book 'for the man, who while not intending to lay every stone with his own hands, would like to be able to exercise intelligent control over the work'. To further this end, the second part of the book gives guidance on the practical use of materials and the third part information on recommended plants.

The numerous illustrations show, among other things, what can be achieved, in widely differing situations, by a combination of good design and an intelligent choice of plants.

TERRACE AND COURTYARD GARDENS

by

DENIS WOOD

DAVID & CHARLES : NEWTON ABBOT

ISBN 0 7153 5001 3

First published in 1965
by W. H. & L. Collingridge Limited
Second edition published in 1970

To
A. J. W.

Printed in Great Britain
by Redwood Press Limited Trowbridge Wilts
for David & Charles (Publishers) Limited
Newton Abbot Devon

Contents

Introduction   17

Chapter   Part One—Planning   23
   I   Terraces   25
   II   Wind, Sun and Butterflies   31
   III   Pavings   38
   IV   Terrace Lawns   47
   V   Fountains and Pools   50
   VI   On Planting in General   56
   VII   Planting the Bed against the House   61
   VIII   The Bed facing West   75
   IX   The Bed facing East   79
   X   The Bed opposite the House and Island Beds   81
   XI   Plants for Town Gardens and Shady Positions   85
   XII   Trees on the Terrace   91
   XIII   Plants in Tubs and Pots   94
   XIV   Pots and Tubs   111
   XV   Window Boxes   116
   XVI   Planting Composts   123

   Part Two—Construction   127
   XVII   Laying Paving and Terraces   129
   XVIII   To Make a Small Lawn   134
   XIX   Electric Pumps and Fountains   137
   XX   Emptying, Overflow and Pump Chambers   146
   XXI   To Make a Pool   152
   XXII   Composts and Feeding   156
   XXIII   Construction of Window Boxes   159

Part Three—The Plants 163

XXIV   Notes on Plants 165

British Standards in Nursery and Horticultural Practice 206

Metrication 209

Books which may be Consulted 216

Professional Institutes and Trade Associations 219

Index 222

List of Illustrations

Photographs

Facing page

1 Interpenetration of indoors and out of doors   28
2 At Pusey House, Faringdon, Berkshire, the wide stone path articulates the house with the terrace   28
3 Fountain in the garden of the Villa Pamphilj near Rome   28
4 Part of the garden at the Villa Lante, Bagnaia, near Viterbo   28
5 A cedar and yew as background to a formal garden   29
6 The formal garden at Knightshayes Court, Tiverton, Devon   29
7 A terrace and part of a balcony in a garden at Hulshorst, Holland   29
8 A scene at University College, Oxford   29
9 Parterre beds seen from a small loggia   36
10 Paving and plants successfully combined   36
11 Paving pattern on a terrace in a garden at Aalsmeer, Holland   37
12 A small courtyard with marble paving at University College, Oxford   37
13 Cobbles and pre-cast concrete paving, with concrete plant containers   52
14 Part of the terrace at Ditchley Park, Oxfordshire   52
15 A terrace-deck of redwood at Woodside, California   53
16 A small courtyard behind the Rye Galleries in High Street, Eton   53
17 Hexagonal paving in a long, narrow garden   76
18, 19 and 20 Three examples of curves where grass meets paving   76
21 A lanai at San Mateo, California   77
22 A lanai with sliding doors   77
23, 24 and 25 Three examples of provision for shade   77
26 Part of the garden at the Villa Pamphilj near Rome   92
27 The Villa Pia in the Vatican Gardens, Rome   92

28 A small fountain in the Alcazar, Seville, Spain 93
29 Lotus fountain in the Generalife, Granada, Spain 93
30 Fountain in the upper garden of the Generalife 93
31 A pool in a courtyard and planting which makes much use of foliage contrast 93
32 A fountain consisting of three low cylinders 93
33 Paving in a Berlin garden with concrete slabs and flint units forming a mosaic pattern 108
34 Paving formed of pebble dashed concrete tiles 108
35 Hexagonal paving with wide joints 108
36 Agapanthus in large white tubs at Pusey House, Faringdon, Berkshire 108
37 Part of the garden at the Palazzo Farnese, Caprarola, near Viterbo 109
38 Villa Medici, Rome 109
39 Italian and English pots 116
40 Vaso da Camelia 116
41 Vaso Normale 116
42 Vaso Festonato 116
43 Orcio ad Anforna Liscio 117
44 Orico da Giardino 117
45 Jardinière Decorata 117
46 Jardinière Festonata 117
47 A fountain in the Vatican Gardens, Rome 132
48 A large Rhododendron Pink Pearl in a square tub 133

Diagrams

Steel edge to lawns 135
A pool with pump operating with flooded suction 138
A pool with pump fitted above water level 139
The overflow and emptying arrangement 147
Alternative overflow and emptying arrangements 148
Overflow and emptying and suction arrangements 149
Small pump chamber 150
Reinforcement for a small pool 154
Window boxes: various types of fixing 160

Preface to the Second Edition

For this revised edition I have included some metric conversion tables to assist readers during the transition from Imperial to metric units.

I have added a chapter on British Standards for Horticulture. These can be of assistance to consumers, whether of plants, materials or contracting services, and I think that they ought to be more widely known and more frequently consulted.

I have tried to assess the real value of container-grown plants and semi-mature trees, the use of which has increased considerably since the first edition was published.

In the course of investigating whether the plants and materials referred to in the first edition are still available, it appeared that some of the seasonal bedding plants upon which we depend so much for scent and colour in the garden are now sold only as mixed, although a fair number of separate varieties and colours is still included in seedsmen's catalogues. To confirm my impression, I wrote to the managers of a dozen garden centres. Their general opinion was that both growers and retailers find it cheaper to sell mixed pansies, for instance, than six or more different varieties, and that, as one of them stated, 'it is impulse buying . . . the public take what is put in front of it'. I hope that readers of this book will not regard themselves as any part of this amorphous, insensate 'public', but rather as discerning individuals wishing to exert a personal and constructive influence on the picture which their gardens are to present.

It is not only the varieties of seasonal bedding plants which are being eroded in the interests of economic production and distribution. The process towards so-called rationalisation has been going on for some time with trees and shrubs and many other plants, and here I would salute such firms as Hillier & Sons of Winchester, and Thompson & Morgan of Ipswich, the seedsmen, who can still provide for a curious gardener distinguished and beguiling plants or seeds which are too often overlooked in the present age of commercial and often vulgar standardisation.

In rewriting the passages on roses I have tried to bring the hybrid polyanthas up to date, but this is an unrewarding exercise because, unlike the trees and other plants which form the bone and structure of a garden and are true enduring sources of delight and content, roses of this kind are employed simply for decoration and are, like mini-skirts or maxi-coats, subject to unpredictable caprices of fashion.

I have included some new photographs of Italian gardens, partly to illustrate details of design and the use of materials, partly also to serve as a reminder of an important stage in the progressive evolution of gardens, and terrace and courtyard gardens in particular; partly too, I must confess, from pure delight and to encourage some who may never have seen them to go one year in June, with Miss Masson's book in hand, and among the splendours of Raphael and Vignola, the cool fountains and shady alleys, hear perhaps, as I have heard, a cuckoo calling in the garden of the Villa Madama, and nightingales singing in the daytime at Lante, and see the wild flowers, the *flos campi*, in the lawns of the Palazzo Farnese at Caprarola.

I have again had the assistance of Mr Colin Allsebrook, this time in rewriting much of the chapter on electric pumps and fountains. I have introduced a new table to show the flow of water required to produce jets of varying heights from different sized nozzles, so that a technically-interested reader will now find all the information necessary to calculate exactly the type of pump and electric motor for his requirements.

I record my acknowledgements to the following:

The Council of the Royal Horticultural Society for permission to draw largely on their *Dictionary of Gardening* published by the Clarendon Press, Oxford, in conjunction with the Royal Horticultural Society, and also to make use of their Classification of Camellias.

The Clarendon Press, Oxford, for verbatim definitions from the *Oxford English Dictionary*.

The Macmillan Company of New York for drawings from *Window Box Gardening* by Henry Teuscher.

I am grateful to the following for providing me with photographs:

Amateur Gardening; *Country Life*; Morley Baer; John Brookes; Cement and Concrete Association; Peter Coats; R. J. Corbin;

J. E. Downward; Sheila Harrison; Kon Kwerkerij, Moerheim; Sydney W. Newbery; Maynard L. Parker; Peter Pitt; Spanish National Tourist Office; and William Wood & Son Limited.

The drawings on pages 135, 138, 139, 147, 148, 149, 150 and 154 are by W. T. M. Williams.

Taplow
February 1970

Introduction

This book is designed to be an introduction to the use in Britain of plants and materials in parts of the garden close to the house, that is, on paved areas at ground level, and on balconies and in window boxes above. It is written for the man who, while not intending to lay every stone with his own hands, would like to be able to exercise intelligent control over the work. For this reason guidance is given in Part Two on the practical use of materials. In Part Three, Notes on Plants, information has been compiled from standard authorities as a check against my own assessments in the main part of the text. Here the height and spread of plants is given, and also, where it has been possible to ascertain them, the size of flowers and leaves, to assist those interested in matching the scale of plants to their surroundings.

The high cost of professional labour and the limited time which the owner himself is able to spare has led to much of the garden being reduced, often with advantage, to the more or less basic elements of grass, trees, and coalescing shrubs on the boundaries; but on a terrace the area concerned is comparatively small and much of it taken up by paving, so that those parts which need regular attention, the planting beds and grass panels, will be of manageable size—the planting in particular being confined to small beds and to pots and tubs, which, if convincingly planted and disposed, can exert an influence out of proportion to their size and much beyond the space which they occupy. The very smallness of the commitment should make it possible for high standards to be reached, not only in design and construction, but also in maintenance. The matter of quality is important, because any plant, as soon as it is put into a container, becomes a cynosure, and also because a terrace will often have in it something of the character of the stage, an unmistakable suggestion of drama which calls for a degree of heightening in its treatment and decoration.

A close-companioned association between organic plant form and fixed architectural shape is in the main stream of garden

17

design going back to Babylon or beyond. In our time in areas near the house where architecture and landscape overlap, we are concerned with a specialised, sophisticated side of gardening, far removed from the softer, water-colour character of daffodils and wild cherries in the garden farther from the house. Its practice requires a different discipline, the use of emphatic colour and line, more meticulous regard for scale. It means coming to terms with geraniums and petunias and learning to deploy plants in pots and tubs.

We have borrowed words from other languages to define those sheltered alcoves and paved spaces which occur where house and garden meet, and share in varying degrees the character of both. Four of these are very much a part of the house, covered with a roof but open on at least one side.

Loggia is an Italian word meaning 'a gallery or arcade having one or more of its sides open to the air'. It is essentially contained within the area of the ground plan of the house, i.e. it does not project.

Verandah, originally Spanish and Portuguese, was introduced here from India. It is defined as 'an open portico or light-roofed gallery extending along the front (and occasionally other sides) of a dwelling or other building, frequently having a front of lattice-work, and erected chiefly as a protection or shelter from the sun or rain'. In contrast with a loggia, it projects from the line of the house and usually has a sloping roof supported on light pillars.

Balcony comes from the Italian. It is described as 'a kind of platform projecting from the wall of a house or a room supported by pillars or consoles and enclosed by a balustrade', in fact a kind of first floor verandah.

The new word *lanai* comes from Honolulu and is becoming common in the southern United States. It is really a deep loggia on a large scale. It is described by the Honolulu Academy of Arts as 'glassed or walled in on the side of the prevailing winds and screened against the invasion of. moths and mosquitoes. The lanai, or outdoor living-room, planned for special living purposes and incorporated into the basic design of the house, has now in Hawaii become the most used living area in most houses and serves as a transition between house and garden'.[1] Some have built-in

[1] Quoted with permission from the *Sunset Garden and Patio Building Book*, published by the Lane Book Company, Menlo Park, California

kitchens and separate dining-rooms. Light, split-cane blinds can be rolled down to keep out the afternoon sun.

For all these, plants can be arranged in large boxes or in tubs at the outer edges where they will get most light, but the existence of the ceiling overhead, resulting in an absence of top light, will restrict the planting possibilities to little more than what can be achieved in a sunny room. Spring-flowering bulbs in boxes at the outer edges will make their display in the same way as bulbs in bowls indoors. Bay trees in tubs will endure for a time, but need to be kept turned. Summer flowers like fuchsias and begonias, which prefer shady conditions, will give fair results, but will not flourish as they would in a cool position entirely out of doors.

The word **patio** has been taken up with such glib facility in the United States and in this country that it may be worth looking briefly at its origin and true meaning. It is a Spanish word meaning 'a court of a house. An inner court open to the sky in a Spanish or Spanish-American house.'

In Spain the patio garden evolved from the Roman atrium. It reached its highest point of development during the Arab occupation of southern Spain, which began in the eighth century. Up to the time of Mohammed the Arabs were a remote and unconsidered people, but soon after his death in A.D. 632 they burst out in an access of tumultuous energy and conquered much of the civilised world. When Persia and Syria were overrun between 633 and 641 the conquering Arabs, to whom the shade and water of the oases in the desert were among the most desired things in the world, found them already idealised in the gardens of Persia and, returning, copied or adapted features of these Persian gardens in their own land. Mrs Villiers-Stuart has pointed out[1] that 'Mohammedan art in Spain drew its inspiration largely from Persia by way of Baghdad and Damascus'. In fact, soon after the invasion of Spain in 711, Abd-er-Raham I began to make in conquered Cordova a garden which would remind him of his grandfather's palace at Damascus. For many centuries afterwards the patios of Cordova, Granada, Seville and other towns were developed and improved, the traditional characteristics even being continued by the Christian kings after the final reconquest of Granada by Fernando and Isabel in 1491.

These patio gardens were always and essentially an integral

[1] C. M. Villiers-Stuart—*Spanish Gardens*—Batsford

part of the house, enclosed on all four sides, designed to bring into shaded rooms at noon the living form and moving shadows of trees and foliage, the scent and colour of flowers, and the splash of water, designed also to make a paradise to walk in at early morning and in the evening, cooled by the spray of water in the fountains. With their painted walls and tiled water channels, their cypresses and peach trees, their oleanders and pomegranates and myrtles, their roses and their jasmines, these gardens were unique.

I think it is a pity that we should now use casually for any area of paving near the house a word that once stood for something which attained a pitch of beauty that has never been surpassed and will probably never be repeated. Misuse of the word in this way has the same pretentiousness which led to cinemas being called Rialto, Plaza, and even Granada. In any case, there is little correspondence between the uses of the true enclosed patios of Spain and paved areas in these islands. The Arabs had a civilised appreciation of the quality of intense sunlight seen from indoors. They were connoisseurs of shade. They would not have understood the ecstasy with which the sun is greeted here, the instinct to tear off clothes, to put on dark glasses, to lie supinely silent, oiled and sweating, gently twitching at the puzzled investigations of visiting flies.

A **courtyard** is described as 'an open area surrounded by walls or buildings within the precincts of a large house, castle, homestead, etc.' It may be enclosed on two, three or all four sides. It may be external to the house, although often connected to it by one or more doors. It was probably not originally designed for luxurious pleasure like a patio, but was just an enclosed space within fortifications where men-at-arms could assemble, and, later, where carriages could turn. Many of them are now made over to garden courts with other small, enclosed spaces which had their origin in the necessity to give light to surrounding rooms.

A **terrace** means 'a raised level place for walking with a vertical or sloping front or sides, faced with masonry, turf or the like, and sometimes having a balustrade: *esp.* a raised walk in a garden or a level surface formed in front of a house on naturally sloping ground'. For our purpose here the word implies a change of level at the side farthest from the house, with steps to the garden beyond. The word is also used for a simple paved area when there is no change in level. In this book I shall use terrace to include not only a true terrace, but any paved area near the house, to avoid repetition of the clumsy 'paved area' and because, although not strictly accurate, it has a fair tradition of usage. It is, I think, natural to say: 'Come on to the terrace', while 'Come on to the patio' sounds false and smacks of estate agent's jargon.

PART ONE—PLANNING

CHAPTER I

Terraces

Before making detailed plans for a terrace it is useful to have at the back of one's mind a broad appreciation of two principles of design.

Unity is defined in *The Oxford English Dictionary* as 'singleness of design or effect in a work of art; consonance of parts with each other and the whole'. In a garden it means a grand design in which, through the juxtaposition of height and breadth and shape and colour, all the elements are in equilibrium. On a terrace the quality of unity may be present if there is a visual balance between the height of trees and breadth of panels of turf, or between the darker mass of flower beds and the lighter expanse of paving. It may be present when the terrace appears as a recognisable entity complete in itself and convenient for human use, also when the planting has a perceptible intention—continuous foliage contour and texture; an evident rhythm in the occurrence of colour; or again if the pots and tubs are disposed in a discernible but not necessarily symmetrical pattern.

Scale is defined in *The Oxford English Dictionary* as 'relative or proportionate size or extent; degree, proportion'. For our purposes it simply means good proportion. A paved area will have scale if it fits into the ground plan of the house and matches its size, if the plants have a character of largeness or smallness which responds to similar characteristics in the house and its surroundings.

In the eighteenth century Capability Brown and others did away with terraces and parterres, and allowed the grass of the park to roll in an uneasy ground-swell to the plinth of the house, which, maintaining its dignity with difficulty, must have viewed with dismay the disappearance of its platform beneath the grassy surge. I think that a terrace wholly of grass, with no stone or gravel paths running across its width, will not mate with the house and fails of its purpose because the contrast of materials is too massive. Where the whole area is not to be paved I feel that there should be a perceptible articulation of hard surface repeating, or at least in sympathy with, the material of which the house is made, in one or more places linking it to the further edge of the terrace.

I suspect that the aim should be to create the illusion that the house was originally built on a base consisting entirely of paving or gravel, and that a pattern of grass plots and flower beds has been superimposed later. In the illustration of the terrace at Pusey House (facing p. 28), the wide stone path 30 feet wide running from the house to the steps at the far edge of the terrace is seen to accomplish this. It is usually an easy requirement to satisfy and will leave adequate latitude to adapt the area of hard surface to practical needs. As a guide, a 6-foot bench needs a space at least 6 feet long and 4 feet wide to allow three people to sit and stretch out their legs; a small table with four chairs needs a space of 8 feet by 8 feet; an area 20 feet by 10 feet will take two benches, a table and six chairs and allow reasonable space for walking about.

Le Nôtre is said to have insisted on a large space next to the house, its width equal to the height of the building from ground level to cornice.[1] This proportion is a fair general guide for calculating the width of a terrace, which could be wider for a house with a pitched roof. It does not necessarily mean that the whole level area must be a uniformly blank surface. In the case of tall houses the corresponding wide expanse of stone or gravel would be too staring for comfort. To prevent this it can be relieved with contrasting materials laid in bands or borders to form outlines to panels and to make compartments. More significant relief is gained by the inclusion of panels of grass, planting beds, fountains and pots and tubs of flowers.

The house and terrace at Wexham Springs, Bucks, do not follow Le Nôtre's proportions. The house is unusually low—about 25 feet—and the width of the terrace was already fixed at 40 feet when Mr Jellicoe was asked to design it. He has said that it was the

[1] Russell Page—*The Education of a Gardener*—Collins.

fact that it was out of proportion to the height of the house that persuaded him to make such a complex design, but in fact by the skilful manipulation of rectangles of grass and planting he has reduced the hard areas of paving to a comfortable human scale, for perambulation, and the use of tables and chairs. He has also in the planted beds, as it were, brought the garden over the terrace wall and into the influence of the house without destroying the recognisable platform on which the house is standing. The rectangular planting beds are given a sharpness and increased significance by a precast edging which raises the level 4 inches above the paving. There is a higher bed raised 18 inches above the terrace level. In this case it is retained by a thin wall of exposed aggregate made of blue Shap granite and Lee Moor sand. Raised beds give an added interest to planting on a terrace. They are particularly useful where the paved area in front of the house constitutes the whole garden. Against a boundary they are a means of gaining height for planting against walls and fences. They are, of course, essential when there is not enough depth of soil below the paved area owing to the presence of cellars or drain pipes near the surface.

When a new terrace is designed it is not only the immediately contiguous surroundings which must be taken into account. Mr Russell Page[1] in referring to a Japanese concept of 'borrowing' features of the surrounding landscape, points out the need, not only to keep the close-at-hand gardening details in scale with a distant hill or tree, but also to make sure that such details do not compete for interest with the elements which are being borrowed. This, I think, is particularly marked in gardens by the sea. I was once taken to see a new house by the side of a tidal inlet of the sea in Cornwall. From the windows one looked out on sparkling sea and white clouds, boats moored, boats sailing, and a ferry coming from the large town across the bay. In the foreground of the garden at the front edge of the terrace there was a bed of red floribunda roses which distracted attention from the maritime scene, and shattered the illusion that one was looking not through a window, but into a marvellous picture inside the room. This could have been avoided if the edge of the paving had been allowed to run unobtrusively off into the grass, and if the roses had been put under the window, where they would have been invisible to watchers indoors, while to those in a boat coming in from the sea the bed

[1] *The Education of a Gardener*—Collins.

of roses would have been seen in natural and expected partnership with the house, and its identification with land and home. This intangible 'borrowing' exists only in the mind's eye, but actual physical interpenetration of house and landscape has for long been a feature of gardens in hot climates, in Pompeii, in Rome, Spain, Renaissance Italy and in India. There, water channels ran through courtyards into rooms, fountains played inside the houses, and patios open to the sky were in truth outdoor rooms.

This interlocking of landscape and house is much in the minds of landscape architects today. It is a feature of new gardens in Latin America and in the southern United States. It is also being adopted in the north of the United States and in this country, although how successful it will prove to be in our wet and windy climate may be open to doubt.

Mr Derek Lovejoy has told me that the design of his house at Woldingham 'was predominantly to achieve a feeling of interpenetration of indoors and outdoors. The polished terrazzo floor in the sitting room extends out on to the terraces, and the planting beds extend into the sitting room. . . . The house has been designed in order to achieve a complete integration between architecture and landscape.' It is interesting to note the primacy given to the landscape over the house. Mr Lovejoy is going nearly as far as Sir George Sitwell when he wrote in 1910: 'The great secret of success in garden making (is to) move the house to where nature is beautiful.'[1]

The idea of interpenetration is like similar trends in the theatre, the use of the apron stage and the theatre in the round, both designed to integrate actors and audiences in one arena of action. This is interesting and stimulating, but it is not achieved without some loss, the loss of the secret withdrawn pleasure of watching unseen as a spectator. In somewhat the same way, when house and landscape are locked in hermaphrodite conjunction, we lose the delight in contrast which exists more strongly when indoors and out of doors are allowed to retain their separate characters, when the relationship between the two is conducted in good-humoured tension, a sort of Mirabell-Millament alliance, in that brief debatable land of transition with which we are concerned in this book.

A terrace will generally be situated on the south side of the house. If it is slanted a little to the east of south it will catch the

[1] Sir George Sitwell—*On the Making of Gardens*—Gerald Duckworth

1. Interpenetration of indoors and out of doors. A polished terrazzo floor in the sitting-room extends out on to the terraces, and the planting beds extend into the sitting-room. Designed by Derek Lovejoy, M.A. (Harvard), DIP. T.P., A.R.I.B.A., M.T.P.I., F.I.L.A.

2. At Pusey House, Faringdon, Berkshire, the wide stone path articulates the house with the edge of the terrace, which was designed by G. A. Jellicoe, C.B.E., F.R.I.B.A., M.T.P.I., P.P.I.L.A.

3. Fountain in the garden of the Villa Pamphilj near Rome

4. Part of the garden at the Villa Lante, Bagnaia, near Viterbo

5. The fine cedar and yew make a good background to this garden. The pots of flowers are well disposed on the terrace. *Photograph by courtesy of the National Trust*

6. The formal garden at Knightshayes Court, Tiverton, Devon. The beds are edged with moulded stone and the foliage contrast is interesting. Designed by G. S. Thomas

7. A terrace and part of a balcony in a garden at Hulshorst, Holland. The paving was made of yellow bricks and concrete tiles. Designed by Mien Ruys, Amsterdam

8. Grass panels and planting beds against the house with a whitebeam tree in the foreground. The brick wall was a York stone coping, and the teak bench has a good clear-cut outline. This walk at University College, Oxford, in front of the Durham Buildings, leads to the new Goodhart Quadrangle designed by Sylvia Crowe, P.P.I.L.A.

sun earlier in the day, and the dazzling glare of low evening sun may be cut off by a corner of the house; if to the west of south there will be some shelter from east winds and the paving will hold the warmth of evening sunshine a little longer.

Where there is an appreciable difference of level between the terrace and the garden beyond there will be a sense of insecurity unless some sort of barrier is made at the outer edge. A balustrade above the retaining wall is appropriate in large gardens, but would be pompous in smaller ones where, instead, a low parapet wall or a closely clipped box hedge of from 15 to 18 inches high would be more in character. The top of this wall or hedge will make a firm horizontal line to define the platform on which the house is standing. It is important that an awareness of this line should be preserved and not smudged by a confused growth of plants in a bed on the inside thrusting up above the level line. On the other hand, this level line will appear uncompromisingly rigid unless it is relieved at intervals with a few apparently casual unregulated sprays of foliage.

After the proportions of the terrace with its paving and other components have been settled and brought into human scale, any thoughts of further decoration should be critically examined. A litter of sun-dials, bird baths, figures, even tubs of flowers or too many chairs can so easily bring to nothing the careful planning aimed at unity in overall design. Anything that is to be added should be introduced in place of rather than in addition to an existing object. The man who is fortunate enough to have a small piece by Epstein or Henry Moore will design his terrace round it. A less-fortunate man would do better to try to find a piece of abstract sculpture than to bring in copies, however good, of renaissance figures.

In general I would beware of 'objects'. Sun-dials can be attractive on walls, but are difficult on pedestals; a fountain is better than a bird bath; instruments of the barbecue and the smell of cooking are best kept to caravan sites; toadstool-like staddle stones are pointless pieces of sentimentality not much better than those smooth concrete children coyly tipping water out of jars.

Chairs and tables on the terrace are up against a larger scale than when indoors. Thin steel furniture, with its spindly legs like stiletto heels and its seats and back rests like maladjusted spiders' webs, is hopelessly overpowered; flimsy folding aluminium picnic chairs and tables covered with shiny, thoroughly man-made fibres in gauche checks and zigzags should be kept locked up in the luggage boots of motor cars and not allowed in the garden. The best-looking and most comfortable are ample wicker seats and chairs with plain-coloured cushions, dark cinnamon red or dark green or, best of all, dark blue.

CHAPTER II

Wind, Sun and Butterflies

Wind is the gardener's most malevolent adversary; it will remorse-lessly flutter the pages of his book, send dust whirling into his eyes, shred petunias and daturas, and murder spring-planted evergreens. It has the devastating, insensate energy of a bossy woman.

On a terrace which faces south, the house itself will provide a wind-break to the north, but unless the house is L-shaped extra screens to east and west may also be desirable. A solid screen such as a brick or stone wall will provide calm conditions in its lee for a length of about three times its height, but beyond this there may be disturbing downdraughts. Thus a screen wall 8 feet high will give good shelter for perhaps 24 feet, but in high winds it will create untenantable conditions at a distance downwind greater than this. None the less, 20 feet or so of terrace will usually be enough space into which to draw chairs and tables and make a warm corner on spring days when the sun is bright and the east wind keen.

A hedge or slatted screen, by filtering the wind, will materially reduce its speed and strength for a distance up to six times its height; such screens are useful out in the open garden where pro-tection for plants is needed, but in this country even filtered wind is lacking in appeal on a terrace where humanity is to congregate.

In the small to moderate-sized houses and gardens which we are chiefly considering, projecting walls will not end in gazebos or dovecotes, so that in the interests of comfort it will be necessary to accept an abrupt end with only a terminal pier, or at best a short

31

right-angled return. Sheltering wing walls should be made of the same material as the house—stone, brick, flint or wood—and at one end bonded into the house fabric. Certainly any idea of making a 'gardeny' York stone wall must be resisted. York stone is good material for paving, but when used for walls it becomes brash and defensively self-conscious with its thin courses of rough-faced quartzy stone, and the fussiness of its detail further emphasised by relentlessly raked back joints.

A wing wall will provide an excuse for growing favourite shrubs —some of those on the verge of tenderness like the Lemon Verbena for instance, and such roses as *Rosa × anemonoides* (*R. sinica* Anemone), or the Banksian Rose. If it is high enough, 8 feet or more, it can provide an excuse, and perhaps also a sound practical reason, for building into it a mysterious, inviting garden door, round-headed, solid-looking in teak or oak.

If instead of a wall it is decided to have a hedge, yew or beech will be the most satisfactory. Both of these when established will make dense screens up to 8 feet high or more and will grow reasonably quickly. A fair formula for the rate of growth of both these plants is: in the first year nothing, in the second year 2 inches, in the third and all subsequent years a foot. Thus plants put in at 3 feet high should reach 6 feet in the sixth or seventh year after planting, if allowance is made for pruning to develop bushiness at the base. Yew is evergreen and beech retains its russet leaves all through the winter. Both can be clipped regularly and hard if it is done at the right time of the year. Yew can be pruned hard for shaping in April, but no more than light trimming or touching up should be done in August. Beech is best pruned in July.

Holly makes a dense evergreen hedge, but is slower growing than the first two. The prickly leaves of the common holly, with their wavy edges and sharp spurs, have too much fussy detail in close proximity to the house, besides inducing a feeling of discomfort on account of the prickles. A better choice would be one of the varieties, *Ilex aquifolium camelliaefolia* or *I. a. hodginsii*, both of which have smooth-edged leaves.

Lawson's Cypress and *Thuja plicata* are planted to make screening hedges. They can be bought and transplanted at a height of 3 feet or more, are evergreen and quick growing, but they are not amenable to being pruned and trimmed like beech and yew; apart from this I find the flat, feathery cypress foliage, packed closely together in a hedge, to be repellent.

Cupressus macrocarpa is a tender exotic from California which, although it will often endure for a time as a tall screen in Ireland or Cornwall, is hopelessly unreliable away from these warm districts. In its maturity it has a habit and shape almost indistinguishable from the Cedar of Lebanon.

A reliable and very fast-growing plant for tall screens is *Cupressus* (or *Cupressocyparis*) *leylandii*, a hybrid between *Cupressus macrocarpa* and *Chamaecyparis nootkatensis* which, once established, will put on height at the rate of from 2½–3 feet each year.

I know of a fine beech hedge, 10 feet high, behind white square mesh trellis fixed in panels between hollow treillage piers, surmounted by carved beasts on white-painted capitals. The live green or russet of the hedge seen through the regular squares of the white trellis is at all times strikingly beautiful. It has the obvious disadvantage of being tedious (for a day) to maintain, but it is a triumphant example of the truth that it is worth going to trouble and expense to achieve something which is handsome and remarkable.

In the United States much use is made of slatted wood fences in natural cedar or painted white. They are decorative and in sympathy with the architectural character of some modern houses. These slatted fences, which, like hedges, filter the wind instead of stopping it entirely, are now popular in the southern states where the summer temperature is regularly above 32°C (90°F.) and where the cooling effect of a light breeze is welcomed. In this country, too, on a long terrace, the absence of turbulent conditions half-way along may sometimes be of advantage. Louvred screens are a further refinement. Here the slats are wider and set at an angle, usually 45°, into top and bottom rails for vertical louvres, or into framing posts in the case of horizontal ones. Owing to the large section of the timbers and their considerable weight, vertical louvres are more satisfactory than horizontal ones because they cannot sag.

Another type of wood screen, known as board on board, or chalet fence, was popular in Japan before being adopted in America. A typical arrangement would be boards of about 6 inches with a space of 4 inches between each board. The arrangement is repeated on the other side so that the fence would look the same on both sides. When the boards are fixed horizontally they admit sunlight and filter the wind but they are viewproof, whereas with the boards fixed vertically the wind is still filtered but there is not a complete visual stop.

These wooden screens have a freshness and sincerity that makes them natural companions to modern ranch or chalet-type houses where traditional English fencing would be out of place. In fact, vertical feather-edged boards on oak or concrete posts, although familiar and sometimes inevitable on the boundaries of a garden, do not associate well with houses of any kind. There is no place near the house or anywhere in the garden, except on the bonfire, for the flimsy interwoven fencing which is so widely advertised and so disastrously used. It is supplied in panels fitted between posts too small in scale, often projecting above the line of the top rail, and surmounted by arch little timber caps. When temporary screens are needed to give shelter while a hedge grows up alongside it, more honest, if a little homespun, are osier or wattle hurdles with their frank acceptance of their transient purpose.

All the screens we have so far been considering will provide varying degrees of shelter from the wind and almost complete visual stop. They are best suited to the eastern end of a terrace where the shelter they provide will often be more valuable than the loss of light and view into the further landscape. But there are situations where less shelter from the wind is needed and where a blank wall would be unbearably confining. In such cases a baffle screen will be suitable. Wing walls can be built with large window-shaped openings covered with iron grilles—plain, rather thick round iron bars might be most interesting, like some of the forged iron *rejas* of Spain. Or brick walls can be perforated by the omission of bricks in a regular pattern.

An open screen is also provided by the comparatively new screen wall units made in coloured concrete or in ceramic material the colour of bricks, red, brown and black. One pattern of mesh is hexagonal and another, perhaps a little effeminate, consists of a grid of circles. The screen walls are built up in panels of from 4 to 6 square yards. Thus, for example, the panels could be 6 feet long and 6 feet high or 4 feet long and 8 feet high, and so on. They are fixed to 9-inch brick piers. At first sight these walls might seem to be best suited to modern houses, but by virtue of their 'transparency' and being unlike any solid barrier, they can be used in other contexts. In the long, narrow garden at Chelsea, illustrated

opposite p. 76, Mr Pasley employed them to give a receding succession of interest. In his exhibition garden at Chelsea, Mr
Brookes made effective use of the circular pattern of screen walls
as a background to planting on the edge of a terrace.

By contrast with the wind, the sun in this country is on the whole
an ally, if an intransigent one. It is necessary for the growth of
plants and the ripening of wood, it warms the air and the paving-
stones of the terrace. Perhaps the greatest benefit which it bestows
is the creation of shadows, hard ones on the undersides of steps and
mouldings, tender and mysterious ones in the shadows of clouds on
mountains or of trees on the lawn towards evening.

In the United States, where elaborate measures are devised to
make outdoor living spaces cool and habitable in the height of
summer, use is made of slatted roofs, sometimes joined to the
house at the back and supported on posts in front like a skeleton
verandah, with bamboo lath-blinds fixed so that they can be raised
or lowered according to the sun's position. Sometimes these slatted
roofs are detached from the house and built out in the garden like
a tent of lath. There are also shelters of canvas like tent tops, open
at the sides, with tent poles and guys which can easily be put up
or taken down. There are also enormous canvas awnings which
can be pulled down to cover the entire width of the terrace.

It is possible to have wide awnings made in this country, too,
like the blinds that are pulled out in front of shop windows in the
summer. They will extend to 8 feet, with the usual hinged and folding iron brackets, and to 12 feet or more if the outer edges are
supported on light alloy poles fitted into sockets in the paving at
the outer edge of the terrace. These poles can quickly be put up
or taken away. Although expensive, this is the best way to shade a
terrace and the windows. Garden umbrellas are much cheaper, but
their gaiety, such as it is, is self-conscious and temporary. They are
better suited to hotel gardens than to those of our own homes.

In the wayward summers of these islands it is not surprising that
we lack the passion for shade and water which inspired the Mughal
gardens of India, planted with sacred Chenar trees, where the
pavilions were cooled by the spray of fountains and built on islands
at the meeting-place of canals. Mrs Villiers-Stuart[1] writes of a visit
before 1914 to the Rang Mahal, the Painted Palace: 'Far below
all the garden seemed asleep in the warm noonday haze. . . . The

[1] *The Gardens of the Great Mughals*—C. M. Villiers-Stuart.

birds were all asleep or else the roar of the waterfalls had drowned their various calls. Only the butterflies and the fountains seemed alive, dancing points of gold and silver.' I read this on a day of unusual heat, sitting withdrawn on the verandah, at times watching a hawking fly catcher, the random progress of a tortoise across the lawn or the play of light on foliage.

I remember when the Humming Bird Hawk Moths used to visit my garden—in the days before all our springs were silent—when we were more or less content to share the garden with our fellow pests, and when even our war against aphids was conducted with conventional weapons. Since then there are no Red Admirals and Peacocks and Painted Ladies floating over the buddleias and marigolds or basking on the terrace stones in the sunlight, opening and shutting their beautiful, intricately patterned wings. Regretting this I later wrote to Mr L. Hugh Newman with no great hope, and feeling that I should be making a fool of myself. To my delight he replied: 'Oh yes, we are supplying live chrysalides all the time to wealthy clients for liberating on their estates.' I learned from him that butterflies can be encouraged into a garden by putting down among the plants a saucer half-filled with a mixture of honey and water, also by allowing pears and plums to ferment on the ground. Flowers which particularly attract butterflies are the common purple aubrieta, yellow alyssum, valerian, lavender, Michaelmas daisies, buddleias, candytuft, mignonette and annual scabious. I found out that the caterpillars of Peacocks, Red Admirals and small Tortoiseshells all feed on stinging nettles, and those of Painted Ladies on thistles, and that therefore there would be no difficulty in providing food plants.

Mr Newman no longer supplies butterfly eggs or chrysalides himself, but I have looked at the price list of Worldwide Butterflies Limited of Sherborne in Dorset from which it seems that for about £10 I could have chrysalides of 40 small Tortoiseshells, two dozen each of Peacocks, Red Admirals, Painted Ladies and Camberwell Beauties. These latter are immigrants from Scandinavia and do not breed here, but would none the less adorn a chosen afternoon. I should hope, though, with generous plantings of nettles and thistles in odd corners, to be able to establish a proportion of the others, if I were not too closely hemmed in by the gardens of those addicted to poisonous sprays.

It will be tempting, too, although without any possibility of

The view from inside an extension to a small loggia. The climbing plants are *Cobaea andens*, and the box-edged parterre beds are planted with white and blue violas. This arden was designed by Russell Page, O.B.E., F.I.L.A.

). In addition to the white petunia Snowcap in the foreground, other plants shown are *hlomis fruticosa*, a Dutch lavender and carpeting Bugle (*Ajuga reptans*). The white wood eats and cane table came from Paris

11. Paving patterns and planting on a terrace in a garden at Aalsmeer, Holland. The plant include campanulas, geums, euphorbias, achilleas, verbenas, artemisias, helianthemums phlox, azaleas, irises and heathers. The hedge is hornbeam. The garden was designed b Mien Ruys, Amsterdam

12. A small courtyard with marble paving at University College, Oxford. A concrete cur has been built round the weeping cherry. The garden was designed by Sylvia Crowe P.P.I.L.A., and photographed by permission of the Master and Fellows of the College

establishing them, to have flying in the garden, if only on a few evenings, some of the large exotic moths. The eggs or caterpillars of these would be kept in breeding cages until the moment of liberation. A pound would buy two dozen or so eggs of the Giant Atlas Moth from Borneo whose caterpillars feed on privet, or about two dozen caterpillars of each of two moths from India which feed on common garden plants; apple, plum and hawthorn for the larvae of the Moon Moth, and Virginia creeper and vine for Golden Emperor caterpillars. A prince who wished for memorable summers would make a butterfly reserve a little upwind of the house. Here he would plant nettles and thistles, and also buckthorn for Brimstones. If he had £50 to spend he could have in the first year 200 each of small Tortoiseshells, Peacocks, Red Admirals, and Painted Ladies, and 50 Camberwell Beauties.

Looking again at the list, I saw the names of hawk moths that were familiar in childhood days, Elephant, Lime, and Privet, but not a special one for which I was looking. In fancy I thought of an evening's entertainment I would like to give to particular acquaintances who, as they came out on to the terrace after dinner, would be greeted with a 'swift whirr of terrible wings' as flights of Death's Head Hawk Moths were released from the darker recesses of the garden beyond.

CHAPTER III

Pavings

Before the final surface is laid a firm foundation (see Chapter XVII) must be constructed, sloping slightly to carry water away from the house. Of all the surfacing materials that can then be used gravel, besides being the cheapest, has important virtues. It provides a safe foothold in nearly all conditions. It is, as it were, flexible and can be laid over difficult levels where stone paving would not only look awkward but might also be dangerous in frosty weather. It throws back little glare in bright sunlight and its unobtrusive good manners make it a fit companion for any house, no matter how large or small or of what materials it is made. Its disadvantages are that it can become temporarily soft after rain and may not then make a firm enough base for tables and chairs; it tends to be picked up on shoes and brought into the house in wet weather; and it needs regular maintenance, brushing and rolling and treatment with weed killer, particularly in corners or on areas that are not regularly walked over.

Binding gravel is a mixture of stone, sand, silt and clay, often in almost continuous gradation. Its composition varies considerably from place to place. It is often referred to as 'hoggin', but in some districts this can be misleading because the word hoggin is also taken to describe any gravel 'as dug', irrespective of the proportion of materials or the size of the particles. Even the word gravel itself can be imprecise. For instance, the well-known Breedon Hill path-surfacing material is not strictly gravel but shale, and materials from the Cerney district of Gloucestershire have no silt content, although when laid and rolled bind very well, due to the fact that under the rolling the soft stone breaks to form a binding medium. It is advisable to rely on trustworthy local experience, and to get path gravel which is known to make a firmly bound surface, material which if necessary will have been specially processed for the purpose.

Concrete makes a firm surface in all conditions of weather, needs no maintenance and will not grow weeds. It has a brusque honesty which is to be preferred to the whimsy of crazy paving. Nevertheless, in its crudest form when laid *in situ*, it is an uncompromising material in the garden, and when finished with a smooth surface and a light colour reflects glare in strong sunlight, most particularly in the early months after laying. This glare will be reduced if the reflected light is broken up by giving a textured or ridged surface to the concrete by tamping or the use of a wood float in the later stages of laying (see Chapter XVII). The use of darker-coloured cements will also mitigate glare, and so, too, will the simple effluxion of time, in the course of which dust collects in the pores, and mosses and algae begin to develop.

Over large areas concrete laid *in situ* may be monotonous, but concrete flags or slabs, with their pattern of jointing, will avoid this. Hydraulically pressed concrete flags are available with a degree of texture on the surface; their usual colour is natural grey, but other colours can be obtained. They are made in two thicknesses in a standard range of sizes (see Chapter XVII).

Precast concrete slabs are not usually hydraulically pressed but vibrated in moulds. They are made with one side smooth and the other with a hand-finished surface, giving variations of texture and non-slip characteristics, although, if desired, the smooth side may be laid uppermost.

Colouring is often mixed with the concrete to make greyish-green, sandy grey, light yellow, pale pink and even sky blue slabs. Some of these are more startling than beautiful and it is safer not to be too adventurous in the choice of colours. Generally, the most satisfactory effect will be obtained from slabs of the same colour, or at most a random mixture of two closely related colours such as grey-green and sandy grey.

The smaller size of these slabs makes them useful for paving a narrow terrace on which pressed flags would be too large and out of scale, but it is easy to go to the other extreme and create a fussy pattern by the use of three or four different-sized slabs. My own first choice for a small terrace would be a perfectly straightforward arrangement of 2-foot square slabs laid with continuous joints, as seen in the illustration facing p. 36. Over medium or larger areas the honeycomb network of hexagonal slabs makes a contented, reassuring pattern.

Concrete paving is seen in its most sophisticated form in the exposed aggregate finishes which are being developed at Wexham Springs in Buckinghamshire, the experimental station of the Cement and Concrete Association. No trouble has been spared to search out strange and beautiful materials for the aggregates which give the paving its special character. On the terrace at Wexham the long walk next to the lawn is made of black and grey flags 3 feet by 2 feet, laid in a key design. The black-coloured flags are made with a dark granite aggregate with a sprinkling of Derby spar and black cement, and the grey flags of ordinary Portland cement and granite aggregate. In the small courtyard garden shown in the illustration facing page 52 the buff tones are obtained with sand and gravel, from Hoveringham in the valley of the Trent near Nottingham, and white cement, and the lighter, creamier colours by mixing Feltham sand, pink Shap granite, Derbyshire spar, white cement and extra light cream cement. The process of exposing aggregates (see Chapter XVII) results in a rougher-textured surface with more character than the normal smooth finishes. It reflects less glare from the sun than ordinary flag or slab paving, and looks well in association with modern houses.

In limestone areas local stone has been and is still used for paving—from Ancaster and Ketton in Lincolnshire, the neighbourhood of Bath, in the region of Ham Hill and Doulting in Somerset, Portland and Purbeck in Dorset and Weldon in Northamptonshire, to name only a few. These have much beauty of texture and colour but they are not always proof against frost when laid flat, and may also become slippery through the growth of moss or algae.

By contrast, sandstone has been called Nature's non-slip material. Stone from the Forest of Dean is quarried in dull blue and grey colours, but the best-known and most widely used of the standstones is natural York stone. This, also, is either buff-brown or smoky blue and can be had as self-faced, that is, split along natural laminations, or sawn-faced. The self-faced stone shows the lamination on the surface where a thin layer has flaked off, leaving irregular depressions of a depth probably less than the thickness of a penny but deep enough to hold, for a little time after rain, a shallow pool of water reflecting sky and clouds. Split stone can be refined a stage further by being worked over the surface with a chisel, or by planing, but for a uniformly smooth finish, sawn stone, which is more expensive, must be used.

There are three ways in which the edges are normally finished. With a fettle edge the sides of the stones are roughly trimmed and when laid need a joint of $\frac{1}{2}$ inch. When the edges are mason-squared, the work is still done by hand, but a finer finish is obtained and the stones can be laid with a $\frac{1}{4}$-inch joint. The finest finish is produced when the edges of the stones are sawn. When this is done they can be laid with a joint of $\frac{1}{8}$ inch.

The width of the joint is important. Wide joints may look rough-hewn in association with precise architecture, but, on the other hand, too close a joint can easily be 'lost' over a wide area, with the result that the pattern cannot be seen and the paving loses character and becomes boring. The joints are best pointed with sand and cement mortar or at least filled with sand and kept clean of moss, pearlwort or other growths. These have their places elsewhere in the garden in grass and under trees, but in the joints of paving they over-emphasise the pattern.

York stone which has been recovered from the pavements of London and other towns is sometimes available. It is generally blackened with age and soot and comes in odd sizes and in varying thicknesses. Its venerable appearance is no disadvantage, but the variation in thickness makes it heavier to handle and more expensive to lay, because the depth of the bed has to be continually readjusted to take stones varying from 2 to 4 or more inches in thickness. It may also have developed depressions on the surface as a result of constant use over many years. It appears at first to be less expensive than new stone, but when its uneven thickness and large variation in size is taken into account it will be found that by the time the paving has been laid there is little difference in cost.

When the stone is laid in what is known as a random rectangular pattern, the mason fits the stones together freehand with possibly every stone of a different size. There should not be too great a variation in the sizes of the stones. Sometimes a mason will make use of a very small stone, perhaps only 6 inches square or perhaps 6 inches by 9 inches, to fill an awkward space, instead of taking time to work out the pattern with larger stones. As a rough guide, on medium-sized and small terraces no stone should have a side less than 1 foot or larger than 2 feet 6 inches. Care should be taken to make sure that the stones are squared before they are laid so that all joints are parallel and at right-angles. It is distracting to stand at one end of a terrace and look along a network of joints running this way and that.

Another way of laying the stone is to have the paving coursed, that is, in even widths in one direction but laid in random lengths. This gives the best effect with all but the most symmetrical houses. The courses can be 2 or 3 feet wide running parallel with the house. The lengths of the stone will be different provided that the joints are 'broken'. that is, joints in adjoining courses over-lap and do not coincide. When the character of the house calls for it, the paving may be coursed along its width and laid in a precise repeating pattern along its length.

For a small house with no special character, self-faced stone with mason-squared edges coursed one way and in random lengths will look the best, and for a larger house, or one of marked char-acter, sawn stone in one colour, again with mason-squared edges and regularly coursed with a repeating pattern and relieved with bands of slate or other contrasting material, may be appropriate.

Paving patterns may be loosely compared with verse forms. Coursed stone with a repeating pattern of joints is like a sonnet which follows an understood formula of rhymes; stone coursed one way and with random joints is like verse with occasional rhymes, and random rectangular stone like blank verse. To com-plete the analogy, crazy paving is perhaps like *vers libre*. This way of laying stone is sometimes satisfactory with certain materials. For instance, the rusty red stones which come as waste from slate quarries in Devon and Cornwall, laid with flush-pointed joints, can make an attractive surface, and so can broken marble if care is taken in fitting the pieces together. But York stone crazy paving seems doomed to disaster, as if the jagged pieces of shattered stone had been put together with the pathetic clumsiness of a child trying to mend a broken toy.

Marble, which was used to adorn the buildings of the ancient world and which still has a continuing everyday use in countries abroad, is in Britain too expensive for anything except the gentlemen's lavatories of railway hotels and the macabre façades of banks and insurance offices. It is a pity that it cannot be afforded for gardens; perhaps it is too dangerously beautiful, too un-English, too unstodgy, to be let out of doors. It has an inward vitality and a lightness which makes York stone look sullen, and it could so often be a perfect material for paving on loggias and verandahs and on some terraces. It has endless variety, never calling for relief with other materials, although sometimes enhanced by contrasting bands of another marble. There are over 300 different kinds found in all the countries of Europe, particularly in Greece, Italy, Spain and Portugal, Belgium, Sweden and Ireland, and indeed in many other parts of the world—Persia, the American continent, New Zealand, and South Africa.

Italian marbles have sonorous names like Portora machia, which is shining black with gold veins; Verde St Denis, dark green, mottled with light green; Rosso levanto, plum-coloured, clouded pale pebble grey, or Breche Rose, like white clouds in a pink sky. From Sweden, Black Polar and White Glacier are good to use together in a chequered pattern paving. Some of the most beautiful of all come from Ireland. The Connemara marble, known as Light Sepia, is veined with grey-green and mauve-brown, like the hills and sky at Lettergesh; there is another dark green, almost black, with markings like grey wavelets. There are marbles from Galway, plain, gleaming jet black, and black with white markings like cumulus clouds.

Marbles that have been used for paving here include many of the near whites: Arabescato—parchment grey with lead pencil shadings; Piastraccia—palest grey with half a hint of pink in it and deeper grey shadings; Sicilian—white with veins the colour of unboiled white of egg; and Calacata machia—cream suffused with apricot. The best known is probably Travertine—pale or dark honey colour, not a true marble but used for the same purposes, and especially for paving, as Thornton Wilder remembered when he wrote of a first arrival in Rome in 1920 '. . . a drive through shadowy streets to the sound of fountains, and the very special echo of Travertine pavements'.

A honed surface is applied when marble is to be laid for paving to prevent it being slippery, but when intended for facing the walls or piers of a loggia, it is highly polished. The rotary polishing heads generate so much heat that a thin vitreous skin is produced on the surface. It is perfectly frostproof. It can be obtained as offcuts in fixed widths and random lengths more cheaply than when specially prepared for a particular contract.

The illustration facing page 37 shows a small courtyard in Oxford paved with marble recovered from the floor of the dining hall when this was taken up and renewed.

Slate comes from many sources. That from Lancashire and Westmorland ranges from pale green to olive-green in colour; from North Wales it is blue or blue-purple; and from Cornwall it is generally grey or grey-green, sometimes with rusty red tones. When dry the colour is a rather dull, fairly light grey; when gleaming after rain it resembles old pewter. It is useful for paving small areas or for copings on walls, but *par excellence* its use is as banding to relieve large areas of York stone. It was so used by Mr Jellicoe on the long terrace at Ditchley, where the two materials make a sober and outstandingly successful marriage. Slates laid on edge can be made to form a chequer-board pattern, as in the porch of the Church of St Fimbarrus at Fowey. For external pavings a finish with a perceptible texture, such as that which is known as frame-sawn, is attractive. The joints should be a uniform $\frac{1}{8}$ inch and pointed with black cement. Wider joints or white pointing would destroy the intention behind the use of this material.

So far we have been considering paving in which the units are comparatively large, but with granite setts, cobbles and bricks we come to smaller units. Granite setts may come from Cornwall, Wales, Scotland or Ireland. They are generally quartz-grey, but pink and red colours are to be found in material from Aberdeen and Shap. Setts, or pitching, as it is known in the North, which once had an entirely utilitarian association in their use for paving the streets of northern towns and for making gutters and curbs, have come back into favour at a higher social level. They are used on terraces for making panels to relieve a broad expanse of paving, or for covering areas next to the house in a deeply shaded northern aspect where plants would not grow. Like gravel, they are flexible in use and can be used to cover slopes which could not be paved with stone. They are excellent for laying round the base of trees to form an interesting contour, and readily accommodate minor differences in level between the base of the tree and its surroundings. Sizes of setts vary from as little as 4 inches square up to 10 inches by 5 inches, but on an average the units are comparable in scale with bricks.

Pebble mosaic was used on the floors of the Arab patios of Spain. It has been revived in western Europe to such an extent that with granite setts it has become a part of the vocabulary of almost every architect. Both are used effectively as patterned inserts to large areas of paving or to cover awkward levels and mounds; both are admirable bases for trees in paving or gravel.

Cobbles can be laid in radiating patterns like fish scales or like the feathers on the breast of a bird. Some of the new cobbled areas have a bristling, assertive appearance, due to the fact that the pebbles have been laid on edge instead of flat, as they were in Spain, and in the alleys and narrow streets of old towns of this country.

Brick paving has a warm, intimate character and an air of immemorial native calm which no other paving material possesses. It is not glaring in bright sunlight. Because the scale of the units is small, interest is added to large areas by bands of bricks of the same or a different kind laid in another sense, i.e. on edge if the bricks in the main area are laid flat, and vice versa.

Stock and wire-cut bricks provide a rough, fairly non-slip surface for walking, and are also hard-wearing and comparatively cheap. In the making of stock bricks breeze is mixed with the clay after it has been dug, and when the bricks are fired in the kiln the breeze in the body of the brick burns, giving to the surface the traditional stock black marking or mottling, and making in the body of the brick an open texture with large air spaces. Contrary to what might be expected, these stock bricks are singularly proof against frost owing to the fact that, although they are readily saturated with water, the passages are large enough to accommodate expansion when water freezes into ice without fracturing the body of the brick. They are also light to handle. Suitable bricks available in the South of England are Wealden rough stocks, which come in a variety of colours blending well together, and ranging from dark smoky grey to cocoa brown and dirty straw, flashed in varying degrees with the blue-black breeze markings. It is only London stocks which are all pale mustard-yellow.

Wire-cut bricks are so called because they are cut out into shape by wires on a frame. They are dense bricks, much heavier than stocks, and of great strength. In some kinds a pleasant, uneven texture is produced on the face by the drag of the wires on the clay. Lunsford blue brindled wire-cut seconds, also made in the South of England, associate well with the rough stocks. The colour is generally a grey-smoky-blue with touches of brindled brown; they can be used as contrasting bands to outline panels in the main body of the paving, which could be made of Wealden rough stocks. The contrast in texture and sharpness between these two bricks is greater than the contrast in colour which, though small, is perceptible.

A joint of ⅜ inch is usual, and in fact essential when a properly bonded pattern is to be laid. I would prefer to see a main area paved with bricks laid flat, that is to say, with the 9-inch by 4½-inch side uppermost, except on very small areas where brick on edge would be more in scale. Bricks on edge also make good borders to beds and gravel paths, and are most effective when laid as a 9-inch-deep band.

Paving bricks—or paviors as they are called—are designed mainly for use on factory floors where resistance to strong solutions is necessary. In the course of manufacture they are subjected to a double pressing which gives them a smooth face, so that when intended for walking over they are made in panelled or chequered designs to provide a non-slip surface. Plain ones are not, therefore, very suitable for general paving on garden terraces, although they have been used effectively to give an interesting contrast in texture with the rougher bricks, as, for instance, when laid as banding or to outline panels.

Quarry tiles also have a smooth-looking surface and are intended for the same purposes as paving bricks. In the garden they are more useful for verandah or loggia floors. They are obtainable in blue and heather mixture colours, and can be interesting when laid with wide joints of up to an inch and pointed with black-, white- or cream-coloured mortar, to emphasise the pattern of the paving. A part of the floor of Coventry Cathedral is paved with blue hexagonal quarry tiles.

CHAPTER IV

Terrace Lawns

The living green of a grass lawn is a good counterpart to the static hardness of a building. Indeed, a new house will often seem to come to life only after the turf has been put down. As has been suggested in an earlier chapter, panels of grass in the stone or brick will generally give a better balance than an entirely grass-covered terrace. These areas of grass are generally so small that the extra cost of laying a clinker foundation (see Chapter XVIII) will not be great. With such a drainage layer the turf will become firm and dry quickly, so that the little lawn can be used for sun-bathing soon after a shower of rain. The free drainage will make it necessary for the grass to be watered often in dry summer weather, but as it is immediately outside the house, and as a tap and a length of hose will be needed to water the flower beds and tubs on the terrace, this will not be an onerous commitment.

The turf should stand an inch above the paving of the terrace so that the mower can be used to the extreme outside without being damaged on the stone. Narrow steel bands (see Chapter XVIII) can be fixed round the outside, $\frac{3}{4}$ inch above the paving to contain the turf, as in quadrangles and courts at Oxford and Cambridge. With these the turf always has a firm edge and will not recede as it otherwise inevitably will under regular trimming with an edging iron.

Laying turf will give a quick result and eliminate many of the anxieties that a freshly seeded lawn can arouse, provided that good inland turf with a high proportion of Fescue and Browntop grasses can be found. The least desirable of all is Cumberland or Sea Marsh turf. Bowlers will go to immense trouble, always in the end unsuccessful, to maintain the character of this turf, which they choose, partly because of its undoubtedly fine-textured grasses, but also because the close-packed, silty nature of the soil in which the grasses grow makes it possible for the turves to be cut from the marsh with uniformity, and to be trimmed and laid on the green with a high degree of accuracy. Although some of its weeds are charming, its grave disadvantage is that under conditions of rolling and close mowing, the silt becomes even more compacted and the vigour of the grasses reduced to such a degree that the turf is attacked by fungus diseases and invaded by volunteer grasses and weeds from outside.

All in all, and if there is a little store of patience, the best lawn will be made from seed (see Chapter XVIII) sown in August after a month of fallowing to allow the seeds of coarse grasses and unwanted weeds to germinate and the resulting plants to be removed.

I suppose that weeds in lawns began to get on our nerves as a nation when we started to take ball games in deadly earnest and allowed them to undermine our sense of humour and our sense of proportion. The tireless aim of the pilgrim of the perfect lawn is to achieve a universal blank by sowing a mixture of Fescue and Browntop grasses in the proportions he learned at his grandfather's knee at Bingley. To preserve these areas inviolate, money and precious time is spent on the invention of poisonous sprays to kill some of the most engaging plants of the garden, the wayside and field.

Elsewhere in the garden we have the opportunity to admire '. . . dappled things . . . things counter, original, spare, strange'— patches of lichen on granite walls, sky-reflecting puddles on paving after rain and fallen blossom on the grass. It is only on the lawn that monotony is *de rigueur*. I would like to make the grass a background to a tapestry of congenial weeds. In the wider lawns beyond the terrace there would be room for constellations of daisies, for hawkweed like shoals of starfish stretching to the ha-ha, and woodrush looking as if it had stolen out of the wood unseen. But in the small lawn near the house I would have only these: self-heal with its mauve-blue flowers and dusky foliage like the shadows of clouds, yellow suckling clover (with the endearing Latin name of *Trifolium dubium*) weaving its network of golden threads through the grass, pearlwort in random pools of parsley green with *gros point* of recondite pearls, and moss pervading all to make a carpet fit for poets' feet to tread.

CHAPTER V

Fountains and Pools

A fountain on the terrace can be a source of cool delight on summer days. It can also be one of the visual masses to be disposed about the terrace in the same way as panels of grass and flower beds. Pools on the terrace will be small, and should always be formal in shape by contrast with those out in the garden and away from the immediate influence of the house, where they may be like small lakes, irregular in outline with grass sloping gently to the water's edge, sufficiently wide and deep to hold the largest-flowered water-lilies and where rushes and waterside irises, with their sharp, upright foliage standing above the level of the banks, may fit well into the immediate surroundings.

In deciding the position of a pool on the terrace it will be wise not to put it immediately in front of the door from the house into the garden. This area should be kept clear as a general gathering ground. There is a natural inclination on coming out of the house to walk straight ahead to look into the garden and it is frustrating to have to dodge and mince round obstacles, whether pools or flower pots, to reach the other side. It is better to have a rectangular pool fitting comfortably into one end of the terrace or a round one half-way between the corner of the house and the end of the terrace, provided always that the pool is placed to receive direct sunlight. A fountain playing, scintillating, throwing off rainbow hazes in the sun, is a miracle, going back to the gardens of Persia, to the Arab patios and the great Moghul gardens of India and Kashmir; but when deprived of its essential partner, the sun, a terrace fountain becomes dank and meaningless in the day-time, although on fine evenings it will glitter palely in the light of the moon or in the fainter beams of candle flames in glasses on the remote verandah.

A pool on a terrace must have a raised coping to act as a warning fender at night, and because without it, when the water level is below the paving on the terrace the pool will simply look like a hole in the paving. The coping can be a fairly substantial moulding of stone or marble, in which case the water should come well up inside, above the paving level but not to the very top, so that there are a few inches of clear rim inside. The effect of a much higher coping can be obtained if the whole pool is raised 2 feet or so above the level of the terrace. Round pools made in this way look particularly well when made of brick, lined with cement rendering, and finished off on top with a coping of double bull-nosed bricks which make a comfortable seat from which to observe pond life at close quarters.

Where the pool is to hold water-lilies, or fish, or both, there are two factors to be taken into account. The first is that the depth of water required by different water-lilies varies from 6 inches to 3 feet or more and that generally those with the largest flowers need the deepest water. The second factor is that in order to survive through the winter fish need a minimum depth of from 18 inches to 2 feet. Thus, in medium-sized pools, in the interests of their co-existence, it may be necessary to accept, within reason, some of the stronger-growing water-lilies, with flowers larger than would have been chosen in the interests of perfect scale. In the smaller pools it may be impossible to combine the two without ending up with a surrealist spectacle of enormous flowers squatting like complacent chamber pots on the water, intimidating the little pool and much of the terrace.

For a small pool I would choose first, white water-lilies for their pale radiance in the dusk, and if the pool were large enough, one or two pink ones also. The following lists will meet most requirements. For 2 feet of water: *Nymphaea* Marliacea albida, white, or Hermine, also white but its flowers tend to stick up 3 or 4 inches above the water:; *N*. Somptuosa, pink; James Brydon, red; and *N*. Marliacea chromatella, yellow. The flowers are generally not more than 6 inches across; each plant when established will take up a space 3 feet in diameter. For an intermediate depth of from 1 to $1\frac{1}{2}$ feet, in which it might just be possible to have some fish:

N. odorata alba, white; *N. odorata turicensis*, pink; Froebeli, red; and *N. odorata sulphurea*, yellow. The flowers of these will not generally exceed 4 inches in diameter: each plant when established will take up a space 2 feet in diameter. For the shallowest depth from 6 inches to 12 inches: *N. pygmaea alba*, white; Pink Opal, pink; *N.* Laydekeri purpurata, red; and *N. pygmaea helvola*, sulphur-yellow.

Water-lilies will establish themselves and grow more quickly if a layer of loam 8 inches deep is spread on the bottom of the pool. After planting—which is done at the end of April or in May—a layer of cobbles spread on the soil between the plants will reduce the amount of clay and silt in suspension which might clog the strainer of a circulation pump. After initial planting, the level of the water should be brought up slowly over several weeks as the plants extend in height.

Water-lilies can also be planted in wire baskets, old tubs or polythene crates, which are lowered through the water on to the floor of the pool. These have the advantage that water-lilies needing different depths can be grown in the same pool; for instance, the pool could be made 3 feet deep, which is enough for the largest water-lilies, and the crates of those requiring a lower depth rested on bricks or piles of stones. But the appearance of these crates or wire baskets seen through the water is not attractive, the rate of growth will not be so fast, and water-lilies in crates have to be lifted and divided every three years to prevent them overcrowding their containers.

The sword-like foliage of rushes and irises is out of place in pools on the terrace. There should be no plants rising much above water level to compete with the vertical principle of the single jet of the fountain, which will compose best in isolation with the floating water-lily pads and flowers. Some oxygenating plants will be essential. Submerged plants not only give off oxygen but provide a sheltering underwater jungle for the fish, who also lay their eggs on the leaves. Submerged plants also help to keep down algae by shading the water beneath them and depriving the algae of mineral salts dissolved in the water. *Hottonia palustris*, the Water Violet, is an oxygenating plant whose leaves float on the water and whose fragrant violet flowers rise only a few inches above. *Callitriche autumnalis* is valuable because its oxygenating activity is carried on even in the winter and also because the fish eat the leaves. Other

3. The contrasted precast and *in situ* concrete paving and cobbles provide an interesting
floor. Concrete plant containers can be made deeper by the addition of extra rings. This
garden was designed by Sylvia Crowe, P.P.I.L.A.

4. The arbutus tree on the terrace near the Orangery at Ditchley Park, Oxfordshire. This
garden was designed by G. A. Jellicoe, C.B.E., F.R.I.B.A., M.T.P.I., P.P.I.L.A.

15. The long-established large trees give good patterned shade to this terrace-deck made of redwood at Woodside, California. It was designed by Thomas D. Church, San Francisco

16. A small courtyard behind the Rye Galleries in High Street, Eton. The photograph was taken by courtesy of the owner, Mr C. H. Spencer, and shows a great amount of detail and interest in a small space

good oxygenating plants are: *Fontinalis antipyretica*, *Myriophyllum spicatum* and *Tillaea recurva*.

Two or three dozen Ramshorn snails will be useful scavengers. Where there is a layer of soil on the bottom of the pool water mussels can also be introduced. They will not survive without this, or if cobbles have been laid over the soil. The Zebra Mussel, *Dreissena polymorpha*, is said to be the most suitable because its larvae do not attach themselves to young fish.

In addition to the common gold-fish, the fish population can include some Shubunkins. These are similar in size and shape to gold-fish but their scales are transparent so that they appear to be scaleless; young fish develop their colour within a few weeks of hatching. They can be had in a selection of colours, red, yellow, brown and blue which, with the rarer mauve, apparently make the most appeal to fanciers. I would also certainly include some Golden Orfe. These are slender, active fish swimming near the surface in shoals and in the summer rising to flies. They are better suited to the larger pools which give room for their active swimming. I would not choose the grotesquerie of the fish world, the fancy Comet Longtails, Veiltails or squinting Celestials.

A guide as to the number of fish that a pool will hold is given by calculating on one fish 6 inches long to 2 square feet of water as the absolute maximum. This would mean that a pool measuring 6 feet by 10 feet would hold up to 30 fish, but in practice 12 would be found to be a good number.

In Chapter XXI guidance will be found on how to make a pool and what action is necessary to prepare it before fish and plants are introduced. The plants should be put in at least a fortnight before the fish and even then it will probably be necessary to feed the fish for another fortnight or so with shredded shrimps, dried daphnia, dried flies, or one of the proprietary fish foods. No more food should be given than will be taken by the fish within a few minutes, otherwise it will decompose and pollute the water.

When first stocked, the water in the pool will be turbid, but after a time, which may vary from two to six weeks, a state of balance should be reached. The flat water-lily pads shade the water and keep down the growth of algae. The oxygenating plants and the scavenging molluscs will be carrying out their functions regularly, the fish will be eating mosquito larvae and the water will then become transparent, although porter-coloured. If it is changed this state of equilibrium will never be reached; it is important, therefore, that this should not be done or fresh water added except to make up for loss by evaporation. It is unnecessary to clean out the pool until after a number of years an accumulation of dead leaves is built up in the bottom. When this happens the water will become toxic and the pool will have to be emptied, dug out, and refilled with fresh loam.

Neither water-lilies nor fish will succeed well in a pool with a vigorous fountain constantly working, but their welfare will not be greatly interfered with by a small single jet working only intermittently, preferably with its fall tempered through a succession of saucers or falling into a fibre-glass bowl, fixed to appear as if it were floating on the surface of the pool, with the water running back into the pool over the sides.

In any case it is not the huge cascading fountains of Italy that we are in search of here but rather the small pensive fountains of Arab Spain, seen at their simplest in the Lotus Fountain in the Generalife at Granada, or the small three-tier fountain in the Cathedral Patio at Seville. In both of these a single jet of no great height is used. For our purposes (see Chapter XIX) a height of 6 feet or less, controllable by a valve in the delivery line, will be all that is needed, but the thickness of the upward stream should be significant, not the thready trickle of the Mannekin-Pis, but a firm pillar of water at least $\frac{5}{8}$ inch thick, going up in one piece and falling off the top.

If the output of the pump is not enough to work a full $\frac{5}{8}$-inch jet, a fair substitute can be obtained by using a jet consisting of six small nozzles round a central nozzle, which gives very much the impression of a solid stream. Thin streams may be unavoidable if there are fish and water-lilies in the pool, but these again are best when single jets; the rose-like sprays, making transparent outlines in the shapes of Prince of Wales's Feathers, or peacocks' tails, are vague and unconvincing. I was interested to see some of Mr Colin Allsebrook's experiments: in one the water is given a swirling movement as it enters the lower end of a wide perspex tube about 2 feet long, so that it emerges from the top as a thin descending veil shaped like a shining dome. In another, which he calls a Spinning Lariat, four jets spinning slowly from a central hub weave spell-bound figures of eight, and he, as he calls it 'sculptures water' to make petalled flowers and to produce turbulent surfaces as if springs were bubbling from the floor of the pool.

Pools intended only as fountain basins, that is, without fish or water-lilies, need only be a foot or so deep. The water can be kept clear and even a little blue by the addition of copper sulphate. These basins may be so small that it would be possible to contemplate making them in precious materials, perhaps with a raised marble coping and a lining of glass mosaic. Smaller effects than a single jet can also provide interest. The illustration facing page 93 shows three low cylinders of exposed aggregate each with water slowly bubbling from its centre. Mr Denis Tegetmeier once carved for me a grotesque stone mask which was set face upwards, and arranged for water to bubble softly from its mouth and course over the furrowed cheeks to disappear and be lost among surrounding cobbles.

CHAPTER VI

On Planting in General

Planting is the indispensable quickening element in gardens. It is like charity, 'the very bond of peace and of all virtues', without which our terraces and tinkling fountains are nothing.

Besides a knowledge of plants and flowers, it needs a sense of scale, a mature understanding of colour, deep reserves of patience, and a degree of idosyncrasy, amounting sometimes to prejudice, ready to break rules on occasion when doing so does not lead to anarchy.

A sense of scale is concerned with the outline or habit of the plant and with the shape and size of its leaves and flowers. The broad leaves and large flowers of the evergreen magnolia may compose perfectly with the garden front of a large house, where the thin, needle-like leaves and small flowers of winter jasmine would be overpowered; but, on the other hand, the relative situations would be reversed on the porch of a small cottage. Similarly, an acacia tree 50 feet high on a wide terrace might accord well with the same large house, while it would not only be too big, but also look too refined in proximity to the unassuming cottage, where a thorn or a rowan would be happily at home. The importance of the size of flowers was borne in on me when, in need of a red colour and influenced by the description in a catalogue, I bought five or six *Heucherella* Bridget Bloom and planted them alongside a group of *Geranium grandiflorum*. The attempted partnership was not just a failure—it was a howler of the first magnitude. The small, pin-headed, brick-red flowers of the unhappy heucherella entirely failed to stand up to the scale of the much larger-flowered, broad-leaved geranium.

Foliage is to be taken into account in its own right. In fact, considerations of scale are more involved with foliage than with flowers, if only because there is relatively more of it and it is in evidence for a longer time. Plants such as senecio, phlomis, rue and santolina are used primarily for their leaves; it happens that the first two have agreeable flowers while those of the last two are better snipped off. Combinations of foliage alone are longer lasting than flower colour schemes; for example, a brown contour of purple sage growing into a wider group of blue rue, both of them against a background of the strange dark green of *Euphorbia wulfenii* and the spiky bluish grass, *Elymus glaucus*. A good foliage-flower combination is made of the feathery, silver leaves and pale yellow flowers of *Achillea clypeolata* with the dark purple-brown bracts and navy blue flowers of *Salvia superba* and the broad, solid foliage and crimson-scarlet flowers of *Monarda* Cambridge Scarlet. Where a contoured mass of foliage threatens to become monotonous, sharp upward-piercing iris blades will give astringent relief.

A mature appreciation of colour is needed to avoid the misunderstanding and mistrust with which the subject is beset. It is misunderstood by those who tend to value it in isolation and in terms of quantity rather than for its quality in a given context. This attitude is encouraged by gaudy seed and plant catalogues, and by insensitive polychromatic planting in exhibition gardens at large flower shows. It is not discouraged by much of the popular gardening press which would do more to educate its readers if once in a while it could bring itself to say something harsh about the more outrageous of the new plants—double petunias, for instance—and allow overworked words like colourful and ideal to lapse into unlamented desuetude. Naturally enough this naïve appetite for colour *per se* has excited mistrust in others, those who, under the influence of the agnostic pessimism of our time, are defensively suspicious of exuberance and enthusiasm.

The truth, I think, is that colour is precious, something to be treated not with familiarity or contempt but with love, almost with awe. Soft colours will be used to blend with foliage to liven a background without taking an assertive part, bright colours will be hoarded and used in small but intense concentrations in pots and vases standing on the paving, or as punctuation points in a lower-toned assembly of plants in beds. Wherever and however it is used it must be clear-cut and definite, in recognisable groups of a reasonable size, seldom in isolated plants. Except for polyanthus, mixed colours are almost always to be avoided. I never buy mixed tulips, pansies, stocks or anything else; I like to think that in my garden any mixing that is to be done will be done by me.

Patience in gardening can have at least two meanings. In one it is a resigned 'philosophic' acceptance of misfortune, as when late frost kills the heliotropes that have been put out optimistically a week too early, when sparrows tweak the crocus flowers, or wood pigeons take the winter aconite corms. In another it is a willingness to wait, to come to terms with a biological time-scale which the advent of container-grown plants has not significantly altered. There are, of course, great advantages in buying plants in containers provided that they are well established in their pots or polythene bags, and are properly watered and cared for in the first months after planting. They may be a little more expensive than plants from the open ground, but they are often larger and bushier. They can be bought and put into a garden at any time of the year, even when in full flower and, once taken home, can await the purchaser's convenience before being planted. But even container-grown small shrubs, such as potentillas and senecios, are unlikely to carry much weight in the first year or two after planting.

And it still takes a line of little beech saplings, whether container-grown or not, all of seven years to make a stout 6-foot hedge. A magnolia may take ten years to reach the eaves of a two-storey house and perhaps another ten to flower regularly. It may also take ten years for a robinia planted at 9–10 feet and costing about two guineas to reach 20 feet. It is true that it is possible to buy a semi-mature robinia at 20 feet and have it planted by experts for £50 or more, but at such high prices trees of this size are unlikely to be within the financial reach of many owners of private gardens with moderate terraces.

In these days such extended intervals of time at once provoke the question, 'Is it worth it?' The answer, of course, depends on how much you want it because, except for the expensive semi-mature trees, there are few real short cuts, and to rely only on annual flowers or herbaceous plants and roses, which reach maturity in the first year after planting, is like being content to play the piano with the right hand alone. If the discipline of patience cannot be accepted, it is better to give up at once any attempt at gardening, to save the few shillings that might have been spent on half-hearted scarlet salvias, and to spend them instead on weed-killers to keep the place respectable.

Planting is a continuing education that is never done. What will have begun as a catholic appreciation will become narrower through increasing critical observation, selection and, even more important, rejection. One of the hardest, but most necessary, lessons to be learnt is when to discard, and to do it ruthlessly. In time a sort of personal style is built up out of preference and prejudice and an increasing faculty of being able to see the bone under the flesh, to penetrate to the essential character of the plant, a character which depends more on outline and habit of growth than on the flowers.

Some plants are immediately recognisable as unquestioned aristo-crats. Magnolias, perhaps, are mandarins, and the arbutus comes from a long line of High Kings, but it takes experience to perceive that the Winter Sweet, in its sober summer dress, is a prince in disguise. It would be a boring, lifeless garden if it were confined to a socially approved list of 'U' plants, without some solid yeoman stiffening of thorns and whitebeams, together with the humbler creation, carpeting bugle and dead-nettle and thyme. But there is one layer of society for which there should be no room, the lurid *demi-monde* of scarlet salvias and dahlias and what a sardonic friend once called 'stockbrokers' teas', meaning the more brassy hybrid tea roses of that time—a collection into which he would now sternly commit many of the floribundas of today.

The serious gardener will derive interest and benefit from keep-ing a commonplace book, not a small diary—useful though this is for its information on when to sow biennials and how to prune shrubs—with its bare inch or so of writing space for each day of the year. What is wanted is a thick quarto exercise book, so that when necessary whole pages or indeed many pages can be given to observations on the performance of plants, the success or failure of groupings, notes made at flower shows, at trial grounds or in other people's gardens, for it is better to choose plants from ob-servation, than from nurserymen's and seedsmen's catalogues or from articles in the gardening papers.

A visit once a month, if possible, to botanic gardens such as Kew, Edinburgh, Cambridge, Oxford, or to the Royal Horticultural Society's gardens at Wisley where plants are seen growing, if not entirely naturally, at least life size, will be better than visits to flower shows where plants are seen as on a stage, larger than life. Daffodils and tulips can be seen at growers' trial grounds, and tulips in any number of combinations at the Birmingham Tulip Festival. The spring-flowering biennial plants, or those treated as biennials, are not so easily seen. The gardener is too often dependent on his nearest garden centre or the local nurseryman, who may have taken the trouble to visit trial grounds in the previous season, but more probably has not found the time to do this and has got into the habit of buying the same seeds each year. Whenever there is room in the garden it will be worth raising one's own spring biennials—forget-me-nots, wallflowers and early stocks. Observation and trial will not only keep the gardener abreast of new developments but enable him to test the value of the newest introductions and compare them with the older ones.

In the following pages suggestions are made for planting in all the possible positions in which planting can be used on the terrace. In practice it will be seldom that all these positions exist in any single terrace—a bed against the house, beds against wing walls on either side, a bed at the farthest edge under the parapet wall, and even an isolated panel bed in the paving—nor is it likely that there will be room against the walls for all the climbers referred to; in fact, many of the plants recommended for one bed can very well be used in others.

CHAPTER VII

Planting the Bed against the House

The bed against the south wall of the house will be close to those living inside, it is also the easiest to look after, so that it should be the place for favourite plants that may need special care, and above all for plants with scented flowers and scented leaves.

In planting a new terrace the first plants to be put in will be climbers against the house. Unless the architecture is of such perfect proportion that it must remain immaculate, climbing plants will make a figure against the walls and may even redeem an undistinguished building. It will be easier to train them in future years if, before planting, wires are fixed to the walls. The first wire can be 4 feet above ground and upper rows fixed at intervals of 2 feet 6 inches.

On a moderate-sized or large house, and where unrestricted cover is accepted, the first choice would be the evergreen *Magnolia grandiflora*. This outstandingly handsome tree is a native of the southern United States where, as in the South of France and Italy, it is generally seen growing free standing. It was introduced into Britain early in the eighteenth century and here is nearly always seen growing against a house wall, where it will reach a height of 30 feet or more, being trained round the windows and up to the eaves. It has large, shining, laurel-like leaves, in some varieties felted with brown on the back, and very large, creamy-white flowers with a strong, but refreshing, lemon scent. If these flowers are picked and floated in a bowl a whole room will be scented. Once established it will grow reasonably quickly, but some varieties may not produce flowers until the plant begins to approach maturity, which may take twenty years. The varieties Exmouth and Goliath generally produce flowers at an earlier age.

The common wisteria of China, *Wisteria sinensis*, makes a dense foliage cover. Once established, and if planted in a well-prepared position with a liberal quantity of manure below the roots, and if never allowed to get dry in the summer, it will grow rapidly. It has large, pinnate leaves and mauve or deep lilac-coloured, scented flowers in long racemes opening in May. Old plants are familiar sights, having been planted many years ago at the corner of a house wall and by now trained all along the garden front, probably with one long branch close under the eaves, informing the character of the house, festooning from window sills and giving shelter to returning generations of spotted fly catchers. *Wisteria floribunda* '*Macrobotrys*' of Japan, generally known as *multijuga*, has blue-lilac flowers in racemes as long as 3 feet; there are white and pink forms, although I prefer the characteristic, lilac-heliotrope colour.

Where a less enveloping climber is needed, the figured pattern of a climbing rose may pay a delicate compliment to the house. For the warmest corner I would choose *Rosa × anemonoides* (*R. sinica* Anemone), which has large, single flowers nearly 3 inches across, pale pink, often with blotches of darker pink at the edges, and sometimes produced as early as April. The leaves are long and shining, almost evergreen. It is a tender plant but in the south of Britain, and certainly in the West, when planted in a warm position it will survive through most winters. Rather more tender is the double yellow Banksian rose which at the end of March pours like golden rain on the hillside banks in the gardens at La Mortola, and which is worth taking a risk with in the south and west of Britain; its small, pale yellow flowers are seen at their best in the angle of a tall stone house.

Among entirely hardy climbing roses for south walls I would recommend the following:

Madame Alfred Carrière, a climbing noisette, which will also flourish on a north wall. The double white flowers are faintly flushed and have a fragrant tea scent. It generally grows vigorously with ample foliage.

The climbing hybrid tea Ophelia. Its rather small flowers, smelling of honey, are the colour of mother of pearl, with high-centred, sensuous buds.

Ena Harkness, another climbing hybrid tea, and for me the authentic 'red, red, rose', a lambent, passionate, deep crimson with a high-pointed, voluptuous centre.

Gloire de Dijon, a tea rose introduced as long ago as 1850 in France and still a fine climber. It looks well against stone walls. It will flourish on east and northern aspects. The large, flattish flowers are buff-coloured, sometimes flecked with touches of rose, and strongly tea-scented.

Lady Hillingdon, another climbing tea, has yellow flowers suffused with apricot, said to smell of peaches. The fine, deep red young foliage is attractive. It will climb high and its rather drooping flowers are best when seen from below.

Emily Gray, a rambler, produces blossoms only once in the summer, but it is a fine climbing rose with deep gold, semi-double flowers and shining, evergreen-looking foliage.

Mermaid, a hybrid between *R. bracteata* and a yellow tea rose. The single, pale gold flowers, unfortunately not scented, are as large as 5 or 6 inches across, with golden anthers. It has shining, dark green foliage which persists well into the winter. It is the best of all the yellow roses and, while best on a south or south-western aspect, it will also grow well on a north or east wall. It will flower from June to October. In Cornwall I have seen flowers on New Year's day.

Zéphirine Drouhin, an old Bourbon rose, is more suitable for training on a trellis or the front supports of a verandah than against a wall of the house. It is the true thornless rose, has medium-sized flat, lightly scented flowers, semi-double, and a bright carmine-pink. It is not so continuous-flowering as many of the others.

Clematis montana rubens, extremely rapid growing and with small, palest pink flowers which it carries with great profusion in May, is better suited to a trellis or arch over a gate than to a flat wall; but the large, three-lobed, pointed leaves of *C. armandii* (which is unusual in that it is an evergreen clematis) can be of value against the house all the winter. The type has creamy-white flowers in April; the variety Apple Blossom has pale pink flowers. This clematis has a tendency to make all its leaf and flower at the top, but this can be countered by training the new shoots outwards as soon as they have made significant growth.

The variety Lasurstern has very large, lavender-blue flowers with cream stamens which appear at the end of May and in early June and often again in September. Ville de Lyon bears large bright carmine-red flowers in late summer; and the best clematis for the evening, Henryi, has very large, pure white flowers at mid-summer with sometimes another crop of flowers in the autumn.

The Passion Flower is a clematis-like plant. The large flowers have a blue centre and creamy-white sepals. According to Bean,[1] '. . . the name of "passion flower" by which this and all the passi-floras are known, was given originally by the Spanish priests in South America because of the resemblance their piety led them to detect between the various parts of the flower and the instruments of Christ's Passion. . . . The three stigmas represent the three nails, two for the hands and one for the feet; the five anthers represent the five wounds; the corona represents the crown of thorns or the halo of glory; the five sepals and five petals stand for ten apostles —Peter and Judas being absent; the hand-like leaves and whip-like tendrils represent the hands and scourges of His persecutors.'

Vines are best suited to pergolas, but can be grown against a house wall with support. *Vitis coignetiae* has very large, shield-shaped leaves turning to burning copper in the autumn.

Parthenocissus henryana is self-clinging and will proceed up the wall of a house under its own arrangements. Its leaves, smaller than those of *V. coignetiae*, are edged and veined with silvery-pink. A useful display can be made by building a light wooden frame out from the house to support vines or other climbers. Some of the outdoor grape vines can be grown over such a structure. Those from which wine can be made after hot summers are Golden Chasselas (also known as Royal Muscadine) and Madeleine Royale, which are usually reliable white grapes, and Pirovano 14, a heavy-cropping black grape.

There is a number of moderately tall-growing shrubs which can be put in against the walls of the house between the climbers. *Lippia citriodora*, the Lemon Verbena, is the best of all the scented-leaved plants. Its place is at the side of the door from the house into the garden, so that a leaf can be picked and pinched and

[1] *Trees and Shrubs Hardy in the British Isles*—W. J. Bean—John Murray.

sniffed at, on entering or leaving the house. The very fragrant leaves are long and lance-shaped. The small, pale purple flowers are by some standards insignificant, but they have none the less a particular elegance when they appear in July and August. Lemon Verbena grows rapidly when established and plants that have survived two or three winters may well reach 10 feet. It is tender, and although it may survive without protection in a mild winter, it is more likely in an average season to be cut down and killed by frost, so it must be protected by such means as building round it a tent of hessian supported on light stakes pushed into the ground and secured at the top to one of the training wires on the wall. An armful of bracken or straw can be packed into this tent and built up round the roots. These protective measures must be taken in good time, certainly before Christmas and preferably at the end of November. I have found that the deciduous leaves fall inside the tent and can be scooped out about Christmas-time. When these are put into a bowl and gently agitated they release all the lemon sweetness that they had through the summer.

Chimonanthus praecox, the Winter Sweet, is an apparently undistinguished deciduous plant with rather large, downward-pointing lanceolate leaves, but for a few weeks at midwinter its bare branches are starred with small, goblin-yellow flowers which give out a smell so sweet and strong that a spray picked and taken indoors will scent the whole house for the twelve days of Christmas.

Choisya ternata, the Mexican Orange Blossom, is a useful evergreen to make a solid mass against the house wall. The leaves, arranged in three leaflets, are dark green, perhaps a little thin in substance, with a smell, when crushed, of rubbery bay. The white, star-like flowers are borne in May and have the scent of orange blossom.

On the other side of the door from the house I would plant a bush of rosemary, either the Corsican kind with its porcelain blue flowers, or the prostrate Spanish rosemary, to spill across the edge of the step and on to the paving. Strictly, I suppose, the small flowers and the rather needle-like foliage will be out of scale with the solid mass of a large house, but the best gardeners will have a set of Private Rules, with escape clauses to provide for this—and who would feel fitted to make the perambulation of his garden without a sprig of rosemary to inform his progress?

Lavender, like rosemary, comes from the Mediterranean region and, also being 'evergrey', will preserve a kind of skeleton of design in the border in winter when the flowers and the bees have departed. The very grey-foliaged Dutch lavender is a rather large plant developing a spread of from 3 to 4 feet and seen at its best in a wide bed where it can sprawl forward on to the paving. In more restricted situations the Hidcote lavender, with its deep purple flowers and a spread of only 1 to 1½ feet, will be a better choice.

Planting cistuses is taking a calculated risk because, although they will often come safely through an ordinary winter, they can be wiped out by a very hard one; but the gardener's life would be dreary indeed if he played for safety all the time, and as this bed which we are now considering is the kindliest in the whole garden I would try to make room for some of these plants, whose foliage and buds are resinous and give off the scent of incense in days of shimmering heat. The flowers of *C. laurifolius* are unremarkable, but the massive solidity of its upright, gaunt habit and the dull, leaden-looking leaves are a splendid foil for other planting. *C. ladaniferus* has much larger, white flowers with a maroon blob at the base of the petals. Its stems glisten with aromatic gum. *C. cyprius* has large white flowers blotched with deep red at the base of each petal. The leaves are olive green, turning darker in the autumn. *C.* × *corbariensis* is a lower, more spreading plant with a crowd of small, white, single flowers.

Salvia hispanica (*S. lavandulifolia*) is another useful plant from the Mediterranean, lower growing and good for the front edge because it soon becomes procumbent and will grow outwards over the paving. Its leaves are greyish-green, like those of the kitchen sage but narrower, and when crushed smell of a mixture of lavender and sage. It is worth growing for the flowers alone, which are pale lilac and come out in June. *S. grahamii* from Mexico is another half-hardy evergreen shrub which may survive in mild winters and is more likely to do so if protected in the same way as the Lemon Verbena. It grows up to 4 feet. In one hot summer in my garden in Berkshire, Humming Bird Hawk Moths used to visit the flowers, which are bright scarlet, turning to magenta as they grow older; they are most delicately poised above the light, apple-green foliage, the balance between flower and leaf being beautifully proportioned. When crushed the leaves have a foxy-black currant smell, not always approved by refined natures but stimulating and encouraging to those of coarser fibre.

At the front edge there could be a few colonies of *Thymus serpyllum*, the fragrant, prostrate, mat-forming Wild Thyme, with minute, purplish-rose-coloured flowers in tiny inflorescences, to creep over the sun-baked paving, irresistibly drawing the bees.

Some or all of these shrubs will give this bed under the house a skeleton and a ground base of fragrant foliage against which and amongst which the patterns of colour and foliage texture are to be disposed; but before considering seasonal planting there are some bulbous plants to be put at the back as close to the wall as can be managed. *Iris unguicularis*, once known as *I. stylosa*, is little more than a foot high and must therefore be planted where there will be an open space in front of it in the winter, for it is in mid-winter that it produces its large, strongly scented, sky-blue flowers with yellow markings. It demands a poor, gritty soil.

Nerine bowdenii is the hardiest of the nerines. Its lily-like flowers are pale pink, with a deeper-coloured line in the middle of each segment, and appear in the autumn before the strap-shaped leaves. A rather coarser plant, taller and with less delicate flowers, is *Amaryllis belladonna*, the Belladonna Lily, which, like the nerines, comes from South Africa. The flowers range in colour from deep pink to white, and are scented. There is a coloured illustration of *A. belladonna* and *N. bowdenii* on the same plate in the *Oxford Book of Garden Flowers*, and they are also illustrated in A. G. L. Hellyer's *Flowers in Colour*. Both of these plants need a position against a wall in fullest sun and will flower best after a thorough baking in a hot summer. Mr Synge recommends that if there is no heavy rain Belladonna lilies should be flooded about mid-August to start the flower spikes into growth, provided that they have been well baked in the summer.[1]

The plants so far mentioned could complete the permanent planting, which should take up about half the space, leaving the rest for seasonal flowers which can and should be varied from year to year, being subject to continual experiment and change, but always with the quality of scent most in mind.

Of all the spring flowers that can be used in this bed, wall-flowers will be thought of first: Bacon wrote of them '. . . they are very delightful to be set under a parlour or lower chamber window'. Against brick walls of a dull red colour I would choose strains with similar tones—Blood Red, the colour of venous blood; Ellen

[1] *Collins Guide to Bulbs*—Patrick M. Synge—Collins.

Willmott, ruby-red; Harbinger, mahogany-brown, and Vulcan, to me the essential wallflower, with larger flowers than many others, of a glowing crimson-brown which lasts all the time the plants are in flower. The best for white walls are full yellows and oranges such as Cranford Beauty and Orange Bedder, although when I last saw this on trial grounds the flowers had taken on a variegated appearance as they began to age. Also Fire King and Scarlet Emperor, towards whose blazing colours one instinctively stretches one's hands on a day of east wind. The primrose or sulphur-yellow colours, such as Primrose Monarch, look well against stone walls. Phoenix, a rich chestnut brown or blood red, and Yellow Phoenix, bloom three weeks before the ordinary kinds, as do earlier-flowering strains of Primrose, Orange, Fire King and Vulcan. I can find no place for the pink wallflowers now being developed; they do not register with me as wallflowers, the colour seems effete, with none of the charm of the older ones. I think that the Persian Carpet mixture is also unfortunate.

The best-known Siberian wallflower, *Cheiranthus × allionii*, is an uncompromising hot orange, useful to give vitality, particularly with blue; there is also a more companionable variety, Apricot Delight. Both flower later than ordinary wallflowers. When they have finished flowering they can be replaced by such beautiful and useful half-hardy 'fillers' as *Salvia patens*, and the delicate Marguerite Jamaica Primrose (*Chrysanthemum frutescens*).

Wallflowers belong to the natural order Cruciferae, all of which will grow best in soils with a high lime content, therefore the pricking in of hydrated lime before planting will be beneficial.

In small nurseries seeds of wallflowers are usually sown in the open ground in May and June, pricked out in rows and either given an immediate shift or put directly into their flowering positions in October. They always resent this treatment. A better way is to prick the seedlings into Jiffy pots and to keep them standing in wooden boxes on stone or concrete to prevent them from rooting into the ground beneath, until October when they are planted out pot and all. The Jiffy pots are assimilated into the root balls and there is no check to the plants.

Wallflowers can be damaged or killed by a very hard frost, and it is a worth-while insurance to raise a few extra plants to be kept in cold frames and used to replace any casualties in the spring.

Forget-me-nots give of their best with a west or north-west exposure although in a cool spring they will often do well enough in a south-facing position. Royal Blue, about a foot high, is a good variety for a bed against a house. Blue Ball has deep blue flowers and, being only 6 inches high, is useful for box-edged beds where it is wished to keep the level of colour below the box to prevent a misty cloud of indeterminate blue smudging the design of the beds.

Winter-flowering pansies are shorter in stature but have larger flowers than either wallflowers or forget-me-nots, so that they are best separated a little from them by groups of the permanent evergreens. Winter-flowering pansies with faces are: Ice King, white with a dark eye, and Winter Sun, golden with a dark eye. Others without faces are: Orion, buttercup yellow; Celestial Queen, sky blue; and March Beauty, a deeper blue.

The stiff habit and packed flower spike of the florists' hyacinths make them difficult to amalgamate with the other flowers in the beds, but their scent is compelling enough to override the rules, so that in some years at any rate two or three groups could be planted. For myself I would have one kind only, a pure white, L'Innocence. Other early ones which should flower at the same time in April are Ostara, bright blue, with deeper blue markings, and Lady Derby, shell pink. City of Haarlem is a good primrose-yellow, but the flowers come out rather later than the first three. For planting out of doors smaller bulbs than those used for indoor forcing are sold. These can be lifted after flowering and put into a rescue bed farther away in the garden or in woodland, but they are not likely to be of much account.

Polyanthus are the outstanding exception to the rule against mixed colours. All the colours speak of spring and it is impossible to find an unhappy combination. They result from crosses between primroses and cowslips and have been known in gardens at least as far back as the middle of the seventeenth century. Flowers of the size which we have been used to for so many years are the ones we should look for in preference to some of the new strains with enormous flowers as large as violas.

Polyanthus are happier in cool, half-shaded positions such as north or north-west aspects. To me they are, with daffodils, the essence of spring. I remember two round tubs of mixed polyanthus by a door of the gardener's cottage in a walled garden in Cornwall Only a hundred yards away from the cottage was perhaps the most beautiful magnolia in the world, and even closer great trees of

Rhododendron arboreum were heaving their blood-red trusses of flower into the sky; but what chiefly remains in my memory are those two tubs of polyanthus.

To return to the bed against the house, in some years I like to put in a cottage mix—about equal numbers of wallflowers, yellow or red, forget-me-nots and polyanthus, planted broadly in drifts of one sort but with some degree of interpenetration. Some groups of the lily-flowered tulip, White Triumphator, planted at the back, will add useful height.

When May is half-way through it will be time to take out the wallflowers and forget-me-nots and polyanthus, and to prepare for the summer. When the spaces have been cleared they can be forked through and dressed with a slow-acting organic fertiliser. At the time of planting the soil should be moist and crumbly, not dry and dusty or sodden.

In the summer as much as in the spring, the emphasis on the planting for this bed against the house, is the scent of flower and leaf. At the back against the house wall I would plant two or three groups of tobacco plants. The new Lime Green strain is a newcomer and looks interesting palely loitering in a shady corner in company with euphorbias and hostas, but *Nicotiana alata grandiflora* is the familiar white-flowered plant with flowers opening at night, very strongly scented. This is the one which we look for, not crimson or pink or, worse, a mixture of colours, or even plants with flowers that remain open in the most brilliant sunshine. Tobacco plants are for the cool of the evening when a new and different scent refreshes our senses, when their white flowers glimmer in the dusk and nightingales begin to sing in the distant woods.

The sweet and spicy scent of stocks makes them indispensable for this bed. The rather spire-like outline of the ten-week stocks, with spikes of closely packed flowers like hyacinths, does not amalgamate easily with spreading or pendulous sprays of other plants, but this habit is less marked in the branching Giant Perfection stocks, which grow from 15 to 18 inches, and come mainly in purple and mauve colours, showing the influence of *Matthiola incana*, but there are also pink, white, and yellow forms available. Being crucifers like wallflowers they benefit from a dressing of lime at planting. They can be planted in wedge-shaped groups extending from the front almost to the back of the bed, the white colour being very effective. I myself would be content with a pale scheme of white tobacco plants, lilac heliotrope, white stocks, blue pansies and a fair weight of grey green foliage lit up by the scarlet candle flames of *Salvia grahamii*. If this is thought to lack strength, groups of pink and crimson stocks would give the scheme more body. Like other stocks, the Giant Perfection strain contains a mixture of double and single flowers, the proportion of double flowers having been steadily increased as new strains are developed. In fact, there is already one Danish strain of 100% double stocks. While it is true that the gillyflower clove scent is strongest in the double flowers, I still prefer a good proportion of the older, simpler, single-flowered plants.

Brompton stocks, if sown in the summer and pricked out, can be put into their permanent quarters, in mild districts, by the end of September, so that if they survive the winter they will flower early the following spring. They can be had in shades of white, pink, rose, crimson, mauve and purple. East Lothian, intermediate, or autumn-flowering stocks in the same range of colours and about a foot high, if sown at the end of February, pricked out and put into permanent positions towards the end of June, will flower in July and August, thus having a rather later period of flowering than ten-week or Giant Perfection stocks.

Heliotrope, or Cherry Pie, came to this country from Peru in 1757. It has been treated for many years both as a tender greenhouse shrub and as a summer bedding plant, when it will reach from 1 foot to 1½ feet during a season. The violet or lilac flowers are carried well above the foliage. It has a spreading habit of growth, and as the summer proceeds and the shoots lengthen they will lean down and trespass with the greatest elegance on the paving. I like to use helio-trope as a continuous groundwork all through this bed, a back-ground which holds together in unity the tobacco plants, the stocks, the pansies and all the scented-leaved plants. Its fresh, nutty scent is delicious, particularly in the evening after rain. Marguerite, which has large umbels of dark-blue flowers, can be raised from seed sown in February in mild heat, the seedlings being potted once before being planted out at the end of May, when they will flower until the first frosts. Princess Marina, which has flowers of deep purple, is raised from cuttings taken in August or in the early spring.

Pansies and violas can be planted at the front edge, yellow in front of the Lemon Verbena and blue or purple close to the rosemary. Here I would choose pansies for their familiar and endearing faces. The soft smell, of yellow pansies in particular, reminds me of Sundays at a private school when we picked them from the garden and wore them in the buttonholes of our blazers for chapel. In later years I have admired an early flowering Swiss Giant with a dark maroon face. For blue I would above all others have Ullswater, a violet-coloured flower with a darker purple, almost black face. There are white pansies with faces, but I do not think that where an impression of whiteness is needed pansies are the best flowers to choose. The petals are a little thin in texture and their dark centre reduces the overall effect. Nor do I admire the crimson and wine shades and I find no place for mixed colours, though I have a sneaking affection for the Felix strain with their cheeky cat faces, whiskered on yellow centres.

When there is no predilection for faces there is still a good choice of faceless pansies in separate colours. The sweet-scented Coronation Gold, for instance, is a fine clear yellow, and in the Clear Crystals strain there are good separate colours, white and red, besides yellow, orange, and light and dark blue. Violas are useful where a solid colour is required, particularly white, in an arrangement where colour contrast is a more important consideration than it is in the amiable disarray which we are planning for this bed under the window of the house. In the garden at Donnington (see illustration facing p. 36), which Mr Russell Page designed, he used violas in box-edged beds—Pickering Blue, bright purplish-blue, and Lady Tennyson, white, with a small yellow eye. These, with the familiar Maggie Mott, a pale lavender-blue, do not come true from seed and are raised from cuttings. Good violas which can be grown from seed are Sutton's Large-flowered Campanula Blue, sky blue, with a small yellow eye; Admiration, violet-coloured; and Chantreyland, apricot-yellow. Miniature violas, with flowers only $\frac{1}{2}$ inch in size compared with the normal $2\frac{1}{2}$ inches, can sometimes be used at the edge of small raised beds or in old stone sinks. There are white, yellow, mauve and blue colours and a black one, as dark as Satan, when the sun goes in.

Planted at the very front edge, some patches of Sweet Alyssum (*Lobularia maritima*, syn. *Alyssum maritimum*) will sprawl over the paving. The small, rather grey-white flowers have a strong honey scent on sunny days. I remember it planted as an edging to two long beds of petunias, and how it pervaded an Oxford quadrangle with its contented sweet smell.

Beside the scent of flowers, leaf scent can also be cultivated here. Second only to the Lemon Verbena already referred to is *Origanum microphyllum*. It grows to about a foot high with small, neglible, pinkish flowers. The grey-green foliage gives off a strong, rather sweet lemon scent at the mildest agitation—if the bed is hoed or even after a shower of rain, when the scent is delicious drifting in through bedroom windows on summer mornings.

Several of the scented-leaved pelargoniums can be planted in this bed. Although the flowers are very small and make little contribution to any intended colour scheme, they have a delicate charm with their white or creamy ground and brownish-purple veining. The fragrance of the leaves is released when the foliage is pinched, crushing certain specialised cells and releasing essential oils, geraniol, citral, eucalyptol and many others, which combine in varying proportions to produce the characteristic scents.

Pelargonium denticulatum, the Pheasant's Foot, with rough, dark green, much-cut foliage, is a vigorous grower and may reach as much as 3 feet in height and an equal width by the end of the summer, when it must be lifted before the frosts come, and if possible put into a pot in the greenhouse to take cuttings from and to be cared for all the winter, before being trimmed and put back to fight again another summer out of doors. When pressed the leaves smell of lemon and rose geranium mixed. *P. tomentosum* grows to about 3 feet and has heart-shaped leaves engagingly hairy and friendly, with a strong, rather astringent scent of peppermint. *P. × fragrans*, 1 foot high, is a good plant for the front edge, with its demure habit and soft grey-green leaves smelling of nutmeg with a background of lemon and menthol. This graceful little plant will merge happily with stocks and heliotrope. *P. capitatum* is a true, rose-scented geranium growing to about 3 feet, with lobed, heart-shaped leaves.

Humea elegans is a tender biennial plant with many coral-coloured flowers in a drooping panicle, particularly decorative when grown in a greenhouse and brought into the house in September and October. It is an uncommon plant now, but was once frequently seen on great occasions in large houses, where it was included among the decorations not only for its flowers but for its peculiarly exciting, spicy smell of incense, a smell which was reputed to have aphrodisiac qualities—certainly once encountered and identified its teasing redolence will never again be mistaken. The scent is freely released from the leaves, there is no need to pinch them—indeed, it is possible to get a form of dermatitis from them and it is better not to touch them with bare hands. In our scented bed the plant can be put out in summer at the same time as the scented pelargoniums.

CHAPTER VIII

The Bed facing West

The common fig, *Ficus carica*, which is deciduous, is a good plant for a warm wall. Its deeply divided leaves form a classic outline against light-coloured walls in summer. Brunswick is probably the hardiest, although even this may prove tender in hard winters and get cut by frost, but when this happens it usually rises again from suckers. It is only in the mild parts of the South and West that its fruits will ripen out of doors.

Ceanothus dentatus russellianus would be worth trying on a warm chimney breast. It has small, shiny, evergreen leaves and smoky blue flowers in May and June.

Wall shrubs for this bed would include some of those already mentioned—the taller cistuses; common English or Mitcham lavender, *Lavandula spica*, which will grow to 3 feet or rather more and have an equal sideways spread; the common, floppy rosemary, *Rosmarinus officinalis*, with pale mauve flowers early in the spring and sharply aromatic leaves; towards the front the smaller cistuses, *C. crispus*, 2 to 3 feet, with purple-red flowers, and *C.* × *lusitanicus*, of less height and with white flowers; the Corsican rosemary; and perhaps also small colonies of the shorter lavenders, all from 1 to 2½ feet high, Folgate Blue, Twickel Purple, and the even darker purple Hidcote. If this bed is fairly narrow, perhaps 4 feet or less, this Mediterranean mixture will be enough. It will need little attention in the way of pruning and in a few years the plants will grow together, forming a coherent and aromatic assembly with no room for weeds.

If there is more room on the terrace, a wider bed can be made for the sort of mixed planting which has superseded the older, purely herbaceous border and which will commonly be found farther out in the garden. For such a bed the choice of plants is wide, but a beginning could be made by spreading out the plants of the Mediterranean collection to make room between them for more colour and a greater contrast in foliage texture. About the middle of the bed a loosely connected backbone of roses could be planted to blend with the grey-green foliage of lavender and rosemary. This backbone would not be continuous but interrupted by mounds of the taller lavenders and cistuses, and by such herbaceous plants as *Salvia sclarea turkestanica, Campanula lactiflora* and peonies.

For roses there is a wide field of choice, ranging from the old roses, most of which will only show their recondite charms for two or three weeks after midsummer, to the brightest of the new hybrid floribundas, which will be in flower continuously from June to' October. For myself, I prefer roses which are rather less insistent, among them some of the hybrid teas, which have, not only in their flowers but also in their opening buds, a grace, a degree of breeding perhaps, which is becoming rare. Ophelia and Ena Harkness have been referred to earlier as climbers, but they made their first glorious appearance as bushes. Others which I like are Apricot Silk, whose name well describes its colour and texture, and the white Message, with its undertones of green. I would try to find room also for a few of the old roses, Queen of Denmark, one of the albas, a warm pink with bluish foliage, Madame Pierre Oger, a Bourbon, cream to rose with cup-shaped flowers, and the beautiful tall Souvenir de la Malmaison, with pink quartered blooms, and for good measure the Old Pink Moss.

For those who want them, there are some good hybrid floribundas. Red Dandy is a solid crimson without the alarming scarlet-vermilion of Super Star (a hybrid tea) or the ashen-coral of that overpraised rose, Fragrant Cloud. Gold Gleam has large bright lemon-yellow fragrant flowers. There are several good pinks, Pink Parfait, slightly scented, and Plentiful, again scented; and the coral-salmon flowers of Pernille Poulsen looked well behind a little hedge of Hidcote lavender in an Oxford college garden. I would give a genuine welcome to Iceberg, taller than some of the others, with a romantic, loose-flaunting habit. The flowers have occasional

7. The screen wall units give to this long, narrow garden a receding interest. The hexagon-l paving has an assuring character and the planting makes good use of foliage contrast. 'his garden was designed by A. du Gard Pasley, A.I.L.A.

Three examples of curves where grass meets paving. Planning curves often invites disaster, but all three of these succeed

18. This garden in Sussex was designed by J. St Bodfan Gruffydd, F.I.L.A.

19. Norham Gardens, Oxford, designed by Sylvia Crowe, P.P.I.L.A.

20. A garden designed by A. du Gai Pasley, A.I.L.A.

21. A view from inside a lanai at San Mateo, California. The whole garden was designed by Thomas D. Church, San Francisco

22. A lanai with sliding glass doors. Also designed by Thomas D. Church

23, 24 and 25.
Three examples
of provision for
shade in the
southern United
States of America.
All the gardens
were designed by
Thomas D.
Church, San
Francisco

pale pink blotches at the edges of the petals and none of the coldly forbidding quality suggested by the name. This is one of the most valuable of all the white roses.

Groups of white lilies will look well near the red roses. *Lilium candidum*, the Madonna Lily, is from 3 to 6 feet high and has pure white flowers in July. *L. regale* is about the same height; the flowers are trumpet-shaped, white with rosy-purple outside and pale yellow at the bases, with golden anthers showing.

Some of the single peonies, with their looser habit and fine-cut foliage, will make good foils to the more twiggy growth and urgent colour of the roses. They grow to about 3 feet. The flowers of *Paeonia* Whitleyi major are lemon-cream, almost white; Victoria has crimson flowers with golden anthers; Eva is a deep pink.

In a really wide bed there might be room for tree peonies at the back. *P. ludlowii* has clear yellow, single flowers and a mass of finely cut foliage and may in time reach a height of 6 feet; Reine Elizabeth has double, bright crimson-rose flowers; and Yano Okima pure white, semi-double flowers.

At the back near the wall the common myrtle, *Myrtus communis*, might reach a height of 10 feet, although it will take many years to do this. It is a tender, evergreen shrub with small, delicate, dark green leaves, slightly fragrant when crushed. The crowd of very thin anthers look almost like a mist in the small white flowers in July. Sprigs of myrtle are to this day included in brides' bouquets and lovingly taken out after the wedding to be struck as cuttings. In the years which follow they grow into large bushes, kept in pots in the greenhouse, for the admiration and astonishment of grand-children.

Teucrium fruticans, the Tree Germander, will not grow much above 4 feet, even in favourable conditions. It is inclined to be tender, but in a middle position in this protected situation its pale blue flowers and grey foliage would be worth a trial. *Hebe* (*Veronica*) *hulkeana* needs the protection of a wall. It has a loose habit and dark, glossy green leaves larger than the leaves of some of the other hebes (veronicas), and pale lilac-coloured flowers in May or June. *Verbascum bombyciferum* (*V.* Broussa), a biennial, will lend a useful vertical line with its fine, virile, grey woolly spikes of pale lemon-yellow flowers. *Salvia ambigens* is of value because its dark violet-blue flowers come out in late September or even October. It is cut down to the ground by frost every winter, but seldom killed outright, throwing out fresh shoots rather late in the spring. It grows to about 5 feet.

A good plant for the edge is *Artemisia lanata* (*A. pedemontana*), which, although it has insignificant, downy yellow flowers, has long prostrate shoots of 'tin-plated' grey foliage which, when crushed, has the acerbity of tarragon.

For the winter one or two deciduous shrubs with good 'bone' rising a little above the sea of evergreen or evergrey foliage will relieve a tendency to monotony. Two of the viburnums will accomplish this and also be of value for their flowers in spring. *V. juddii* has a strong, twiggy outline in winter and pinkish-white, clove-scented flowers in April; *V. tomentosum* Lanarth Variety has tiers of outward-spreading branches, which are as lovely when studded with diamond drops of rain in winter as when the large, greenish-white clusters of flowers appear in May.

Some of the more upright-growing Japonicas also have a good winter framework. *Chaenomeles* (*Cydonia*) Hollandia, with scarlet flowers, and Minerva with crimson ones. As with all the Japonicas, the flowers are chiefly borne in March, but appear on and off at odd times from early February until the summer.

For the corner of this bed farthest from the house and at the outward edge of the terrace I would choose either a clump of *Romneya trichocalyx* or *Yucca gloriosa*. The former is a herbaceous perennial and therefore deciduous, but in summer it has large, poppy-like, single white flowers with a centre of golden stamens in July and August and fine, deeply cut, rather glaucous green leaves reaching perhaps to 6 feet. The evergreen *Yucca gloriosa* pierces the sky with its stiff, sword-like leaves and conjures thoughts of remoter lands and clearer light.

CHAPTER IX

The Bed facing East

Where there is open country to the west, or if the view in that direction is of particular interest, it may be wisest to leave the terrace open on that side, but if there is a reason to make a screen there, a number of plants will grow well on a south-eastern aspect. In fact, except for those which are undoubtedly tender and with which a recognised risk is being taken, nearly all of those suggested for the south-western-facing bed at the other end of the terrace can be grown in the bed we are now to consider. If both beds are to be made it will be more interesting, to make a contrast between the two, to plant this one in a lower key, with all green and no grey foliage.

For climbers against the wall pyracanthas are obliging and versatile. They are evergreen, have handsome red or yellow berries, are tough and hardy, and can easily be trained in horizontal lines to form a living trellis pattern against the house walls. They are not self-clinging and wires must be fixed to the wall to train them successfully. *Pyracantha atalantioides* (*P. gibbsii*) has large, oval, shining leaves with dark red berries. *P. rogersiana* has yellow berries and smaller leaves.

Hydrangea petiolaris (*H. scandens*) is a deciduous, self-clinging climber, better perhaps on a north or east than a south-east wall, with large, dark green, heart-shaped leaves, large flat corymbs of greenish-white flowers in June and July, and bright, reddish-brown young wood. This is a fine cover for old walls and, for instance, is in perfect accord with the stone of Oxford quadrangles.

The Knaphill Scarlet variety of the common Japonica, *Chae-nomeles speciosa*, has orange-scarlet flowers in April and, although it will endure on a north wall, will grow more quickly and produce more flowers on a south-eastern aspect.

Of the roses previously mentioned, Madame Alfred Carrière and Mermaid will succeed in this position.

A skeleton of evergreen plants can be laid down in the bed. *Fatsia japonica*, the Figleaf Palm, when it is established may reach a height of 10 feet and makes a good figure against the background of the wall. It has large, ivy-like leaves and pale, greenish-white flowers. *Viburnum* × *burkwoodii* is a distinguished evergreen with dark green, oval leaves, of good size, and pinkish-white, carnation-scented flowers in April. *Euphorbia wulfenii* will grow to 4 feet and has dark green foliage, with long, narrow but thick leaves, and pale, greenish-white flowers.

All or some of these will make a contrast with the border at the opposite end of the terrace and provide a framework more green than grey for other planting, which could be subdued in tone.

Potentilla arbuscula is a low, quickly spreading shrub. Two or three will make a comfortably rounded group, with pale yellow flowers in abundance all through the summer.

Geranium pratense has bluish-purple flowers in June and July, and a well-contoured foliage outline. *Salvia* × *superba* (*S. virgata nemorosa*) has navy blue spikes of flowers with brownish-purple bracts which last for a long time. It makes a good combination with *Achillea clypeolata*, with its feathery grey foliage and pale lemon-yellow flowers.

Hemerocallis (Day-lilies) have light green, very narrow leaves and lily-like flowers clustered at the tops of flowering spikes. The variety Hesperus has citron-yellow flowers in July and August and will liven up the weight of evergreen.

The clear-cut silhouette of iris leaves will make a contrast with other foliage. I. Aline, which is strongly scented, and Jane Philipps, are good sky blues; Arabi Pasha, darker blue; Ola Kola, deep golden-yellow; and Cliffs of Dover, a good creamy white.

Finally, and to mark the approach of autumn, I would have some plants of the Japanese anemone *A. japonica alba*, with vine-like leaves and ascending spikes of large, saucer-shaped, white single flowers with golden anthers.

CHAPTER X

The Bed opposite the House and Island Beds

If there is no change of level between the outer edge of the terrace and the garden, the paving can run directly into the grass, but where there is a drop in level, a parapet wall or balustrade is advisable to give a feeling of security. The hard junction of paving and wall will be softened by a bed, which can be from 18 inches to 4 feet wide, or even more if the terrace is a large one. This bed will be in constant view from the windows of the house and when sitting on the terrace. Much more care, therefore, must be taken in the visual effect of foliage texture and the use of colour, than in the case of the bed under the windows, which is not seen from inside the house and which has been planned for scent and without great regard to flower colour and scale. Low-growing plants will be needed so that they shall be largely contained below the height of the parapet wall. A balance must be struck between tempering the hardness of the horizontal line and entirely destroying the visual purpose of the wall by allowing a continuous bristling fuzz of tall foliage and flowers to thrust itself into the air along the whole length.

For the few plants which are designed to send an occasional unregulated spray above the wall I would use *Senecio laxifolius* which, although it could in time reach a height of from 3 to 4 feet, can be kept in control by pruning with a knife in April. It has very grey, felted leaves and a charming, loosely spreading habit. It is one of the grey-foliaged plants which is grown much more for its foliage than for its flowers, although in this case the pale, lemon-yellow flowers are acceptable.

The Jerusalem Sage, *Phlomis fruticosa*, is another good plant for this purpose. It grows to about the same height, but has a less-spreading habit. It has large wrinkled leaves, elephant grey above and paler grey on the undersides. The flowers, which are formed in whorls, are the colour of dull lacquered brass and combine superlatively with the foliage.

There is a number of small evergreen shrubs which in time may reach from 2 to 3 feet, but which can be kept down by thoughtful pruning with a knife in the spring. *Ruta graveolens* Jackman's Blue, a variety of Rue, or Herb of Grace, is one of these. It has finely cut, lacy-looking foliage, smouldering blue like tempered steel. It is ruefully acrid when pressed, Its spikes of yellow flowers do not do it justice and are better snipped off when they appear in the early summer. The Purple Sage, *Salvia officinalis purpurascens*, has dull, brownish-purple, wrinkled foliage and makes an excellent contrast with grey-leaved plants.

A good, dense, low-growing evergreen shrub with dark green leaves to contrast with so much grey foliage is *Viburnum davidii*. Although its flowers are a nondescript grey-white, it is an excellent foliage shrub with its large, oval, pointed leaves, and its shining metallic blue berries in the autumn give it an added interest.

Deciduous shrubs for this position are *Potentilla nana argentea* (*beesii*) with bright buttercup yellow flowers almost continuously during the summer, grey foliage and an easy lax habit of growth; and *Chaenomeles* × *superba* Simonii, a very short variety of Japonica, with deep crimson flowers and a twiggy structure.

For the very front edge the prostrate, evergreen foliage of helianthemums will lap on to the paving. *H. rhodanthe carneum* has silver, variegated foliage and soft pink flowers; *H*. Supreme has dark crimson and *H*. Wisley Primrose has pale yellow flowers, again with silver foliage.

This framework of shrubs, chiefly evergreen but with some deciduous ones, can be bodied out with herbaceous and other flowering plants. The herbaceous *Geranium* A. T. Johnson has large, soft blue flowers well poised above finely cut foliage; *G. endressii* Wargrave has pale pink flowers. *Anchusa officinalis angustifolia* has bright blue flowers in sprays, beginning in June and continuing all the summer. *Anaphalis triplinervis* has silvery-white foliage and whitish 'everlasting' flower heads.

Nepeta faassenii (*N. mussinii*), Catmint, has smoky blue flowers and grey foliage which will billow over the edge of the bed on to the paving, and *Stachys lanata*, Lamb's Tongue, with thick, exceedingly hairy leaves and ascending spikes of small royal blue flowers, is another good plant for the forward edge. So, too, are *Geranium cinereum*, only 6 inches high, with grey foliage and pale purple-pink flowers with darker veins, and *G. grandiflorum alpinum*, which has blue flowers and finely divided foliage.

Some of the garden pinks can be used in this company. They are mat-forming plants with glaucous foliage. Earl of Essex is fringed, deep pink; Inchmery is a paler pink; Paddington is a shorter plant, deep browny-pink and laced with a dark purple eye; and Mrs Sinkins and White Ladies are white, strongly scented with a characteristic clove-pink smell.

If there is a vacant space in the bed in May it could be filled with two or three plants of the pelargonium (geranium) Verona, in which there is a singularly delicate harmony between the pale gold of the leaves and the pale, fuchsia-purple flowers.

Generally I think it is best for the colours in this bed to be kept fairly low-toned so that the bright, hard colours of geraniums or petunias in tubs on the terrace shall stand out.

In an island bed, whether raised up or at terrace level, low-growing plants will again be chosen so that they shall not block the view across the terrace or be seen against the sky. These beds also will be seen from the house not only in the summer but all through the winter, so that for permanent planting a good proportion of low-growing evergreens will cover the bare earth and maintain some interest in the winter.

Salvia hispanica, the Purple Sage, and Jackman's Blue Rue will make a good framework, with helianthemums at the edges to fall downwards over the sides of raised beds. The rest of the bed could be filled with the small *Potentilla nana argentea*, *Viburnum davidii*, and herbaceous plants such as *Monarda didyma* Cambridge Scarlet, *Anchusa officinalis angustifolia*, *Achillea clypeolata;* at the edges *Nepeta faassenii* and *Stachys lanata;* and towards one corner, to pierce through the level contour, a small group of *Iris pallida dalmatica*, with silvery foliage and pale lilac flowers.

If there is no great objection to the appearance of bare earth all through the winter, island beds can be used entirely for seasonal bedding. The early tulips referred to later (Chapter XIII) will give a fine mass of colour, but, if there is reasonable shelter from the wind to protect their rather tall stems, some of the Darwin hybrid tulips will be much more spectacular. They are the result of a cross between Darwin tulips and Tulipa fosteriana. They are the largest and most brilliant tulips so far raised. They flower earlier than Darwins and, although tall, do not have quite the same pinheaded appearance. Holland's Glory, 22 inches high, has enormous dazzling scarlet flowers, and Golden Springtime, even taller, 26 inches, was very beautiful in one year in an enclosed garden at the offices of Penguin Books at Harmondsworth. Hyacinths will give colour, and scent as well. Spring flowers last for such a short time that these beds can be planted with solid blocks of colour without any fear of their becoming tedious. In summer, by contrast, when the planting will be in full view for about five months, I would choose softer colours for these island beds—heliotropes, stocks and violas.

CHAPTER XI

Plants for Town Gardens and Shady Positions

IN TOWNS

Gardening in London and other towns is difficult for several reasons. Pollution of the atmosphere leads to poisonous deposits on leaves and soil. Poor conditions in the soil itself are caused partly by these deposits, but aggravated by the fact that the soil has been in use for a long time and has had its reserves severely depleted without proper regeneration with organic bulk materials and fertilisers; and, finally, because of shade from tall buildings and trees, and drip from the latter.

Therefore, before looking at a selection of plants for towns the first thing to consider is how to improve conditions as far as possible. For perfection, the soil should be dug out to a depth of 3 feet and replaced. This will be expensive over large areas, but it may be possible to afford it in the comparatively small beds of a terrace. If the full depth cannot be renewed at least some of the top, coated with soot and grime, could be taken away. The fresh soil should be good country loam reinforced with cow dung and peat laced with bone meal, hoof and horn meal and sulphate of potash.

Where shade is due to tall or overhanging trees on one's own property, an assessment can be made as to which is needed most, the shelter and protection from being overlooked which is afforded by the trees or the success of the plants in the garden. Sometimes the removal of one or two trees, or even of a large limb, may make a significant difference to the amount of light that reaches the beds and the lawn. Entire removal of some trees will also put a stop to competition by the roots.

There is nothing that can be done to mitigate the 'fall out' in the atmosphere, but syringing and even sponging the leaves and stems of favourite plants will reduce the clogging of the pores. Some of the worst sufferers, particularly in London fogs, are yews, laurustinus and many of the grey-foliaged plants.

Generally, deciduous trees and shrubs which renew their leaves each spring will endure conditions in towns better than evergreens. Among the smaller deciduous trees which will succeed is the common almond which normally grows to about 20 feet; as it matures, its rather erect habit mellows into a rounder shape. The very pale, single-flowered almond is the one to have, not the darker, double-flowered *Prunus communis* Pollardii. *Laburnum alpinum*, the Scotch Laburnum, flowers in early June, two or three weeks after the common laburnum. It is deciduous and will not grow much above 30 feet. It has long hanging racemes of yellow flowers, cool-looking on a hot day, but on wet days it seems to partake of the nature of the streaming rain. Two deciduous magnolias, *M. denudata* and *M. soulangiana*, will appreciate having their branches and twigs washed from time to time to keep the bark clean. *Sorbus aria lutescens*, one of the whitebeams, is a deciduous tree which may in time reach from 30 to 40 feet. Its particular charm is in the grey underside of its leaves, which flash in the sunlight when the wind blows them up. Its flowers are whitish-grey with a heavy scent and come out in May, succeeded by red berries.

For large terrace lawns there is a number of taller deciduous trees which have been found to succeed well in smoky districts. *Ailanthus altissima* (*A. glandulosa*), the Tree of Heaven, will grow to 60 feet or more. The large, pinnate leaves and its rounded head of branches when mature make it a distinguished tree. *Robinia pseudoacacia*, which may reach an ultimate height of 70 feet and have a spread of 30 feet after many years, has a spare framework and elegant feathery foliage. The fragrant white flowers are borne in long racemes in June. *Gleditschia triacanthos*, the Honey Locust, is like a robinia in outline and habit with pinnate leaves and a light, thin framework. *Catalpa bignonioides*, the Indian Bean, which will reach 30 or 40 feet and in time develop an even greater spread, has large heart-shaped leaves; its yellow-white, spotted flowers are borne in pyramidal panicles like those of the horse chestnut. It is a good tree for a lawn where its shade is grateful on a hot day.

Deciduous shrubs that will generally flourish in London and large towns are *Forsythia* × *intermedia* Lynwood, with bright yellow flowers in March, possibly reaching 8 feet in height; *Philadelphus microphyllus*, a small plant growing to about 4 feet, with small white, scented flowers and *P.* × Sybille, a little smaller, with mauve-purple centres to the white flowers. (The larger philadelphus are rather gaunt and tall for planting on a terrace.) Also the following, referred to elsewhere in this book and in the notes on plants beginning on page 165: Chaenomeles (Japonica), hibiscus, rhus, syringa (lilac) *Viburnum juddii*, *V. tomentosum* and most roses.

Among the evergreen shrubs already referred to, camellias, fatsias, hollies, pyracanthas, *Viburnum* × *burkwoodii* and yuccas will tolerate an urban atmosphere. Others are *Cotoneaster conspicuus decorus*, 2 feet high with a spreading habit, dark green leaves, white flowers in June and bright red berries, and *Euonymus radicans*, a procumbent plant with dark green, smooth leaves. This grows to about 6 to 9 inches and can be used as an edging; there is also a variegated form with a band of white at the margin of the leaves. *Phillyrea decora*, which will grow to more than 5 feet high, has pointed leaves, shining dark green above and paler on the undersides. Its small, pure white flowers appear in April. *Skimmia japonica fragrans*, about the same height as *Phillyrea* but wider spreading, has white scented flowers early in the spring.

Many of the herbaceous plants already mentioned will show a reasonable tolerance of smoky conditions, particularly *Achillea clypeolata*, hemerocallis, iris, and *Salvia* × *superba*. The following plants are also useful for this purpose. There is *Acanthus mollis*, from 3 to 4 feet high whose evergreen leaves with their strongly characteristic shape gave rise to the acanthus leaf decoration in Greek architecture. The flowers, which appear from June onwards through the summer, are whitish or pale violet-rose. These stately and very beautiful plants once grew in elegant profusion in the steeply sloping churchyard of St Just-in-Roseland. *Saxifraga umbrosa*, London Pride, grows from 1 to 1½ feet high, with rosette-like, rather leathery leaves and loose panicles of small pink flowers.

Bergenia cordifolia has very large, almost circular leaves, turning deep pink in winter, and spikes of rose-pink flowers in March and April. *Ceratostigma plumbaginoides* is low growing, almost prostrate, and has bright blue flowers in autumn. The leaves turn brownish-purple before they die. *Lysimachia nummularia aurea*, the Golden Creeping Jenny, has small round leaves and small yellow flowers, and is an unassuming but endearing ground-cover plant.

IN SHADE

The following smaller trees will endure a degree of shade from taller neighbours—almond, arbutus, bay, laburnum, magnolia and sorbus; as well as *Cotoneaster frigidus*, deciduous, reaching to about 30 feet, with long, thin leaves and spreading habit, rather unimportant white flowers, and bright red berries, and *Cotoneaster salicifolius*, growing to 12 feet, and having long, willow-like leaves, white flowers and red berries.

Certain evergreen shrubs could be described as shade specialists. These include box, camellias, fatsias, hollies, mahonias and, for carpeting, *Vinca minor*, the Lesser Periwinkle, a creeping plant rooting from its shoots, with dark green, shining foliage and small, bright blue flowers in spring. Other evergreen shrubs which have already been referred to and which will succeed in conditions of moderate shade are—*Cotoneaster conspicuus decorus*, *Skimmia japonica* and *Myrtus communis*. There is another cotoneaster, *C. dammeri* (*C. humifusus*), which is good for ground cover, with dark, glossy green leaves, small white flowers and red berries. *Osmarea* × *burkwoodii*, which is evergreen and in time may reach as high as 10 feet but will take many years to do this, has shining, pointed, dark green leaves and small tubular, creamy-white flowers.

Deciduous shrubs for conditions of moderate shade are—*Daphne mezereum*, the Mezereon, growing from 3 to 5 feet, with rather light green leaves and very sweetly scented, purple flowers on bare branches in February, followed later by red berries. This plant, with Madonna lilies and polyanthus, was a favourite in cottage gardens. *Deutzia* × *elegantissima*, 4 to 5 feet high, with dark, reddish-purple flowers in May and June; and also *D. gracilis*, about the same height, with white flowers. *Fuchsia magellanica riccartonii* is liable to be cut to the ground in hard winters but usually springs again and makes growth from 4 to 6 feet. The rather small but abundant red and purple flowers radiate a quietly optimistic cheer in late summer and autumn. *Hydrangea macrophylla* (*H. hortensis*) is the plant with huge, bobble-headed flowers, blue and pink and white, seen bedded out at Ascot and Henley. These unfortunate plants have been so relentlessly bred for grossness and vulgarity that there is no longer any place for them in a private garden, and even in public places they cause nothing but dismay. The blue colour is only produced naturally in acid soils where iron is freely available. In most soil conditions the plants have to be doctored with strong potions of aluminium sulphate if the blue colour is not to lapse into a washy pink. By contrast some of the lace-cap hydrangeas, looking like true woodlanders, have considerable charm. These have flat, more open panicles with smaller fertile flowers in the centre, and larger sterile ones in the ring on the outside. In the variety Blue Wave the fertile flowers are purplish-blue and the large outer sterile ones pink (or blue in naturally acid soils). It will grow to 5 to 6 feet. Other deciduous shrubs for moderate shade are: forsythia, philadelphus, potentilla and a number of viburnums, including *V. juddii* and *V. tomentosum* Lanarth Variety.

Herbaceous plants for conditions of half shade are:

The hellebores, whose foliage is retained in the winter: *H. corsicus* has green flowers in March and good, blue-green foliage. *H. niger* is the Christmas Rose, with good foliage and pure white, cup-shaped flowers with yellow anthers in mid-winter. Its variety *altifolius* has longer stems so that the flowers are held up out of the December mud. *H. orientalis*, the Lenten Rose, has purplish-pink or white flowers in March which are long-lasting—I have had them continue into May.

Hostas, with large, broad-bladed leaves and delicate spikes of flowers in the second half of the summer. *H. fortunei* has blue-green leaves and mauve-blue flowers. *H. sieboldiana* has grey-green foliage and white and pale lilac flowers. *H. undulata* has green leaves splashed with white and pale lavender flowers.

Alchemilla major, Lady's Mantle, has fairly large, downy grey-green leaves gracefully poised and crowds of very small green-yellow flowers in loose panicles. *Epimedium grandiflorum* has heart-shaped leaves, sometimes spotted with yellow and purple. In the variety Rose Queen the flowers are crimson; in *violaceum* they are violet-blue.

Lily-of-the-Valley (Convallaria), with its demure sprays of white bells, very sweetly scented, and dark green, unfolding sheaths of spear-shaped leaves, and the Japanese anemone, *A. japonica*, are also suitable for these conditions.

Ferns no longer enjoy the popularity they had fifty years or more ago, but it is perhaps time for a revival, and certainly they can have an agreeably softening effect in hard angles and dark corners. *Osmunda regalis*, the Royal Fern, is deciduous. Its fronds will grow from 2 to 6 feet and have a width of from a foot to 3 feet, depending on conditions of growth. It requires a position where water is readily available to the roots. *Blechnum spicant*, the Hard Fern, is evergreen. The fronds are of two different kinds. The fertile ones rise from the centre of the plant to a height of as much as 2 feet; the outer fronds are rather shorter and become horizontal. This fern requires a peaty, acid soil and resents watering with hard tap water. *Phyllitis scolopendrium* is the Hart's-tongue Fern. It is also evergreen and its long, strap-like fronds, often frilled throughout their lengths, are familiar in the cool, damp, sunken lanes in the West Country and Ireland.

Crown Imperials (*Fritillaria imperialis*) have been known here since before 1597, when Gerard wrote of them: '. . . the leaves grow confusedly above the stalke like those of the white Lilly but narrower: the floures grow at the top of the stalke incompassing it round in form of an Imperiall Crowne . . . hanging their heads downward as it were bels. . . . In the bottom of each of these bels there is placed sixe drops of most cleare shining sweet water in taste like sugar resembling in shew faire orient pearles. . . . The whole plant as wel roots as floures do savor or smell very like a fox.' There are varieties with yellow, bright orange and almost red flowers.

I have Crown Imperials growing where the flowers catch the level evening sunlight: to me they are one of the things in a garden which I cannot do without. Why they should have such a strong attraction is difficult to say. Perhaps it is their great strangeness with their ring of bell-shaped flowers hanging below the wild crown of foliage, perhaps their long wanderings from the Himalayas and Persia to Tudor England, or only their robust, rude, earthy smell of lusty spring . . . 'a faint rank taint like April coming. . . .'

CHAPTER XII

Trees on the Terrace

Trees and houses seem to be infallibly complementary. Certainly nearly every architect longs for mature trees to put his building in scale and give it a helping hand into the landscape.

Almost any tree that will match the width of the terrace and the size of the house can be chosen. At Pusey House the scale is so large that a mature oak is in perfect proportion, although in my view a little savage so near the house. I would have preferred the False Acacia, which has an altogether lighter character and a spare, spreading habit. Its elegant, feathery foliage casts a thin shade and its white flowers in June are delicately scented.

Perhaps 15 feet is the narrowest width of terrace on which a small tree can be grown and even this would mean planting it well towards the outer edge so that its branches should not grow into the house as the tree develops. The common almond has a quality of beauty which graces alike the poor bricks of the plainest little by-pass house and the reasoned symmetry of stone pediment and arcade. By contrast the highly ornamental Japanese cherries are too sugary, too pretty to bring near the house. The Winter Cherry, *Prunus subhirtella autumnalis*, which grows to about 20 feet, has a wider-spreading, more rambling outline and would be a good tree for the far end of a fairly long terrace where the wilder garden begins. Its white, semi-double flowers begin to appear in the autumn, continue through the winter, and have a resurgence in the spring. *Rhus typhina*, the Stags-horn Sumach, is a small, angular tree growing only to 10 or 15 feet high, with large, fern-like leaves which turn orange-red in the autumn; and *Cotinus coggygria* (*Rhus cotinus*), the Smoke Plant or Wig Tree, though usually a bushy shrub, can be pruned to make a small tree 8 or 10 feet high, with a very elegant, sometimes contorted, outline, which would look well at one end of the terrace against a wall with no tall planting at its base to detract from the visual value of the stem. The Judas Tree (*Cercis siliquastrum*) is a good tree for small terraces. It also normally has a shrubby habit, but can be pruned, to a clear stem to form a tree perhaps 20 feet high. It is deciduous, with roundish, pale green leaves and bright purple-rose, pea-shaped flowers borne on the joints of the old wood in May.

Perhaps the best of all small trees for a terrace is an arbutus. The illustration facing page 52 shows *Arbutus unedo* on the terrace near the Orangery at Ditchley Park. It can be pruned to a clear stem of 10 feet or so and the trunk will often lean and develop an attractive twist. It will form a crown of dark evergreen foliage, making a perfect source of shade in the summer. The small white, or palest pink, flowers appear in the autumn and are on the tree at the same time as the strawberry fruits resulting from the previous autumn's flowers. This arbutus is entirely hardy at Kew; but for more favoured districts in the South and West, another one, *A. menziesii*, the Madrona, a native of California, could be tried. This may grow to a greater height than *A. unedo*, possibly as much as 30 feet when fully grown. It has large, oval, evergreen leaves and small, dull white flowers, but its special distinction is its cinnamon-coloured stem and branches.

Neither the arbutus nor the Judas Tree can be transplanted in sizes much above 3 or 4 feet, because they make tap roots early in their young lives and have to be grown in pots. The result is that it takes many years before they become substantial trees; but patience is immeasurably rewarded, and it would be an act of affirmation to plant one of these trees even if it is necessary to protect it with a tree guard while it grows.

I would suggest to every father that, instead of, or as well as, laying down port for his children, he should obtain an arbutus and a Judas Tree in pots and cherish them for twenty years, moving them steadily into larger pots and then into small tubs and on into large tubs, so that when the child comes of age he or she will have plants 15 or perhaps 20 feet high in large tubs ready to be planted on the terrace of a new house.

26. Part of the Garden at the Villa
Pamphilj near Rome

27. The Villa Pia in the Vatican
Gardens, Rome

28. A small fountain in the Alcazar,
Seville, Spain

29. Lotus fountain in the Generalife,
Granada, Spain

30. This fountain is in
the upper garden of
the Generalife

31. This pool is in the corner of a courtyard; panelled quarry tiles are used for the coping. The planting makes much use of foliage to provide contrast. It was designed by A. du Gard Pasley, A.I.L.A.

32. The fountain shown consists of three low cylinders made of exposed aggregate materials using different granites. Water is circulated by an electric motor of fractional horse power installed in a chamber alongside. The water bubbles out of holes in the middle of each of the cylinders and runs over the edges to the pool below the cobble filling. The fountain was designed by Eric Peskett

If there is no room on the terrace itself a tree can sometimes be planted in the garden just beyond the paving, probably at one corner. A tree in such a position may not be conveniently placed for sitting immediately underneath, but if it is a spreading one its branches will throw a pattern of shade across one end of the terrace. The most improbable trees can be unexpectedly successful in these positions. When I first came to my own garden I found a tall, bushy yew at the south-eastern corner of the terrace and a wide, spreading hazel at the other end, both entirely wrong choices according to the rules, but first intentions of removing them were never carried out and the trees remain. One, beside providing a nesting-site for thrushes, makes a good visual vertical terminal at that corner of the terrace and is a bastion against the full force of the east wind. It has a disadvantage in that it casts dense shade over the corner of the bed and some of the plants, including Madonna lilies, lean away from the darkness of the yew.

The hazel spreads its branches outside my bedroom window. In autumn it is visited by nuthatches and in winter it is a perch for all the birds of the garden waiting their turn at the bird table. As the days decline towards mid-winter and then begin their slow ascent the catkins lengthen until, at the time of Candlemas, they swing and dance through flurries of snow drifting down to powder the first aconites below.

Though far removed from the native yew and hazel, magnolias can also be planted near the terrace. I think that the first sight of the Asiatic magnolias cannot fail to arouse a feeling of incredulity, largely, I suppose, because of the unaccustomed size of the flowers. We think of them chiefly in the half shade of thin woodland, as in the wild woods of Caerhays Castle, Cornwall, but they can be planted with dramatic effect close to buildings. A specimen of *M. sargentiana robusta* near the house at Trengwainton in the same county, and a *M. soulangiana* near the terrace at Stoke Court near Slough are examples of this. *M. sargentiana robusta* is a rare plant and only likely to succeed in milder counties, but two perfectly hardy magnolias for general use are *M. denudata*, the Yulan of China, which has pure white, chalice-shaped cups on bare black boughs in March and April, and *M. soulangiana*, which has similar flowers with stainings of purple towards the base.

CHAPTER XIII

Plants in Tubs and Pots

So far we have been considering trees growing in the ground at terrace level. Such trees can be large enough both to give shade and to provide a visual foil against the house, a function which can also be performed on a smaller scale by trees growing in tubs or large pots—portable trees which can be deployed at will and, when necessary for their survival, be taken into a greenhouse for protection in the winter.

The relationship between a plant and its tub or pot can be considered to fall into three classes. In the case of mop-headed standards, that is, trees with clear stems and foliage trimmed into a spherical shape, the silhouette is like an unequal dumb-bell, the head of the tree having a diameter of perhaps 3 feet and the tub a diameter of 2 feet or even less. This provides a satisfying balance in which a subordinate, but recognisable, role is played by the tub or pot, which will have been designed with shape and size chiefly in mind and without much ornamentation. Round wood tubs or plain square wood ones are the best for this purpose. They can be painted, preferably in a dark colour, dark grey, dark blue, bottle green or even black, or they can be made in hard wood and left in the natural colour.

In the next class in which shorter plants are used the contribution of plant and pot or tub is equal. In Italy lemon trees make a perfect marriage with their classic terracotta pots. The lemon trees are too tender for our country, but their height and form are a guide to the kind of plants best suited by pots with a fairly high degree of ornament, whether in design or colour or both. In Britain good plants are yuccas and, in mild districts, *Phormium tenax* and agapanthus. Large terracotta pots are the best, but round or square wood tubs can be used, painted in rather lighter colours.

In the third class the plants are shorter than lemon trees or yuccas and will almost always be chosen for their flowers. Here the tub must be as self-effacing as possible. For pelargoniums (geraniums) and petunias, which have little significant height, a low concrete bowl tapering from rim to base is suitable, particularly for ivy-leaved pelargoniums and the stronger-growing petunias, whose tumbling sprays of flowers make a good marriage of opposites with the firm circle of the rim of the bowl.

There are six entirely hardy plants, four evergreen and two deciduous, which can first be considered. The Portugal Laurel (*Prunus lusitanica*) is a distinguished shrub and must not be confused with the common or cherry laurel (*P. laurocerasus*) which has rather oblong, shining leaves. The Portugal laurel has oval, pointed leaves, rather smaller and of a darker green, in fact with some resemblance to a bay leaf. This evergreen tree could once be found as a ready-made, mop-headed standard, 6 or 8 feet high, with a head 4 or 5 feet in diameter. But now it would be necessary to buy a large bush, perhaps 4 feet high, and, having planted it in a tub, to prune it, at first lightly and then progressively more severely each April, to form a clear stem and rounded top.

Some of the larger parks keep a few rhododendrons in tubs on hand for display on special occasions and nurserymen use them for forcing and to give height at the back of a group at flower shows. Although not much in evidence at nurseries, they can sometimes be obtained at a high price and with a degree of pertinacity. They are not everyone's choice for a standard tree on the terrace; indeed, the sight of rhododendrons, by nature plants of thin woodland shade, trimmed into standards and grown in tubs, will make good men shudder, though they will reflect with relief that it is only the hardy hybrids which are treated in this way, raddled queans like Cynthia and Doncaster, offspring of that disastrously prolific mésalliance in Surrey a hundred years or so ago. In London I once saw a pair of standard Pink Pearl, much larger than life, 11 feet at least, with enormous heads lolling with flowers. They had a surrealist quality, the strangely sinister attraction of the world of

Ronald Firbank. They might have been standing one on either side of the door of the Strangers' Hotel in Valmouth.

A lower-growing evergreen with a different character is *Yucca gloriosa*, which has already been referred to as a plant for growing in a bed at ground level. It is equally impressive in a tub or large pot, and in fact is, in my opinion, one of the few really hardy plants entirely suited by Italian terracotta pots. A specimen looks well placed at the outer edge of the terrace. With its thick stem, creamy, bell-like flowers on a central spike, and radiating cockade of sharp, upward-pointing leaves, it is compellingly exotic.

The last of the entirely hardy evergreens is *Camellia japonica*. I do not think that the romantic, looser-growing camellias like *williamsii* are so well suited to a tame life in tubs as the familiar, formal *japonica* varieties. Camellias succeed best facing north-west or north because they need shelter from the early-morning sun and from the full strength of the sun at midday. A large, well-grown bush in the open can be a significant mass in the landscape, but when grown in pots or tubs camellias seem amorphous, with no valid form or contour, and look best placed close to the house wall, where the shining, dark green foliage is handsome, and the plant as a whole is useful in giving evergreen height. I have found them to be notorious calcifuges (intolerant of lime) and have found that they will diminish and die if planted in a bed of calcareous soil, but I see that Mr G. R. Wakefield in his book, *Camellias for Every Garden*, has had more encouraging results even on calcareous soils.

Fortunately the use of a tub makes it possible to create perfect artificial soil conditions, good drainage, a cool, dark rooting medium full of leaf soil and peat and with no lime. All this careful forethought, however, can be undone by watering with cold tap water if it contains lime, and ill effects will be intensified in a hot summer when it is necessary to water often. When camellias are to be grown in hard water districts it is advisable to instal a rain-water barrel and to give the camellias and other calcifuges first priority for soft water at air temperature.

Round barrels are a little too casual for these high-born prisoners, but otherwise camellias seem to grace every kind of tub or pot. I have seen them in the darker approaches to the Boboli Gardens in Florence grown in large terracotta pots, and they are as well suited by square wooden tubs in natural teak or painted a dark colour.

As plants, camellias are at least as hardy in Britain as the common laurel, but the flower buds may be killed by hard frost. It is therefore prudent when possible to move the plants in their tubs to a greenhouse for the winter. If this is not practicable, protection can be given to the flower buds if the whole plant is covered with a temporary tent of hessian supported on stakes, the material being unfastened and let down to allow of the circulation of air on genial days. I have heard it said that if the buds survive up to the time of Christmas they will not suffer from hard frost afterwards. I have not been able to verify this.

In 1957 the Camellia Sub-Committee of the Royal Horticultural Society issued a classification of camellias. In this there are six classes, ranging from single to formal double flowers. For plants in tubs I prefer the fuller flowers with their greater concentration of colour. For a small collection I would suggest the following. For white, Nobilissima in class 3 (anemone form—flat flowers with one or more rows of larger outer petals, the centre a convex mass of petalodes and stamens intermingled. This is the official description proposed by the Royal Horticultural Society and reproduced with the Society's permission). It flowers from November to the end of January and is most suited to mild southern or south-western districts. In less-favoured areas, although the plant is perfectly hardy, the flowers will too often be spoilt by frosts.

A later, white-flowered camellia is Mathotiana alba in class 6 (a formal double—fully imbricated, petals overlapping spirally like the tiles of a house, many rows of petals rarely showing stamens), pure white, late-flowering from March onwards.

For pink, Elegans (Chandleri elegans) in class 3 (anemone-flowered), mid-season, flowering from February to March, rose-pink, up to 4 inches in diameter.

For red, Mathotiana in class 4 (peony form, a deep rounded flower with several rows of outer petals, the centre a convex mass of twisted petalodes and stamens), with turkey red flowers 4 inches across, flowering from March onwards. And also Althaeaflora in class 4 (peony form), dark crimson, mid-season to late, flowering in February and March.

Besides these evergreens I would have two deciduous trees—lilacs and hibiscus. Lilacs can be bought trained as half-standards, with clear stems of 4 feet or so, and with thin, unconvincing little heads of about 1½ feet; with patience and devotion they will fill

T.C.G.–G

out and in a few years develop wide, dense heads. Farther out in the garden shrubberies, the single-flowered kinds will flaunt their looser blossoms, but here, captive and regulated in tubs, the more solid, double-flowered lilacs will be better. Charles Joly has deep purple flowers; Katherine Havemeyer is the familiar, true lilac colour; and Madame Lemoine a good, dense double white, although I would have reservations about using white-flowered lilacs in this context. They are excellent out in the garden by the gate, for instance, but as standards in tubs I have a feeling that more weight of colour is wanted. They make unexpected trees in tubs, bringing close to the house and in through the windows their unforgettable scent, the essence of early summer, tinged a little with sadness like memories of a first love which, like the torrents of spring, hurried away.

Standard hibiscus are grown in Holland and sometimes imported here. Well-grown trees develop good solid heads, well able to balance a 2-foot tub or pot. Like the lilacs, they are deciduous but more twiggy—mine were so rounded that in winter they reminded one of enormous lavatory brushes, the old, round-headed kind. They must be some of the latest of all trees to come into leaf, it being well into May before the oval leaves appear. Hibiscus belongs to the same Natural Order, *Malvaceae*, as the hollyhocks; their flowers are similar in size and shape, coming out in August and September. *H. syríacus* Monstrosus has single white flowers with a dark purple centre; Woodbridge has rich, rose-pink flowers with maroon blotches; Hamabo is paler pink with a crimson blotch at the base of each petal; but the strangest, and to me the most fascinating, is Coeleste, whose mauve flowers stare coldly from the green fastness of the foliage. Both lilac and hibiscus look well in square wooden tubs painted a dark colour, dark grey or dark blue.

There are four plants which are just not hardy and will need protection against frost in all but the mildest climates. Bays are the most familiar trees seen in tubs for the decoration of terraces and the entrances to hotels and large houses. Many of the plants seen in this country have been imported from Belgium, meticulously trimmed into pyramids or mop-headed standards. It is the latter which are so useful on terrace areas. Their compact head and comparatively thin stem in a tub rather smaller than the diameter of the head produce the typically diminished dumb-bell shape.

When they come from Belgium they arrive in tiny wooden tubs. They should be taken out of these and carefully potted on into 2-foot tubs which will balance a tree with a head of 3 feet. After this it will be many years before the trees need moving on again into larger tubs. The traditional, and the most suitable, tub is a half-barrel painted dark green with black hoops. If the plants are well watered, well fed with an organic fertiliser three or four times a year, taken into a frostproof greenhouse or even a shed in the winter (they can be killed outright in hard weather if left out of doors), and trimmed each April or May, the heads will steadily increase in size.

On a wide terrace a line of perhaps four large standards at the outer edge will give height where it will be effective and in focus. On a narrower terrace the trees can be stood at the sides of the garden door, or at any rate well back against the house wall. To stand them half-way between the house and the front edge of the terrace is to put them into the middle distance, a position for which they are unsuited. The pyramid shapes look well on either side of doorways or at the bottom of steps leading down to the garden from the terrace, provided that the tips do not project above the level of the top step.

The aromatic leaves are used as flavourings, discreetly in a bouquet garni or in a rice pudding, more emphatically in sausages. It was once known as the Poet's Laurel; the Romans called it *Laurus nobilis* and used the leaves to make chaplets for poets and emperors. Before leaving them let us pause to salute their good temper in submitting to the unnatural treatment we impose upon them. We think of bays largely as tightly clipped Noah's Ark silhouettes, to be moved about the terrace like chessmen, but in nature bay is a full-scale tree with a native majesty approached by few others. Bean wrote of 'beautiful woods of primeval bay laurel'.

I would like to think that, in the same way that there are organisations for taking care of old horses, there will one day be a society for the rescue of London bays. How often they are seen, the neglected playthings of an architect's fancy, with grimed and sadly thinning foliage, having endured winters of fog and continuing frost. For many their only hope of survival would be a swift translation to country air, where their leaves can be sponged, their parched roots watered, the wicked crust of London grime scraped off the top of the soil, and where in time they can be transferred to larger tubs and topdressed with country earth and cow dung, and in winter given the grateful shelter of a cold greenhouse.

The Pomegranate, *Punica granatum*, seldom ripens fruit in Britain, although it was grown for its fruits in the south of Europe and as far east as Persia and India. Here it will produce its striking scarlet flowers from June to September. I do not know whether it can still be found ready trimmed into standard form, but plants are still included in nurserymen's catalogues and small ones could be grown on and pruned and trained. I once had a pair of standard pomegranates in tubs. Their tall, loose-haired, pre-Raphaelite outline was a major pleasure on summer days before 1939. Like bay trees, they need protection against frost in the winter by being taken into a cold greenhouse or a frostproof shed. The pair that I had were in half-barrels painted white, but they would have been better suited by a square tub in natural hard wood.

Lemon Verbenas, already referred to, can be trained to make small, round-headed trees and be kept in tubs to be moved into a greenhouse in the winter. A small half-barrel painted dark green suits them best. The flowers seem to show up more when the plants are in the open than when grown against a wall, and the combination of these pale lilac flowers with the light green, scented foliage is of rare elegance.

The bright violet-blue flowers of *Agapanthus africanus* (*A. umbellatus*) float above the arching, strap-shaped evergreen foliage, the flower stem being more than two feet long. This plant is surely the one for the difficult middle distance position on the terrace; not so tall that you cannot see over it, and with enough bulk and weight of colour to become a significant mass. The plant came from South Africa in the middle of the seventeenth century. It is tender, and for protection in the winter the tubs are best taken into a cold greenhouse. I like them best in round wooden tubs painted white all over, including the hoops.

There are four plants often seen in tubs (species and varieties of citrus, *Datura cornigera*, the Oleander and the American Aloe) which are undeniably tender and must be kept in a warm greenhouse for the winter and not put out in the garden until all danger of frost is over. In practice this means that such plants appear on the terrace between June and the middle of September.

The most admired plants ever to be grown in tubs must be

orange trees. From the seventeenth century they have been regarded as indispensable in gardens of any consequence, so much so that, in order to have them in colder climates such as our own, glass-fronted orangeries were especially designed to house them in the winter. Sir John Hanmer of Bettisfield wrote of the orange in 1659:

'It becomes here in England, with great care and industry, to a tree of two or three yards high. It hath many branches, and growes naturally with a fine round handsome head. The leaves are smooth, pointed at the top but smooth below, of an excellent chearful greene color, and at the foote of each leafe there is the shape of a little heart, whereon the leafe stands, which distinguishes them from the Lemmon tree. The leaves smell well, but the flowers are deliciously and comfortably sweet, of a pure white color, and consisting of five little leaves. The fruite is well knowne in England, better than the tree, which is only kept in curious gardens by reason of its tenderness. . . . The best kinds wee know here in England are the China Orenge, a sort lately had from Portugall, whither it came not many yeares since from China. . . . The SEVILL Orenge, which is of two sorts, sweete & sharpe and comes from Spane, and the BERMUDA Orenge which is brought from the Island soe called in the West Indyes, and is the greatest and best I thinke, of Orenges.'

Large trees in huge tubs are still to be seen in the gardens of great houses, more in France than in this country, where the need for a tall, spacious greenhouse to keep them in the winter, the considerable weight of the tree and tub together, with the consequent difficulty of moving them in and out of the orangery, have resulted in their becoming fewer and fewer. None the less, they will always attract a gardener who has the means and the space to take care of them.

The species and varieties which have been grown in tubs in this country are: *Citrus aurantium*, the Seville orange from tropical Asia (not from Spain, as Sir Thomas Hanmer thought); *C. nobilis* from China and Cochin China; *C. nobilis deliciosa*, the Mandarin orange; *C. sinensis*, the sweet orange from Asia; and the smaller *C. bergamia*, the Bergamot orange, from the peel of which is expressed an essential oil used in making eau de cologne. In France the one chiefly grown is the sweet orange, *C. sinensis*, grafted on to the Seville orange, or Bigarade as it is known there.

When grown in tubs the trees are pruned to a short leg of 1½ or 2 feet and above this into a loosely rounded head. The shining evergreen foliage, the fruits hanging on the tree nearly all the year, and the delicious scent of the blossom in summer all make them trees of outstanding attraction. Many of the trees in France are of great age, and there are four trees now at Mereworth Castle which came from Wrest Park by way of Ditchley which must be at least a hundred years old. They are now from 15 to 18 feet high and have recently been transferred from their old slate tubs into new teak ones, made to the pattern of the classic Versailles 'caisse' measuring 3 feet 6 inches by 3 feet 6 by 3 feet 6 high, a perfect cube. These tubs with trees in them are so heavy that a specially designed trolley has to be used to move them out of the orangery in June and back again in September.

Orange trees live for so long that it is necessary to make the tubs in such a way that the sides can be taken off. When this is done a thin layer of the old soil is removed and some fresh compost put in to take its place. A good routine is to treat two sides in this way each year. More detailed notes on the choice and use of tubs are in Chapter XIV and on the filling materials in Chapter XVI. When required for ornamental purposes it is only necessary for the temperature in the greenhouse or orangery to be kept a few degrees above freezing-point, but if they are required to provide good-quality fruit a much higher temperature, 7°C. to 10°C. (45°F. to 50°F.) in February, rising to 21°C. to 24°C. (70°F. to 75°F.) later in the spring, is needed.

Datura cornigera (*D. knightii, Brugmansia knightii*), a beautiful extremely exotic-looking and poisonous plant, is a native of Mexico. It has large, soft leaves and enormous white or cream, trumpet-shaped flowers, very strongly—to some people over-whelmingly—scented. Its natural habit of growth is shrubby, but it grows very quickly, and can be trained into a standard with a clear stem of 6 feet or more, ending in a head of three or four spreading, slightly ascending branches. This is the best form in which to grow it, because it enables one to look up into the hanging flowers. It is another greenhouse plant which can be brought out on to the terrace in the summer, but its flowers particularly, and to some extent also its leaves, being soft, are liable to be battered and torn by winds, so that a well-sheltered position close to the angle of the wall should be found for it. Some years ago I had a tall plant which reached a height of 8 or 9 feet and carried hundreds of these strongly scented white flowers each summer. It looked well growing in a round wood tub painted white all over.

The Oleander (*Nerium oleander*) or Rose Bay, also poisonous, is a native of the Mediterranean, but has been grown in this country since the end of the sixteenth century. In a tub it will grow to about 5 feet. It has long, leathery leaves and very beautiful rose-pink, crimson, yellow and white flowers between June and October. Sir Thomas Hanmer described it: '. . . Hath long narrow light greene smooth leaves, like the OLIVE tree, but much longer and broader. The BRANCHES shoote out from the roote, soe that this shrubb will not bee kept with a handsome stemme or body. The Flowers are large and tubous, the leaves lying spread open. . . .'

The American Aloe, *Agave americana*, needs a large greenhouse to house it in the winter, its rosette of long leaves taking up a good deal of room. It also needs enough space all round it on the terrace so that the sharp spines at the ends of its leaves can be given a wide berth. If these conditions can be met, it is one of the most spectacular foliage plants, suggesting the limitless sand, burning sun and clear air of Mexico. The flowers are greenish-yellow, on a tall inflorescence rising from the centre. They will take upwards of eight years to appear. The plants die after flowering. They look well in a wide, shallow tub, a barrel cut down to 14 or 15 inches in height instead of the usual 18 inches, and painted dark grey. They look even better growing at ground level. I think this could be arranged by having the plant growing in a large pot or tub which in summer would be sunk into the ground at a prepared place on the terrace, a place where one of the paving stones had been taken up and the ground dug out to allow for the pot to be sunk. Loose cobblestones could be used to fill up the space between the paving and the pot. For the winter, after the plant had been taken out, the vacant space could be refilled with cobbles.

The plants so far considered are primarily useful for introducing height, their flowers being to some extent incidental. So far, too, in all the plantings for beds at ground level against the house, or against wing walls, colour has been used sparingly, as sharp punctuation points against a base of foliage or softer colours, but now, for pots or tubs on the surface of the terrace itself we are in

search of concentrated, and often hard, colour, generally, though
not always, undiluted.

For the beds on the terrace in the spring we shall use wallflowers
and forget-me-nots, and probably the garden beyond the terrace
will be filled with the pale colours of daffodils and almond blossom,
so that for the pots or tubs on the paving we shall need the brightest
colours we can find. The Early Single and Early Double tulips,
with their short stature and stouter stems, will be able to stand up
to gusty winds better than the taller Darwins and Lily-flowered
tulips, and their proportions are better suited to low bowls such
as the concrete ones with tapering sides. These are now made
smaller and finer in section than the first large and rather heavy
models which came out at the time of the Festival of Britain. In
hard winters there is a danger that the outer bulbs, those nearest
the rim of the bowl, will get killed by frost, but if flowers are to be
there in the spring the risk will have to be taken. It can be reduced
by packing straw or straw bales round the outside of the tub in
hard weather.

Of the Early Single tulips, Couleur Cardinal, 13 inches, is a full
crimson; Prince of Austria, the same height, is orange-scarlet.
There may be years in which nothing will do but white, in which
case I would plant Diana, 12 inches, or, if one were expect-
ing a mauve year, Van der Neer, 12 inches, with very
large, deep-mauve flowers, of good shape and on strong
stems.

The Double Early tulips are an acquired taste, but, if their
rather spiky petals can be accepted, the plain coloured ones at any
rate exercise an unexpected charm. They are a little shorter even
than Single Early tulips and, being double, last much longer.
Vuurbaak, for instance, is 12 inches high and a good solid crimson;
Scarlet Cardinal, a little shorter, is more crimson than scarlet and
has yellow on the inside; Orange Nassau is the one that I find hard
to resist with its smouldering, dusky scarlet flowers.

Some of the tulip species can also be used in these bowls; I
have had good results with *Tulipa fosteriana* Princeps, 16 inches
high, which has very large, true scarlet flowers, possibly a little
thin in substance. Two large bowls of these gave great vitality to
the terrace after a winter of much discontent. I believe that other
species and hybrids of species could also be used. Mr Teuscher in
his *Window Box Gardening* suggests a number as suitable for

window boxes. Included in his list are: *T. eichleri*, 10 to 12 inches, scarlet with bluish-black base; *T. greigii*, 10 to 12 inches, orange-scarlet with darker yellow margin at the base; and *T. ingens*, 8 to 10 inches high, vermilion.

When decisive colour patterns are wanted it is best to keep to one colour only in each bowl or tub, but colour combinations can be made by bringing the containers close together to form a group of three, in which one is raised on bricks to stand a few inches higher than the other two. The golden-yellow, Single Early Bellona could be planted in the upper bowl in close alliance with the dark purple Van der Neer in the two lower ones, or, if Early Doubles are to be used, Schoonord in the upper one with Orange Nassau in the two lower bowls.

Hyacinths look better in bowls on the terrace than in the bed by the house, because in bowls they are isolated from plants with a softer outline. They will certainly provide a change from tulips in some years. Those listed as 'hyacinths for bedding' are suitable and much less expensive than the prepared forcing bulbs. An early-flowering set could be: Ostara, blue with deeper blue marking; Lady Derby, shell pink; and L'Innocence, pure white; and some to flower later are: King of the Blues, indigo; City of Haarlem, primrose-yellow; and Queen of the Pinks.

One day at the end of May, when all the tulips have gone and the last of the blossom has fallen, there is a special shower of rain which certifies the end of frosts, and is the signal for the appearance in the streets of barrows and stalls of geraniums and salvias and petunias, and suddenly we are in Zuleika Dobson's world of window boxes and summer eights. In the summer we shall be confronted for four or five long months by the bedding plants that we choose to put into pots and tubs on the paving, so it is advisable to make as sure as possible that we shall be able to live contentedly for all that time with whatever we decide to have.

The qualities required for plants in tubs are:

(1) Bright colour, including white, as has already been suggested.

(2) Large flowers. Very small flowers like lobelias and *Phlox drummondii* are out of scale even in a moderate-sized tub because, as we are aiming at a high concentration of colour, a number of small flowers (colour units), besides being restless, will not give such a vivid impact of colour as a smaller number of large flowers.

(3) A sound and adaptable constitution to enable the plant to thrive and produce an abundance of flowers in the variable conditions of a British summer—for instance, hydrangeas are sensitive to dry conditions, and particularly to drying winds which can cause them to collapse, but these are not garden flowers; they are rather the last resort of decorators who have run out of ideas.

(4) A long flowering period, at least for the entire months of June, July, August and September.

(5) A medium height, preferably between 1 and 2 feet, or a semi-prostrate habit, because we shall not want them trespassing into the skyline.

If the five conditions above are fulfilled it will mean that a large number of summer bedding plants is excluded, and that those which best fulfil the requirements are zonal and ivy-leaved geraniums, petunias and some of the marigolds.

Double geraniums give a greater weight of colour than single-flowered ones, although the flowers are inclined to go black in the middle in rainy weather. The crimson Double Henry Jacoby is easier to live with in the garden than the strident orange-scarlet of Gustav Emich, which is more suited to public gardens where it is seen momentarily in passing, or at the worst for a few hours. A. M. Mayne, another double, is magenta-purple, a little dark and lifeless on its own in a tub but good as a pot plant mixed with other kinds such as Double Jacoby, Mrs Lawrence or Hermine. King of Denmark is a salmon-pink, double-flowered variety, excellent where a softer, more feminine colour is wanted, but without the bite of some of the stronger colours. It is good on its own, but is not a good companion for flowers on the blue side of red. Hermine has double, blue-white flowers.

Paul Crampel is the best-known of the singles. It must surely be the essential 'geranium', indomitably weatherproof and long-suffering in neglect. It is a true scarlet and in many ways the most satisfying on account of its open habit of growth, its free flowering and good constitution. Doris Moore, another single, has attractive, cherry-red flowers, but it just lacks the quality of harshness which is needed to make flowers 'tell' when out on their own on the terrace. Maxim Kovalevski has a touch of mustard in its orange-scarlet, even hotter than Gustav Emich, and difficult to mix. For a single white not likely to have its flowers spoiled by rain the Queen of Whites will do well.

In small bowls **Red Black Vesuvius** can be exceedingly telling. It is a short-growing plant with small, bright scarlet flowers and dark green leaves with black zones, giving an impression of inky darkness which contrasts sharply with the intense colour of the flowers.

So much for the older, well-known zonal geraniums. In the last few years, largely through the enterprise of Mr S. E. Lake of Ashdown Forest Nurseries, some new zonals have been introduced from the United States. They are known as the Irene strain, from the name of the first outstanding seedling to be developed by Mr Dave Adgate of Elm Road Greenhouses, Ohio. The important characteristics are large trusses of flowers beginning early in the spring and continuing well into the autumn, and compact, short jointed growth. Experience of them in this country so far is limited, but it would appear that these geraniums are most successful in hot summers and where there is some restriction of root growth as in pots and tubs. In cold, wet conditions, in rich soil, in partial shade, and where the roots have free scope, growth can be too free for full flower production, and the blooms show a tendency to be spoiled by heavy rain.

Irene itself is described as rich, semi-double, red. In 1964 I used it experimentally in plantings at London Airport. Although it was bedded out in open beds, in the hot summer of that year it proved to be very successful; the colour, though without the punch of Paul Crampel or Gustav Emich, was warm and solid, and in October, when in nearby beds Paul Crampel was looking leggy and passé, Irene continued compact and as full of colour as at midsummer. Others which I have seen at Trulls Hatch and which I shall try in future years are Genie, semi-double, rose salmon-pink—a greenhouse full of these was a beautiful sight—Pink Bouquet, semi-double, a rather pale lilac-pink, something like Mrs Laurence; Trulls Hatch, a very promising semi-double salmon-pink; and Toyon, a single scarlet with perhaps a little more orange in it than Paul Crampel.

I think that geraniums are seen at their best in clay pots stood about on the terrace as in Spain and Italy. A group could be made up of three plants in 12-inch pots and five or seven plants in 5-inch pots. These put together would make a significant mass of low colour on the terrace. Such a group could be cooled off with a pot or two of the grey-foliaged *Senecio cineraria* (*S. maritima*), or diluted with some pots of *Pelargonium crispum variegatum*, with its spire-like growth and curly, gold-variegated, lemon-scented leaves. Zonal geraniums are also often planted in tubs or shallow bowls in which the colours can be kept separate, as suggested for the early tulips. If it is thought that *en masse* they look a little gawky and *parvenu*, the situation can be saved by including a procumbent plant like *Helichrysum petiolatum*, whose wide-spreading grey foliage has a gently civilising influence. The softer colour of Double Henry Jacoby is well set off by the scented leaved *Pelargonium tomentosum*, with its downward-spreading habit and affable, grey-green, hairy, peppermint-scented leaves.

The ivy-leaved geraniums (varieties of *Pelargonium peltatum*), have spreading, prominently jointed stems, some reaching to 3 feet horizontally, and smooth leaves. The flowers are smaller and rather less bright than those of the zonal pelargoniums. Their greatest use is in urns at some distance above the ground, on piers at the edges of steps, on ledges or pilasters, even above eye level, where their trailing habit can be fully apprehended. They are *par excellence* the plants for hanging baskets. Galilee is a double pink variety often used in hanging baskets, where its blue-pink flowers combine well with the scarlet of Paul Crampel. Audrey Clifton is a darker cerise-crimson, and there are attractive mauve-pink varieties, especially La France. The most interesting ivy-leaved geranium is L'Élégante, which has dark green, ivy-shaped leaves with grey and pale mauve variegation. The single flowers are white with purple veining. The plant has a wide-spreading, very graceful habit; its pale, unassertive colour makes it well suited for mixing with some of the zonal pelargonium in large bowls, where its truly elegant, down-sweeping leaves and flowers make an impressive foil to the hard edge of the bowl.

I think the best plant for urns is the scented-leaved *Pelargonium* Clorinda, a vigorous grower that soon takes on a spreading, prostrate habit. The foliage is softly hairy and strongly rose-scented. The flowers are exceptionally large for a scented-leaved geranium and silvery-cerise in colour. The whole plant is much more graceful than the ivy-leaved geraniums, with their rather gauche jointed stems and shiny leaves.

Petunias are well adapted to growing in tubs or bowls. They flourish in hot weather and within reason seem to enjoy hot soil conditions, provided they are kept watered. They grow so strongly

33. In this garden in Berlin concrete slabs are used in the paving with much smaller flint units in a mosaic pattern

34. The paving is of pebble dashed concrete tiles. The contrasting foliage and flowers are also of interest. The garden was designed by Mien Ruys, Amsterdam

35. Hexagonal paving with very wide joints has been used here. Designed by Arne Jacobsen

36. Agapanthus in large white tubs by the swimming bath at Pusey House, Faringdon, Berkshire. The little pavilion was designed by W. Godfrey Allen, M.A., F.S.A., F.R.I.B.A.

37. Part of the garden at the Palazzo Farnese, Caprarola, near Viterbo

38. Villa
Medici, Rome

in good summers that they soon become procumbent and tumble over the edges of their tubs with exuberant abandon. It must be recognised, though, that they are far less successful than geraniums in cold, dull, wet weather.

Until lately the colours of petunias, except for some of the striped ones, have been difficult. The blues have had a good deal of violet or mauve in them. Alderman, for instance, so much used, is a dark navy blue, a lifeless colour, and Rose of Heaven is a washy pink, but with the arrival of the F₁ Grandiflora hybrids we now have a beautiful series of very large flowers in new colours. The best of these are mentioned in the chapter on window boxes (see p. 116): Capri, so far the bluest of the blues, but still with some violet in it; Red Ensign and Candy Apple, crimson-scarlet; and Glacier, white. The flowers of the last-mentioned are very large, frilled and vanilla scented. One year I used it to follow the *fosteriana* Princeps tulips in two shallow bowls on the terrace, to which they lent a cool distinction all through the summer. When bowls are grouped together I would try Glacier in the high bowl with either Capri or Red Ensign in the two lower ones, but not one in each. A red, white and blue combination, though patriotic, is better appreciated in a public park.

If yellow is called for in these middle-distance tubs or bowls, some of the marigolds will give all the colour needed, but without the charming growth of petunias. Orange Glow and Lemon King are single-flowered French marigolds 8 or 9 inches high. Two double-flowered African marigolds are Spun Gold, 9 to 12 inches, and Hawaii which grows to 3 feet. If they are to flower freely and not run to leaf, the amount of fertilisers given during the growing season should be restricted.

Lilium auratum will bring not only great beauty of flower but delicious scent to a terrace or verandah. This is the golden-rayed Lily of Japan. Each plant will grow to 4 feet or more and have half a dozen or so funnel-shaped flowers up to 8 inches across, with waxy white petals covered in varying degrees with crimson and yellow spots and rays. The scent is exceedingly strong, of a kind that indoors is called overpowering by those of nervous sensibility, but which out of doors is heady and inspiring. *L. speciosum* has more reflexed flowers like a martagon or Turk's-cap. There are many varieties: *album-novum*, pure white with golden anthers; *magnificum* has deep crimson spots and petals so suffused with rose as to appear blushing all over except at the tips; *rubrum* and Melpomene have similar colour characteristics. Both *auratum* and *speciosum* require a lime-free soil. A good mixture would be the same as that recommended for camellias (see Chapter XXII) above a drainage layer of broken crocks in the bottom of the pots. The bulbs should be planted from 4 to 6 inches deep soon after they are received, usually some time in January. Three bulbs will be enough for a pot or tub 1½ to 2 feet in diameter. Single bulbs should be put into 7- or 8-inch pots. *L. auratum* flowers normally in August and September and *L. speciosum* a little later. *L. candidum*, the Madonna Lily, prefers some mortar rubble at the bottom of the pot and an alkaline soil. The bulbs should be planted in August, singly in large pots. When they come into flower a year later the plants can be brought to the verandah or loggia where, as in mediaeval paintings, their austere, tall beauty still speaks of continuing Grace.

Many climbers such as clematis, climbing roses and jasmine can be grown for a time in deep boxes. *Cobaea scandens*, however, is possibly a better choice. It is a tender perennial from Mexico, but is treated as an annual; it will make from 10 to 20 feet of growth in a single summer. It may survive a mild winter, but more often will be cut to the ground or killed. When this happens the opportunity can be taken to change the soil in the container, and little effective time will have been lost, because of the plant's ability to reach the top of the house from a standing start each year. The flowers appear late in the season, bell-shaped, green at first but later turning a mysterious dim violet-purple. There is also a white form. The large seeds are sown on edge in gentle heat and young plants kept in a cool greenhouse until they can be hardened off before being planted out at the end of May. It climbs by twining branched tendrils, and is seen at its best on the supports of a verandah or against a trellis on the house wall.

Pharbitis tricolor (*Ipomoea rubro-caerulea*), Morning Glory, is another twining plant which is well suited to cultivation in large pots or deep boxes. Its success depends entirely on the weather in the summer. In dull, cool summers it will at first do nothing and then die, but in really hot, sunny weather it will flourish and produce its large, innocent, China-blue flowers in profusion.

CHAPTER XIV

Pots and Tubs

Clay pots were some of the earliest containers to be used. For our purposes today the ordinary ones made in this country range from 3 to 18 inches in diameter. Up to about 12 inches these pots are satisfactory for geraniums on the terrace, but above this size the pot plays a greater part in the ensemble and the design of the pot begins to have significance.

The illustration, fig. 39, facing page 116 shows the difference between English and Italian clay pots of roughly equal size, one tight-lipped and a little uncertain, the other smiling, remembering its native Tuscan sunshine.

Plants in pots of less than 5 inches will be susceptible to drying out in hot weather and may have to be watered twice a day in such conditions.

For pots above 12 inches Italian terracotta pots, variations of the classical lemon pots, will be most suitable. One of the simplest is the Vaso Normale (fig. 41, facing p. 116), with a rounded lip and single moulding. It can be had in sizes varying from about 12 inches up to nearly 30 inches, and so also can the entirely plain Vaso da Camelia (fig. 40, facing p. 116), and the Vaso Festonato, with its swag relief and thicker mouldings. The Orcio da Giardino (fig. 44, facing p. 117) and the Orcio ad Anfora Liscio (fig. 43, facing p. 117) are best as pure ornaments or as water jars, because their height is greater than their width, making them too tall for planting.

Italian terracotta is also used for jardinières, long, low, rectangular-shaped boxes in which hyacinths or tulips, and later, any of the summer-flowering plants, can be grown and stood on the terrace, perhaps on either side of a flight of steps, or by the side of a garden door from the house. A Venetian pattern is illustrated in (fig. 45, facing p. 117), and a Florentine design in fig. 46.

Similar in intent to terracotta but centuries away in execution and feeling are the many imitation stone and concrete bowls and tubs. Artificial stone is concrete in which either coloured cement or natural stone dust is used in the aggregate. Some of the patterns are coarse in section. Concrete is used for many of the modern containers designed to match present-day buildings. The low, flat design, with clear-cut sharp taper, was first seen at about the time of the Festival of Britain in 1951. It is useful for petunias and ivy-leaved geraniums which spread outwards and downwards towards the terrace.

The taller concrete tub is not a good partner for a bay tree or a pomegranate; its real advantage is that its height renders plants in it safe from the salutations of all but the tallest dogs.

Uncouth materials such as polythene and asbestos cement are being used to make containers in whose design the primary intention must have been egregious ugliness, with cheapness only a secondary consideration. Some of them, strongly suggestive of spittoons, chamber pots, and bedpans, must be intended for one's most hated plants.

Round wooden tubs are still commonly used as plant containers. The old beer casks like the splendid Guinness tubs referred to in the first edition of this book are no longer available owing to the increasing use by brewers of metal barrels. Instead new tubs are being made of oak or an imported hardwood such as iroko. Two useful sizes measure 20 inches in diameter by 18 inches high, and 16 inches in diameter by 14 inches high. Tubs will last longer if they are painted inside with bituminous paint, or the insides charred like the insides of window boxes. Drainage holes of $\frac{1}{2}$ inch diameter should be drilled in the bottom of the tubs about 6 inches apart. When in use they should be stood on blocks of wood or on bricks, the weight resting on the actual bottom of the tub and not on the lower ends of the staves. Tubs to hold flowers are best painted all over white, hoops and all. White flowers, and particularly daturas, look very well in them. Dark blue or dark grey tubs suit standard lilacs, hibiscus and agapanthus, but green should, I feel, only be used for bay trees.

For the trees square wooden tubs are needed. Even the larger wooden tubs do not hold enough soil, nor do they carry enough visual weight, to balance a heavy-headed tree. Orange trees for some reason look best in tubs of the shape of a perfect cube, but for most others a 'low cube' seems more suitable. The tubs can be made of untreated hard wood such as teak, which is very long-lasting, or cedar, or they can be made of a soft wood if they are to be painted.

When full of soil and with their tree in position they are so heavy that it may be necessary to use rollers to move them. Four of these will be needed, round stakes about 2 inches in diameter, or iron pipes. As the tub is moved forward the roller from the back will come free and is picked up and carried round to the front before another forward move is made. Another method is to tip up the tub and spread a strong piece of hessian underneath one corner and then, by raising the other corners in turn, as it were, screw the whole tub on to the hessian. If two edges of the hessian are then picked up it will be found that the tub can be dragged across the terrace comparatively easily.

Really large trees which will remain in their tubs for many years must be housed in a container from which the sides and the bottom can be removed so that, in order to make room for fresh compost, the size of the ball (the soil in which the plant is growing, held together by the mass of roots) can be reduced from time to time by cutting away one or two inches from the outside to remove some of the old soil. This is best done in the spring, two sides being dealt with each year. The method is to lever up one side of the tub with two crowbars, and then to insert a wooden bearer so that when the crowbars are withdrawn the tub remains tilted with one side clear of the ground. This side can then be removed and the outer edge of the ball shaved away to a thickness of about an inch with an old scythe blade. When this has been done the side of the tub is replaced, the crowbars again inserted, the bearer removed and the tub gently let down to a level position. The whole process is then repeated for the opposite side. The newly-made spaces between the edges of the ball and the inside of the tub are then filled with fresh compost mixed with fertiliser.

When each side is off, the bottom should be examined to make sure that the drainage material is not clogged with silt. If this is so the old crocks or ballast should be carefully pulled out and replaced with fresh material pushed in from the edges. When the bottom of the tub has to be renewed, it will be necessary to suspend the tree and tub together a few inches above the ground by means of a block and tackle and shear legs. When this is done the base of the trunk of the tree must be carefully padded with sacking before the rope is fixed to it. The rope is then led up through the branches to the hook of the tackle chain.

The typical Versailles caisse is an example of this sort of tub. In France they are usually made of oak and painted. They are constructed as four panels secured to the four corner posts by eight flat iron bands, which drop into slots formed by upturned pieces of metal, of the same section, fitted into the posts. When the side of a tub has to be removed, the upper bar is first tapped upwards with a hammer out of its slots and then the lower bar removed in the same way. This makes one side of the tub free so that it can be tapped away, exposing one side of the root ball. I have seen this done to an orange tree which had been in its tub for very many years, and certainly it had been growing in tubs for at least a century. The exposed face of the ball glistened like brawn in a glass and was so compacted that it was difficult to push a knife into it. It impressed me with the importance of an open texture in the growing compost and the absolute necessity of good drainage at the bottom.

Urns are seen at their best when rather above eye level on piers or the copings of terrace walls, when they are filled with petunias or ivy-leaved geraniums, possibly mixed with *Helichrysum petiolatum* or a scented geranium with a spreading habit, like *Pelargonium tomentosum*. The fibre-glass copies of old lead garden urns are entirely convincing and, as far as is known, unaffected by frost, or indeed by anything the weather can do. It is childishly amusing to pick up one of these very large fibre-glass 'lead' urns in one hand and whirl it round one's head. The makers are now also producing a fibre-glass 'lead' tank which is useful to get a little added height for planting by a door, for instance.

The standard recipe for a hanging basket is a wire cage stuffed with moss, a little soil, one Paul Crampel, one white marguerite, three Galilee, two *Fuchsia* Marinka and half a dozen trailing lobelias. The maintenance requirement is formidable. In really hot, windy weather it may be necessary to water them twice a day. But apart from this I do not regard hanging baskets as attractive ways of growing plants. In fact, I find it a little unnerving to see them swinging above my head. When used in attempts to 'brighten' streets, in large towns, they are hopelessly out of scale. In any case I do not believe that streets need brightening in that sense. What they so often need is grass and large trees. I would like to suggest to the authorities concerned that they should save the money budgeted for these brightening operations until they can afford to plant street trees like planes or limes and, by laying waste a few garages and shops, make room for some cool stretches of turf.

Hanging baskets are most at home on house boats on the river where, to those old enough to remember, they will bring back memories of Maidenhead in the early years of the century, memories of cigar smoke and Ayala Champagne, of the sound of the Merry Widow Waltz floating through the open windows of Murray's Club, and of electric canoes gliding away into the amorous dusk.

CHAPTER XV

Window Boxes

Window boxes have two separate functions. In one they are minia-ture gardens and can be used for almost any plant that will exist for a limited time in 7 inches of soil with a favourable aspect. A wide variety of plants from wildings like daffodils, and even snowdrops, to auriculas and dahlias, are grown and cherished in such boxes to give pleasure to invalids or to old people confined to the house. The other function, and the one with which we are concerned here, is to decorate the outside of the house by using the colour and organic form of flowers.

The window box itself is a specialised form of plant container. Its shape and size are dictated by practical considerations of weight and by convention. It provides minimal conditions for the growth of plants raised high above their natural environment, exposed to the circulation of air on all sides and from below, seldom watered by rain, and crowded together at a density which would not be contemplated in the open ground.

Window boxes are now made in metal, plastics, asbestos and con-crete, but the traditional construction (see Chapter XXIII) in wood, painted to match or to contrast with the colour of the house, is still the one most generally employed. Ivory or cream colours will reduce the amount of heat absorbed and will go well with white or nearly white walls. Dark blue or blue-green go with brick walls and grey stone. The hard woods, oak and cedar, when unpainted look best against wooden houses of the same materials but, apart from teak, hard woods do not merit their extra cost on grounds of durability.

39. *Above:* Italian (left) and English pots of about 12in. in diameter

40. *Right:* Vaso da Camelia (23in. in diameter)

41. *Below left:* Vaso Normale (23in. in diameter)

42. *Below right:* Vaso Festonato (31½in. in diameter)

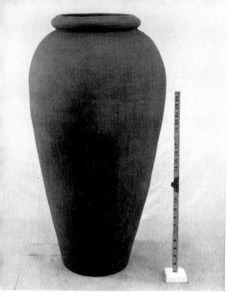

43. Orcio ad Anfora Liscio (31½in. high)

44. Orcio da Giardino (27½in. high)

45. Jardinière Decorata (19½in. lo[ng] 11¾in. wi[de] and 9½in. high)

46. Jardinière Festonata (23½in. long, 7½in. wide and 8in. high)

There must be adequate drainage and the box must be firmly attached to the house. It is obviously of great importance to make absolutely certain that it is securely fixed and cannot fall and cause possibly serious injury.

Before filling the box with soil, each drainage hole should be covered with a broken crock. It is not usually advisable to add coarse drainage material, ashes or gravel, before the growing medium is put in. With air circulating all round the box, plants in window boxes are much more likely to suffer from drought at the roots than from excessive moisture, and if the soil is changed at least every two years there will be little danger of waterlogged conditions setting in at the bottom of the box. The change of soil is necessary for another reason—the fertilisers used for topdressing leave toxic residues which must be got rid of. In the case of an unusually deep box or of one on a western aspect (where it will be exposed to more rain), a thin layer of weathered ashes or gravel could be spread on the bottom and covered with sphagnum moss or thin grass turves placed grass downwards. The final filling, which will be the growing medium, is then put in and pressed down to leave an inch of clear space below the top of the box. Growing composts are discussed in Chapters XVI and XXII.

Zonal geraniums should be planted 9 inches apart and ivy-leaved varieties possibly a little closer; petunias 4 to 6 inches apart; and smaller summer flowers like French marigolds 4 inches apart. When small plants are put in there will be gaps between them at first, but with proper treatment they will soon grow together to form a coherent mass of colour. After planting the box should be well watered and then allowed to dry out to some extent. This is done for two reasons—first, because roots will not thrive in cold, saturated conditions, and second, because the creation of temporarily dry conditions at the roots in the early stages will compel the plant to push out its roots in search of moisture, and thus form an extensive root system. The period of partial water starvation must be controlled, the plants carefully observed and water applied at once if they appear to be seriously flagging.

In the first month after planting no fertiliser will be needed, but when the box is well filled with roots, in from four to six weeks, a soluble, quick-acting fertiliser with a high nitrogen content should be applied. In the case of petunias particularly, and also geraniums, feeding with artificial fertiliser should be repeated about once every ten days, because, to a greater degree even than plants in tubs, or pots, those in window boxes are being asked to produce their flowers under highly artificial conditions. Their root run is drastically restricted, they are grossly overcrowded, and subject to buffeting by wind and rapid drying out at the roots. Certain plants, notably the French and African marigolds, should be kept on a lean diet to discourage excessive leaf production at the expense of flowers. The soil in the box should be thoroughly soaked with water before fertiliser is applied and the fertiliser itself should be watered in. Weeds must be removed, otherwise they will compete for the plant nutrients. Fading flowers and seed pods must be cut off and removed so that the energy of the plant shall be concentrated on producing flowers rather than seed.

On the terrace, plants and flowers exist for the delight of those who, as it were, belong to the house. By contrast, the planting of a window box is a vicarious exercise in that the flowers are intended as much for the pleasure of those outside the influence of the house, perhaps even for strangers who may be passing the house for the first and only time. There are certain definite, if rather limited, requirements for the flowers in window boxes. The first is colour, which must be bright, and if not always hard, at least firm and unequivocal. This is not the place for pastel colours. The size of the window box is generally small in relation to the scale of the house, but if the flowers growing in it envelop the box and expand its apparent size, the proportions will be improved. The flowers, or the trusses of flowers, should be of significant size, because the masses of colour should appear as solid as possible—a *pointilliste* effect will be restless and even disconcerting. The plants chosen should also have a sufficiently long period of bloom to merit the expense and the trouble that has to be taken, and they must also be robust and adaptable enough to survive in the highly artificial conditions which are imposed on them.

If all these requirements are to be complied with, it is evident that the range of plants which can be used in window boxes is considerably narrowed. A number of plants will satisfy nearly all these conditions in the summer, but the value of spring flowers in window boxes is open to question. For formal and official buildings where decoration is considered essential, blue and white florists' cinerarias in the spring and yellow Jante Wells chrysanthemums in the autumn, bedded out for an occasion, will do what is needed, but for private houses there is a good case for the removal of window boxes when the summer flowers have faded. Then for a few months the house can resume its true character, stripped like trees in winter.

If the window boxes are built into the structure of the house, or for other reasons cannot be removed, it will be better to plant them with spring flowers than to leave them stark and staring. Stripling · conifers, Lawson's or Fletcher's Cypress, and variegated aucubas are often used to give greenness and some height through the winter, but baby box are more civilised. In front of them colour is obtained from the Double Early tulips referred to earlier. (The Single Early tulips are too liable to have their petals blown off by rough winds in exposed positions.) Aubrieta along the front and spreading downwards will do something to enlarge the container.

Window boxes come into their own in early summer when men in baize aprons are bedding out the parks and squares. They belong essentially to the Mayfair of Michael Arlen, where 'South Street becomes North Street and Grosvenor Square is but a step in the right direction. . . .'

Zonal and ivy-leaved geraniums have a long flowering period, good firm colours, are long suffering and are probably the most reliable. They have been discussed in Chapter XIII in the context of their use in pots and tubs; they can also be used in window boxes, and it should be remembered that in window boxes double-flowered geraniums are less likely to have their heavy flower trusses spoiled by rain than when growing in the open ground. This is because in window boxes very little direct rain ever falls on the box: the buffer effect of the house creates eddies and upsurges of wind, which keep the rain a little distance away. Double Henry Jacoby is a good solid crimson which will mix much better with whites than Paul Crampel or Gustav Emich. This latter, which is double-flowered, is a hard-hitting signal-red; it is the geranium which has been planted in recent years in the large beds by the Victoria Memorial outside Buckingham Palace. King of Denmark, another double, produces large salmon-pink trusses of flowers with great generosity, and is effective against white walls or where there is a hint of ochre in the lime-washing, but less good where the background has mauve or magnolia tones. These are the best zonal geraniums for the purpose, but if soft or unusual colours are preferred, Mrs Lawrence, another double-flowered one, is lower growing and a pale lilac-pink, a feminine colour without the aggressiveness really needed in a window box. A. M. Mayne, another double, has flowers the colour of pickled cabbage, interesting and unusual in flower beds at ground level, but a little dark and just not sufficiently alive for our purpose here. Some of the American Irene geraniums, already referred to in Chapter XIII, should also be very successful for window boxes.

The variegated zonal geraniums are useful because their foliage colour provides interest when the plants are not in flower. Caroline Schmidt and Chelsea Gem have silvery-white margins to the foilage. The first has rather small cerise flowers and the second paler pink. Mr Henry Cox is known as a golden tricolor. It has pink flowers, but its chief interest is its golden leaves variegated with purple, red and cream.

Ivy-leaved geraniums planted in front of the zonals soothe away the rather stiff upright habit of the latter. They also grow forwards and downwards, contrasting with the hard outline of the box. They have the same good constitution, adaptability and length of flowering as their zonal cousins, so that the combination of the two is much used. The double pink Galilee is often seen alone or in association with Paul Crampel in London window boxes. It is a hackneyed combination, but it has stood the test of time and taste for many years. Other associations are King of Denmark with the ivy-leaved Madame Crousse, rather paler in colour than Galilee. L'Élégante is a beautiful, wide-spreading ivy-leaved variety with white flowers of no great significance, but very attractive leaves with pale mauve margins. The grey *Helichrysum petiolatum*, with its spreading, horizontal growth and leaves green above and silvery beneath, associates particularly well with King of Denmark. *Senecio cineraria* has deeply cut, silvery, hairy leaves and can also be used; but on the whole an admixture of grey in a window box tends to reduce the impact of solid colour and is less effective there than at ground level, where instead some dilution of hard colour may often be welcomed.

Petunias are some of the few plants which thrive with hot soil conditions at the roots. They will carry out both the upright and the trailing functions required of plants in window boxes. They will grow upwards at first for a foot or more, but very soon begin to fall forward and so downwards over the edges of the boxes, which they entirely cover with graceful sprays of foliage and flower. Gipsy Ballerina is a very bright F_1 hybrid grandiflora, fiery scarlet with an overlay of a darker red which at times seems to have something of black in it. It was very successful in one year in the urns along the edge of the terrace at Pusey House. Other good F_1 grandiflora hybrid petunias are Candy Apple, vivid scarlet; Capri, blue-violet; and Glacier, white, which can be mixed either with the blue or the red, but preferably not with both, except for beds in a yacht-club lawn.

French and African marigolds are useful where yellows and oranges are needed; it should be remembered that they will produce most flowers if kept on a lean diet. Spun Gold is an African marigold, double-flowered, growing from 9 to 12 inches high; and Hawaii, also double-flowered, grows to 3 feet. A place can be found in many arrangements for *Campanula isophylla*, a pendulous plant with lilac-blue flowers of much charm.

Where a significant impact of colour is intended, it is a mistake to use more than two, or at the very most three, different plants in one container, but once this intention has been abandoned there is an immensely wide field open to experiment. In his book, *Window Box Gardening*, Mr Teuscher gives 28 different suggestions for effective plant combinations on the American continent, for such conditions as full sun, light shade, and a northern exposure.

Foliage effects are sometimes attempted by making use of the large bronze leaves of *Begonia rex* and coleus, and the Chinese lanterns of *Abutilon megapotamicum*. Asparagus fern is also used, but its fine, needle-like foliage is no match for the massive blankness of a house wall and succeeds only in looking thin and fussy. Generally it is better to approach these window-box cocktails with caution.

On balconies and roof gardens larger, wider boxes can be used, and almost become raised beds. On roof gardens subject to wind it will be prudent to avoid the more delicate plants. Petunias, although enjoying dry conditions, are too easily shredded by harsh winds, so that pelargoniums once again will be the standby, and some of the African marigolds will also be useful. Here, too, once in a while a thoroughgoing clash might be interesting—a mixture, for instance, of the scarlet pelargonium Paul Crampel with white marguerites, mauve *Verbena rigida* and yellow French marigolds.

On balconies and verandahs there is often good shelter from winds and a degree of shade. Here for the spring I would try for one year a cottage mixture of polyanthus, wallflowers and forget-me-nots, with a few of the white lily-flowered tulip White Triumphator; and in other years I would confine a whole box to some of the 'broken' tulips. There are two bizarres which I think of as furniture-coloured: Absalon, yellow, flamed and feathered with mahogany, and Insulinde, yellow-bronze, deep purple and again mahogany. The Bybloem tulip May Blossom also has great distinction with its creamy-white flowers veined with bluish-purple. In these quieter surroundings forget-me-nots will do better than in tubs out in the open.

For the summer the planting in these wider boxes can be designed for a contemplative mood. Gentle and interesting fuchsias, which appreciate partial shade, are: La Bianca, pearly-white with pink stamens; Keystone, a rather warmer pink; and Marin Glow which has a fuchsine-blue corolla with white wing-like sepals. Other combinations could be white stocks and heliotrope, making an all-scented mixture; the white *Antirrhinum nanum grandiflorum* Majestic Avalanche, *Ageratum* Blue Mink and a rose-pink-flowered, tuberous-rooted begonia. Although nearly always sold in mixed colours, tuberous-rooted begonias can with perseverance be obtained in separate colours, among them white, rose, crimson, scarlet, yellow and copper. For a balcony with black railings at its edge and facing the sun, the white flowers of the petunia Snowcap pushing outwards through the railings may be more distinguished than any mixture of colours; or, if the railings were to face a little away from the sun, then a white regal pelargonium like Duchess of Teck would do instead.

CHAPTER XVI

Planting Composts

The filling of a pot or tub will begin with material to ensure drainage, to prevent stagnant, waterlogged conditions developing at the roots. In window boxes this will often consist only of a broken crock, with the convex side upwards, over each hole in the bottom. In other containers a layer of broken crocks can be used, the thickness depending on the depth of the pot or tub. For a 5-inch pot the layer of crocks will be about ½ inch thick; for a 2-foot tub the depth of the layer will be not less than 2 inches; and deeper still for the very largest tubs. The size of the crocks should be from ½ inch to 1 inch.

In tubs and large terrace pots a layer of grass turves placed upside down, or 2 inches of sphagnum moss on top of the crocks will prevent the soil from washing down and clogging the drainage. There will not be room in pots less than 12 inches deep for grass turves but a thin layer of sphagnum moss would be useful.

The soil or compost provides the purely mechanical stuffing to keep the plant in position, the medium into which the roots spread and take hold, an environment of air and water, and a reserve of plant foods.

Where the plants are changed every year one of the standard composts will be satisfactory. The John Innes composts (see Chapter XXII) were developed at the John Innes Horticultural Institution between 1933 and 1939. The object of the experiments was to establish standard formulations of seed and potting composts for greenhouse plants such as antirrhinums, cyclamen, primulas and others, but the principles which underlie the recommended composition of the potting compost are generally valid for plants in pots or tubs out of doors. It is an essential part of John Innes composts that the loam should be partially sterilised by heat in some form, because these composts were designed for plants growing in the artificial conditions of a greenhouse through which disease, if it appears, can spread rapidly. The process of sterilisation is a fairly critical one. Too little heat will accomplish nothing useful; too much may kill all the life in the soil, including beneficial bacteria. It may also produce, possibly temporarily, excessive nitrogen, making it necessary to allow the sterilised soil to rest before it is used to make into a compost. When made with partially sterilised loam the composts should be used within a month or two of mixing because if stored beyond that time they may become too acid for some plants. These factors could, I think, lead to defects in the compost in course of production and possibly through delays in distribution, and therefore—although I know that some of the experts will not agree with me—my preference would be to use unsterilised loam in making up composts for plants grown in pots and tubs out of doors.

Because loam is the most variable and the most difficult to standardise of the constituents of a compost, experiments have been carried out to produce composts which do not contain loam. Some of the formulae used by the University of California are set out in Chapter XXII. Work has also been done on loamless composts at the Fairfield Experimental Horticulture Station at Kirkham, near Preston in Lancashire. Here it has been found that loamless composts, consisting of 50% or more of sand, are very free draining and inclined to dry out completely in the summer months; also that the nutrients are quickly leached out of these sandy mixtures. On the other hand, composts containing more than 75% of peat are retentive of moisture and apt to remain very wet in a wet summer or in the winter months. The Fairfield loamless compost, which contains 75% peat and 25% sand, has been found by the Experimental Horticulture Station to be the easiest to manage from the watering point of view, and if loamless composts are to be used for plants such as petunias grown out of doors during the summer months this would seem to be the most suitable. John Innes composts are probably better for large containers, and, particularly where shrubs and trees are grown in tubs exposed to wind, because the clay fraction of the loam binds the compost together to form a well-knit base for root anchorage.

When trees and shrubs remain in their tubs for many years, considerable compression is developed in the growing compost, largely as the result of repeated watering. To counteract this the addition of broken crocks or charcoal ⅛ inch in size right through the body of the compost is recommended (see Chapter XXII).

For other occasions where the plants are changed every year, and consequently the composts can be completely changed also, John Innes Potting Compost No. 3 or one of the loamless composts will be suitable.

After filling, and when the plants are in position, a space should be left above the compost and below the top edge of the container to allow the surface to be flooded when watering, and to make room for a topdressing of fertilisers. After about six weeks when the tub or window box is well filled with roots this feeding with fertilisers will be necessary, except for such plants as African and French marigolds which will make leaf growth at the expense of flowers if treated too generously. A topdressing of John Innes Feed at the rate of 1 to 2oz. per square yard or another fertiliser with a high nitrogen content should be used.

The Versailles caisse, which is used for orange trees and other very large plants, was designed so that the compost in the containers could be regularly renewed. I am indebted to M. A. M. Chasseraud, L'Ingénieur Général des Eaux et Forêts, Ingénieur Général des Services Paysagers de la Ville de Paris et du département de la Seine, for an interesting letter on the growing of orange trees in France. In translation this reads:

'. . . The orange trees are contained in square boxes with detachable sides for reboxing. This is done after the winter. The soil is made up mainly of turfy loam mixed with horse manure and sand. Re-potting is carried out every three years. In the interval the soil is aerated by raking the surface once a year. In summer the orange trees are put on terraces in the sun and sheltered from the wind. They are liberally watered with liquid fertiliser while the new growth is being made.

'As soon as they are taken out of doors a layer of well-decayed cow manure is spread on the soil in the tubs.

'In winter the plants are kept almost completely dry; they must not be forced or the young shoots formed when inside and under cover will too easily shrivel when the tree is put out. If young branches are formed while the tree is indoors it is better to let them grow on under glass and then transfer them to a sheltered place before placing them in their final summer positions.

'In the Paris area orange trees are only grown for their foliage and their flowers. Two kinds are cultivated, *Citrus bigaradia* and *C. sinensis*.'

Special composts containing no lime must be prepared for calcifuges. A mixture for camellias and rhododendrons is set out in Chapter XXII. Acidity or alkalinity in the soil is expressed in terms of hydrogen ion concentration, written for short as pH. A pH reading of 7 is neutral, readings above are alkaline, lower readings are acid. For camellias and rhododendrons an acid soil with a pH of from 5·0 to 5·5 is needed. Most other plants will succeed best in a soil with a pH of 6·5 to 7. After mixing a compost it is always desirable to check the pH of the finished product. Generally, the addition of peat will counteract alkalinity in the loam, but it is well to make sure by carrying out a test with one of the inexpensive testing sets. In an experimental compost in which I used leaf soil the pH of the final mixture came out at 3·0, which is much too low. When this happens Dolomite lime (magnesium limestone) or calcium carbonate can be added to increase the pH; but it is more satisfactory to arrive at the correct pH naturally without recourse to added lime by a careful pre-selection of the ingredients, slightly acid loam, peat and a lime-free sand.

PART TWO—CONSTRUCTION

CHAPTER XVII

Laying Paving and Terraces

In making a new paved area against the house first find the damp-proof course. This can be recognised as a line of slate or bituminous felt between courses of brickwork a little above ground level. The finished level of the paving should be at least 2 inches below this, and the surface of soil beds 6 inches below. If there is difficulty in locating the damp-proof course it would be wise to ask a builder to point it out, because if, by mischance, the terrace is made above this course there could be serious trouble with damp inside the house. The thickness of the materials to be used must be reckoned in calculating the depth of excavation.

In the recommendations given below the net depths of the excavation necessary to provide for foundation material and finished surface are stated. These depths may have to be adjusted to provide for 2 inches or so below the damp-proof course; the amount of adjustment will depend upon the level of the soil relative to the damp-proof course when excavations are started.

(a) To lay a gravel surface excavate the area to a depth of 7 inches, lay a consolidated depth of 4 inches of hard filling material such as clinker, gravel or brick hard core, and ram well. Then cover with path gravel graded from stones 1 inch in size downwards, water and well ram to a final thickness of 3 inches, cover thinly with fine shell or grit and roll again.

In districts where path gravel is not available, such as Cornwall, parts of Derbyshire, Lancashire, Lincolnshire, and Yorkshire, for example, local crushed granite shale or stone from $1\frac{1}{2}$ inches in size downwards can be used. The dust which comes with these materials will assist in the binding, after watering and rolling.

(*b*) To make a terrace with concrete laid *in situ* on firm ground, excavate 2 inches deep and ram or roll base. On soft or made-up ground excavate 7 inches, consolidate base and lay a 4-inch layer of hard filling material as previously described. With strings attached to long nails mark out a grid of 6-foot squares. Round at least two of the squares fix boards 1 inch thick and of a depth equal to the intended thickness of the concrete. Mix concrete in proportions of 1 part cement, 2 parts sand, and 3 parts coarse aggregate by volume. Lay the concrete within an hour of mixing 2 inches thick on firm ground, 3 inches thick above the hard filling on the soft ground. If the soil base is dry, damp it before placing concrete. Lay the concrete in alternate bays. After laying a bay next to one already laid, remove dividing board to provide joint to prevent cracking. Compact the concrete with a punner or a length of board laid across the forms. To produce a rippled surface work the cross board with a chopping motion and then with a sawing action. Another way to produce a textured surface is to use a wood float with a rotary motion.

Refix boards to proceed to next grid squares until terrace is covered. Remove boards when concrete hardens. Protect newly laid concrete as soon as it has set with wet sacks or with a covering of polythene sheeting or building paper for several days. For exposed aggregate finish, brush surface with a soft broom to remove surplus mortar an hour after the concrete has been placed. Brush surface with stiff broom when it has hardened sufficiently so that stones are not dislodged, and spray with water, leaving the stones slightly proud of the surface.

(*c*) To lay concrete flags or slabs 2 inches thick on firm ground, excavate to a depth of 2 inches and consolidate base. On made-up or soft ground excavate to a depth of 6 inches, consolidate base and lay 4 inches of hard filling material as described above. Fix strings to boundaries. Either mix mortar in the proportions of 1 part cement and 6 parts of sand by volume, use within an hour of mixing, and bed the slabs on this material laid to a depth of 1 inch; or lay bed of sand or fine ashes to a depth of 1½ inches and spot bed the stones with five dabs of mortar, one at each corner and one in the middle. Use small distance pieces of wood between the slabs to maintain even joints or lay slabs closely jointed. Tap each slab into position until any tendency to rock is eliminated. Check level of each slab before bedding next one. Where joints are left remove wooden distance pieces after laying and fill joints with mortar, ramming it well in. Smooth the surface of the joints with a trowel, and finish by rubbing with a stick to reduce level of mortar slightly below surface level of slabs. Alternatively, fill joints with sand. If mortar is dropped on surface, clean it off at once before the next slab is laid.

In pointing paving much time can be saved in protecting the surface from mortar if a sheet metal tray is made up with a long slit in the middle of the bottom and with the edges turned slightly down to fit in to the joint. The mortar mix is then spread on top of the tray and pushed down through the slot into the jointing. My friend Mr Boakes of the Cement and Concrete Association, tells me that he has seen this method employed at St Nazaire in Brittany.

Precast concrete flags are made in two thicknesses, 2 inches and $2\frac{1}{2}$ inches, to a standard width of 2 feet and in lengths of 3 feet, 2 feet 6 inches, 2 feet and 1 foot 6 inches. The usual colour is natural grey, but tints of buff, pink and red are also obtainable. The standard surface textures are mesh face, pimple face, bar face and chequer pattern.

Precast concrete paving slabs are made in the following sizes:

9in × $4\frac{1}{2}$in.
9in. × 9in.
1ft. × 6in.
1ft. × 1ft.
9in. × 9in.
9in. × 1ft. 6in.
1ft. × 1ft. 6in.
1ft. × 2ft.
1ft. 6in. × 1ft. 6in.
1ft. 6in. × 2ft.
1ft. 6in. × 2ft. 3in.
2ft. × 2ft.

Thickness of slabs varies with the size between $1\frac{1}{2}$in. and 2in.

(d) To lay natural stone, prepare base as for concrete slabs 2 inches thick but adjust depth of excavation to conform to the thickness of the stone. New stone will probably be about 2 inches thick, but recovered paving stones may range from 2 to 4 or 5 inches in thickness. In laying to a random rectangular pattern make sure that all the stones are trimmed to true rectangles. Provide bed of fine ashes 1½ inches thick and consolidate. Spot-bed the stones with five dabs of mortar, tapping them into position as described above. Joints should be ½ to ⅛ inches and pointed with mortar as above. Iron back with a thick wire or rod bent at right-angles to produce a depression of about ⅛ inch.

In laying stone coursed one way in random lengths make sure that the stones which are cut on site are true rectangles.

(e) To lay marble on firm ground and for light foot traffic, excavate 3½ inches, lay concrete base 2 inches thick with a mix of 1 part cement, 3 parts fine sand, 6 parts of ⅜-inch aggregate. (If ground is not firm or consists of a cohesive soil, or if there is to be heavier traffic, excavate 5½ inches and lay 4-inch thick concrete base.) Spread ¾-inch to 1-inch bed of mortar made up of 1 part cement, 6 parts of sand by volume, bed the marble with joints of from 1/16 to ⅛ inch and point with a slurry of white cement and sand. Marble is supplied ¾ inch thick for paving. When supplied as off-cuts in fixed widths but in random lengths to be cut to fit on the site with a craft saw it costs about 7s. a square foot less than when specially cut at the yard for a particular contract. Broken marble will cover about 20 square yards per ton, depending on the width of the joint.

(f) To lay slate, prepare base as in (e) for marble, but adjust depth of excavation to conform with the thickness of the slate, probably 1 inch or 1¼ inches. Obtain slate slabs ready cut to pattern and size, and lay with ⅛-inch joint pointed with black cement.

Slate is supplied in thicknesses of 1 inch or 1¼ inches and finished as frame-sawn, natural riven, sanded and fine rubbed. Slab sizes range from 2 feet by 1 foot 6 inches downwards.

(g) To lay granite setts, prepare base as for concrete slabs, but provide mortar bed 2 inches thick. Lay setts by pushing them into the mortar before it hardens. The width of the jointing will be governed by the irregularity of the sides of the setts. After laying, brush in a dry mixture of 1 part of cement to 3 parts of sand to a level about ¼ inch below the top of the setts, and then water carefully with a watering-can fitted with a rose.

The British Standard allows for the following finishes: Fine

47. A fountain in the Vatican Gardens, Rome

48. A large Rhododendron Pink Pearl in a square tub

picked, Fair picked, Single axed or nidged, and Rough punched.

(*h*) To lay cobbles, prepare base as for setts above. Lay cobbles either flat or on end by pushing them into the mortar bed before it hardens so that the cobbles stand about ½ inch above the mortar bed. Brush in dry mix as for setts.

(*i*) To lay bricks, prepare base as for concrete slabs, laying bricks on 1 inch of mortar, or lay the bricks dry on a consolidated ash bed 3 to 4 inches thick. Bricks can be laid flat with the frog downwards or on edge as stretchers. Joint should be ⅜ inch. Either fill joints with sand or point with mortar made of 4 parts of soft sand and 1 part of lime. Point with trowel, strike off and leave rough.

(*j*) To lay quarry tiles, prepare base as for slate. Joints can be as wide as 1 inch. Point with lime mortar as for bricks, or mortar made of coloured cement. Pointing should be flush.

CHAPTER XVIII

To Make a Small Lawn

Ensure that there is not less than 6 inches of good topsoil. For seeding, fix battens of thin wood or building-board all round to stand 1 inch above paving, secured to wood pegs 3 feet apart. (This is so that the finished level of the grass shall stand $\frac{3}{4}$ inch above paving level when lawn is established, to enable it to be mowed out to the extreme edges.)

Fork through topsoil, remove weeds and large stones. Bring to true level by raking. Consolidate by treading (heeling), and leave soil flush with top of battens. Rake in base fertiliser. Sow seed. Lightly roll. When the new turf is strong enough to hold up on its own, remove battens and pegs.

Grass seed can be sown at the rate of 1½oz. per square yard. A mixture of 70% Chewings Fescue and 30% Browntop will make a good lawn. If pedigree strains such as Highlight Chewings Fescue and Holfior Browntop can be obtained they are worth the extra expense. When established a lawn made in this way can be mown as close as $\frac{3}{16}$ to $\frac{1}{2}$ inch. Where close mowing is not insisted on an admixture of some rather coarser-leaved grasses will give a more interesting texture. Such a mixture might be made up of: Pedigree Creeping Red Fescue S.59 30%, Highlight Chewings Fescue 30%. Holfior Browntop 20%, *Poa pratensis* (the Kentucky Blue Grass of America) 20%. The turf resulting from this sowing should not be mown shorter than an inch.

If the lawn is to be turfed, the same preparatory operations will apply except that it is not necessary to fix battens or to carry out a

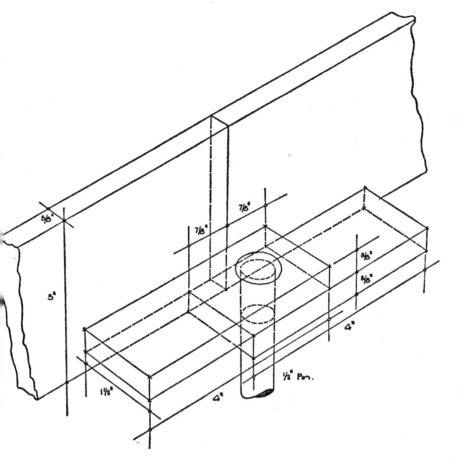

STEEL EDGE FOR LAWNS

fallowing. The turf will be laid in the autumn, winter or early spring, generally not in the summer, because it is often impossible for it to be cut and lifted in hard, dry weather, and also if laid in these conditions the turves will shrink before they are able to knit together, leaving gaps between individual turves.

To make a clinker foundation remove topsoil and lay it aside; excavate subsoil to a depth of 10 inches below intended finished level of grass; remove excavated subsoil. Construct a drain consisting of a line of 3-inch tile (agricultural) drains from the excavated level to an outlet, either the edge of the terrace, or a soak-away. This is to conduct water out of the clinker layer and prevent the latter acting as a tank. Then spread clean clinker ashes grading from $\frac{1}{2}$ to 1 inch to a consolidated depth of 4 inches and roll the surface. Replace topsoil to a consolidated depth of 6 inches if the lawn is to be made by seeding; to 5 inches if it is to be turfed, because the turves will be about 1 inch thick. Consolidate the topsoil in 3-inch layers by treading, then proceed as above for seeding or turfing.

Steel edging when used consists of bands of steel 3 inches by $\frac{3}{8}$ inch in lengths of about 10 feet. Each length has lugs welded to the lower part of each end drilled to take steel pins 12 inches long which are driven into the ground to secure the edging.

CHAPTER XIX

Electric Pumps and Fountains

These notes are intended to give to the private owner some preliminary information to assist him in discussions with his chosen experts. Advice should be obtained from a water engineer, the maker of the pump unit or a reliable contractor. It is particularly desirable that the electric installation should be approved by the local electricity board, because the motors of most pumps are run at mains voltage, and inexperienced workmanship or a bad connection could be dangerous.

There are two main types of pumps generally used for pool fountains: the dry motor surface pump in which the unit is outside the pool, and the submersible pump in which the unit is under water inside the pool or sometimes, for special reasons, in a flooded chamber alongside the pool and connected to it by pipes.

To consider first the surface pumps: the most generally used are not self-priming. They work best when fitted below the level of the water in the pool in conditions of what is known as flooded suction (see diagram I). When the pump is fitted above the level of the pool, as shown in diagram II, it is necessary to fit a valve in the pipe line so that the water in the pump body and the suction pipe will not empty back into the pool when the pump is stopped. The usual method is to fit a foot valve with a strainer at the end of the suction pipe in the pool. This will often work well for a time,

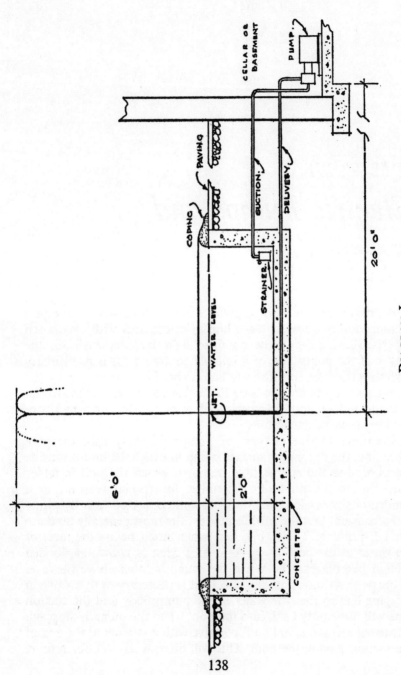

DIAGRAM I

Pool with pump operating with flooded suction

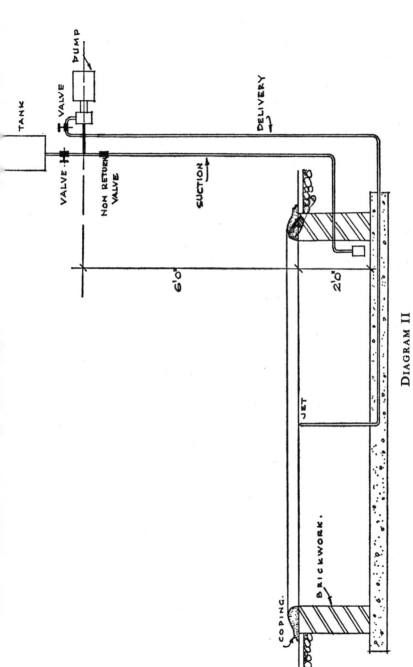

DIAGRAM II

Pool with pump fitted above water level requiring priming tank

139

but if a small piece of grit should get lodged in it the valve will not close properly, with the result that the suction pipe will be emptied. A useful arrangement is to fit a priming tank rather above the level of the pump to fill the system, as indicated in diagram II. The non-return valve is fitted in the suction pipe immediately below the connection between the priming tank and the pump so that the tank shall not empty itself back into the pool. The capacity of the priming tank should be at least half as much again as the capacity of the length of suction pipe. For the 20 feet of 1¼-inch suction pipe in the typical installation shown in diagram II the capacity of the priming tank should be 2 gallons. It has, of course, to be filled in the first instance by hand. Since this priming tank will be above the level of the jet it would be possible for water to run back to the pool through the delivery pipe by way of the pump. To prevent this, a valve should be fitted in the delivery pipe as close as possible to the pump. This valve will also serve as the controlling valve for the height of the jet—there should in any case be one valve for regulating each jet or pipe feeding water into a pool or fountain.

The output of a pump is stated as so many gallons per minute against a given head. This head, which is expressed in feet, is the resistance that the pump has to overcome to force the jet to the required height. It is referred to as total head from all causes and is made up of the forces of gravity and friction. Head due to gravity is approximately equal to the height of the jet. When the pump is fitted above the pool, head due to the static lift of the water from the pool to the pump must be added. The reduction of output due to frictional losses in the pipe runs is calculated from tables based on the diameter of the pipes, the length of the pipes, and the output through them in gallons per minute. The loss of head due to friction is very sensitive to the size of the pipe and the volume of water passing through it. The table below indicates frictional losses per 100 feet of pipe in different circumstances.

Gallons per minute	Pipe size	Frictional loss per 100ft.
2	½in.	30ft.
2	¾in.	4ft.
10	¾in.	80ft.
10	1 in.	20ft.

Gallons per minute	Pipe size	Frictional loss per 100ft.
10	1¼in.	7ft.
20	1 in.	70ft.
20	1¼in.	25ft.
20	1½in.	10ft.
20	1¾in.	4·5ft.

Two typical arrangements can be considered, assuming in each case that a vertical jet of 6 feet is required from a nozzle $\frac{3}{8}$ inch in diameter. In making calculations it is wise to allow generous margins above theoretical performance to provide for contingencies such as a reduction in voltage or partial clogging of the strainer. Therefore the calculations which follow are based on a jet 10 feet high instead of the 6 feet actually required. The output needed to operate jets of various sizes at various heights is calculable from tables. The following examples indicate the gallons of water per minute required to provide jets of water through nozzles of the diameter referred to in this book.

DISCHARGE FROM JETS

Nozzle size inches	Gallons per minute			
	Height of jets in feet			
	5	10	15	20
$\frac{1}{8}$	·537	·758	·929	1·07
$\frac{3}{16}$	1·21	1·71	2·09	2·41
$\frac{1}{4}$	2·15	3·03	3·72	4·29
$\frac{5}{16}$	3·36	4·74	5·81	6·70
$\frac{3}{8}$	4·83	6·82	8·36	9·66
$\frac{7}{16}$	6·58	9·30	11·4	13·0

$\frac{1}{2}$	8·59	12·1	14·8	17·2
$\frac{5}{8}$	13·4	18·9	23·2	26·8
$\frac{3}{4}$	19·3	27·3	33·4	38·6
$\frac{7}{8}$	26·3	37·1	45·5	52·6
1	34·4	48·5	59·4	68·6

In this case 19 gallons per minute are needed to force the $\frac{5}{8}$-inch jet to 10 feet. Frictional losses should also be generously allowed for. Initial exuberance in the height of the jet can be controlled by a valve in the delivery pipe; this valve will in any case be advisable to reduce the height of the jet in windy weather. No harm will come to centrifugal pumps by throttling down their delivery to as little as a quarter of their maximum output, but restriction in the suction is not desirable.

In the first example, shown in diagram I, a non-self-priming pump is installed in a cellar at a lower level than the pool, with a flooded suction. The suction and delivery pipes are each taken to be 20 feet long. The friction loss through 40 feet of $1\frac{1}{4}$-inch bore pipe at 19 gallons per minute is equivalent to a head of about 10 feet. To allow a margin this could be called 15 feet. There is in this case no suction lift, so that the total head from all causes is equivalent to 25 feet (i.e. 10 feet for the height of the jet plus 15 feet for frictional pipe loss). Having made these calculations, the next step is to choose a pump capable of delivering 19 gallons per minute against a total head of 25 feet.

In the second example, illustrated in diagram II, a non-self-priming pump is mounted 6 feet above the level of the pool, that is without a flooded suction so that a priming tank is also provided. Here the equivalent head due to pipe friction is assumed to be the same, namely 15 feet. The delivery head is also the same, 10 feet, but there is this time a suction lift of 6 feet. In this installation, therefore, the total head from all causes is 31 feet—it will probably be prudent to calculate upon 35 feet as the head against which a pump would be required to deliver 19 gallons per minute. The pump chosen should also be capable of a static lift of not less than 6 feet.

Pumps to carry out these duties would be driven by induction electric motors of between $\frac{1}{2}$ and 1 horsepower, depending on the efficiency of the pump and the head against which it would be working. Most motors of this kind run at about 2,900 revolutions per minute and are reasonably quiet in operation. Where silence is important a motor running at only 1,450 revolutions per minute may be chosen because it is usually quieter, but both its size and its cost are likely to be larger. In the case of the typical requirement referred to earlier, that is a jet 6 feet high from a $\frac{5}{8}$-inch nozzle, a motor running at 1,450 revolutions per minute would need to be of at least 1 horsepower.

Modern electric pumps and motors need little attention, but the motor must never be allowed to get wet or even damp. In this country the normal mains electricity supply to private houses is 230/250 volts, single-phase, A.C. supply, which is perfectly suitable to drive small motors up to about 3 horsepower. Industrial and other large premises are supplied with electricity at 400/440 volts, 3-phase, A.C., and this type of supply would anyway be necessary where motors above 3 horsepower are to be driven, and there are advantages in using this supply for all but the smallest motors where it is available.

Motors must be provided with switch gear to start and stop them and to protect the circuit from overload. Advice on the type of starting switch should be obtained from the local electricity authority, and especially if it is to be fixed out of doors or in a pump chamber below the level of the pool.

A self-priming pump will, when working within the limits of its designed suction lift, do away with the necessity for a foot valve or priming tank. In one type a specially designed pump body is kept always partly filled with water. When the pump is started, this water is circulated by the impellor from its discharge side through a venturi and back to its inlet: this draws water up the suction pipe and dispels the air. Some models have a valve which automatically closes the circulating system when the pump is fully primed. Another type works on a centripetal principle: it appears at first sight very much like a centrifugal pump, but has different characteristics and can be overloaded if run against a closed valve. Self-priming pumps are available with motors from a $\frac{1}{4}$ horse-power upwards, but in order to perform the duty taken in these notes as a standard one, that is to operate a $\frac{5}{8}$-inch jet to a height of from 6 to 10 feet, a more powerful motor would be needed.

Where there are fish and water-lilies in a pool, it will be advisable to confine the water effects to rather thin, low jets, except in cases where the pool is large enough for the fountain to be at some distance from the water-lilies. An example might be a jet 6 feet high—to be calculated as 10 feet—from a nozzle $\frac{1}{16}$ inch in diameter. The output required for this is 2 gallons per minute. It is assumed that the pump would be below the level of the pool in a ventilated chamber under the paving and that the suction and delivery pipes would each be 10 feet long. The equivalent head due to frictional loss in 100 feet of $\frac{3}{4}$-inch pipe at 2 gallons per minute is only 4 feet, so that for 20 feet of total run this factor can be regarded as negligible. There will be no static lift and therefore the total head from all causes is 10 feet. Here then a pump should be chosen capable of delivering 2 gallons per minute against a total head of 10 feet. Such a pump might be driven by an electric motor of as little as $\frac{1}{80}$ horsepower. It would be of the induction type, running at about 2,900 revolutions per minute and normally supplied wound for single-phase A.C. electric supply, and at least one type on the market can be specially wound for D.C. supply down to 12 volts.

In all cases a strainer must be fitted on the end of the suction pipe in the pool. The mesh of the strainer should be of a size small enough to exclude particles as large as or larger than can pass through the waterways of the pump and the nozzle of the jet.

Submersible pumps are installed under water. They therefore need no pump chamber or external piping and never require to be primed. They are also extremely silent. Industrial types, having been chiefly designed for pumping from bore holes, are very compact. One of the smallest is only 7 inches in diameter and 15 inches high. It is driven by an induction electric motor of $\frac{3}{4}$ horse-power running at 2,700 revolutions per minute wound for either single-phase or 3-phase supply. It has an output of 25 gallons per minute at a head of 30 feet. This is, of course, much more than is required to operate a $\frac{5}{8}$-inch jet to a height of 10 feet, and if only one jet is in use it will be necessary for the pump to be throttled down by a control valve. This could be set once and for all after initial experiment, but adjustment later would make it necessary to wade into the pool. To avoid this a better arrangement would be to fit the pump itself in a flooded chamber alongside and connected to the pool. A small length of piping would be required to connect to the delivery nozzle. The control valve fitted close to the pump on this delivery pipe would be easily accessible by lifting the cover slab of the chamber.

Much smaller submersible pumps are made for the express purpose of working small garden fountains. One has a capacity of 5 gallons per minute and will throw a $\frac{1}{16}$-inch jet to about 4 feet. It is driven by an induction motor of about $\frac{1}{16}$ horse-power wired for 200/250 volts, 50 cycle, single-phase supply. This little pump is supplied with a length of waterproof cable sealed into the unit. When the pump is in position in the pool, the cable is led along the bottom and over the side to a waterproof connector, from which another length of cable leads to a three-pin outlet on the house. The pump should be stood on a small platform of bricks or stones on the bottom of the pool of sufficient height to allow for the jet to stand just above the surface. The unit, including the prominent strainer, is visible through the water. Some of it can be partly concealed by mounding cobble-stones around it, but the strainer will always show.

Earlier in these notes mention was made of the importance of having the electric connections approved by the local electricity board. This is an absolute necessity where cables carrying 200/250 volts are run into the garden and under water, more particularly if there are children in the family.

To sum up, the following might be the order of preference in choice of electric pumps:

(1) Where silence in performance is all-important, a $\frac{3}{4}$ horse-power submersible pump.

(2) Again with silence in mind, a non-self-priming pump with a flooded suction driven by a motor running at 1,450 r.p.m.

(3) Rather less silent, a pump with a motor running at 2,900 r.p.m., again with flooded suction.

(4) Where a flooded suction is not desired or is impossible, a self-priming pump mounted above the pool level running at 2,900 r.p.m.

(5) In similar circumstances, less expensive, a non-self-priming pump mounted above the level of the pool with priming tank, non-return valve in the suction and throttle shut-off valve in the delivery pipe, the motor running at 2,900 r.p.m.

(6) Where only thin low jets are wanted, either (a) a small, dry, motor surface pump or (b) a small submersible pump.

CHAPTER XX

Emptying, Overflow and Pump Chambers

Diagram III When there is no layer of soil for water-lilies at the bottom, a chamber 18 inches square and of the same depth as the pool is constructed alongside the pool. Concrete as for the pool or bricks can be used. A pipe is connected from the bottom of the pool through the pool wall to a stop cock in this chamber, the stop cock being operated by a removable long arm key. The stop cock is connected at its other end to a pipe leading to a permitted drain or to a soakaway. Copper pipe is fitted under the coping to take overflow water from the pool to the chamber, from which it is dissipated in a small soakaway.

Diagram IV Another method is to have specially made a 3-inch-wide pipe flared out at one end to make a bell mouth. This pipe is screwed into a socket at the bottom of the pool, with a connection to a drain leading to a soakaway or ditch. Excess water will lap over the edge of the pipe and be carried away; when the pool has to be emptied completely the whole pipe is unscrewed and lifted out.

Diagram V When there is a layer of loam on the bottom for water-lilies a different method of emptying is recommended. A baffle wall about 20 inches high is built round the suction end of the pipe to make a small silt-collecting area about 18 inches by 18 inches. The suction pipe is fitted 12 inches above the bottom of

146

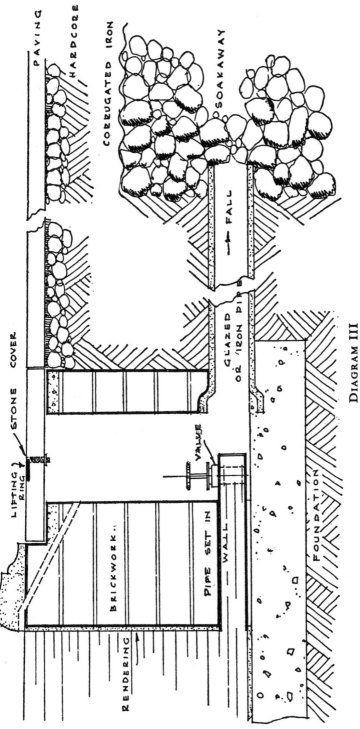

DIAGRAM III
Overflow and emptying arrangement

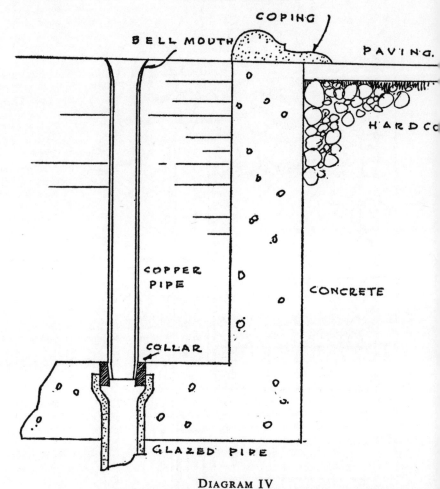

DIAGRAM IV

Alternative overflow and emptying arrangements using bell-mouth copper
pipe

the pool inside this little pen. Alongside an overflow and emptying
chamber are constructed. It will not be possible to drain the pool
dry by this method because of the soil in the bottom, so that the
last 8 inches of mud and water will have to be dug out by hand.
Diagram VI To make a pump chamber below the paving of the
terrace, excavate as for the pool itself, construct the chamber of
concrete or brickwork, ensure that it is watertight; if necessary

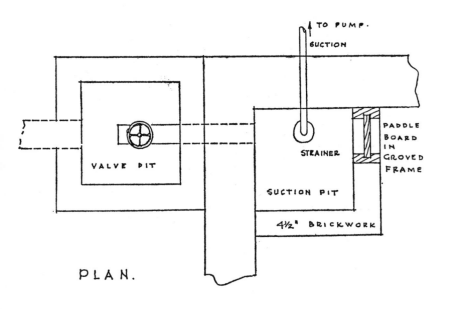

PLAN.

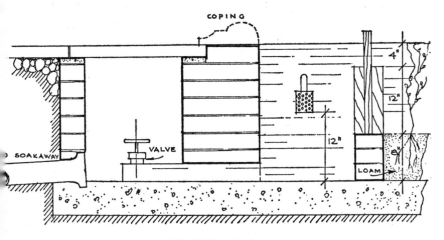

S E C T I O N.

DIAGRAM V

Overflow and emptying and suction arrangements in pool with loam in the bottom for growing water-lilies

149

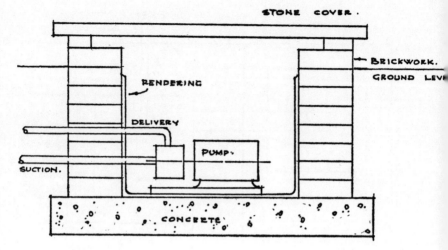

SECTION.

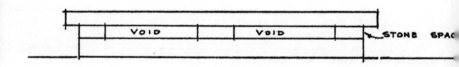

ELEVATION.

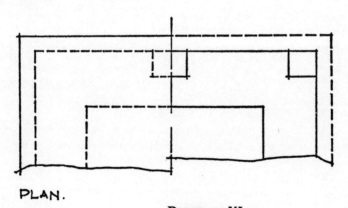

PLAN.

DIAGRAM VI
Small pump chamber
150

arrange for asphalt lining by specialist contractor. In course of construction lead delivery and suction pipes through to pool. Arrange a 4½-inch brick lip all round top edge of chamber to prevent water from washing into the chamber from the paving. Make raised corners so that cover slab when fitted shall stand about ¼ inch above the top of the brick coaming, to allow for circulation of air.

The top of the chamber will therefore stand about 6 inches above the paving level. Its position should be arranged so that it either comes under a seat or can have a tub put on top of it, otherwise it might be a dangerous hazard in the darkness.

CHAPTER XXI

To Make a Pool

Remove topsoil and keep for use elsewhere. Decide on size, and on the depth of water, probably 2 to 3 feet, in the finished pool. Excavate to allow for wall and floor thickness of 6 inches, ram, and consolidate bottom. If required, fix emptying and overflow pipe (see Chapter XX). Lay floor slab to a finished thickness of 6 inches, with concrete made up of 1 part cement, 2 parts of clean sharp sand, 3 parts of coarse aggregate (crushed stone or gravel varying in size between $\frac{3}{4}$ inch and $\frac{3}{16}$ inch). As the concrete begins to harden, roughen the outer edge by brushing or raking to make a key for the bases of the walls.

Construct and fix in position formwork of boards 1 inch thick fixed to 3 inch by 2 inch battens spaced 16 inches apart. This formwork should be securely braced at the top and bottom, and the end panels secured to prevent any movement or bulging during the placing of the concrete. Surfaces in formwork in contact with the concrete must be given a coat of oil or limewash before the concrete is placed, in order to prevent it from sticking to the formwork. This formwork will now form the inner shuttering, it being presumed that the earth walls will stand up without support during construction, but, to prevent soil being pushed down over the outer edge and getting into the concrete and possibly being responsible for porosity and future leaks, it is advisable to lay a sheet of roofing-felt or polythene against the outer wall and to fold it along the top edge. Planks then laid on top of the folded-over material will retain it in position and keep the outer wall clean of soil and dirt. Before placing the concrete for the walls, clean the roughened outer edge of the floor slab and spread a layer of mortar ½ inch on the surface. This mortar should be made of 1 part Portland cement and 2 parts sharp sand, with just enough water to give a 'fatty mix'. Place the concrete in position all the way round in layers about 3 inches thick, consolidate each layer by tamping down with a piece of wood to ensure compaction. Remove the formwork after two to three days, fill the pool with water. This will help to 'cure' the concrete. The coping is then laid and bedded on mortar appropriate to the material, stone, precast concrete, brick or marble.

On firm ground it is not necessary to use reinforced concrete for pools of the sizes under consideration. But if the pool is constructed on made-up ground or on clay, it will be advisable to reinforce the concrete. For the floor, steel fabric for concrete reinforcement should be used to British Standard 1221/64, which means material with a mesh of 6 inches and No. 4 gauge. It will weigh 5 to 6lb. per square yard. It should be cut before the slab is made, and put into position in the middle of the thickness of the slab as the concrete is being placed.

Reinforcement for the walls should be fixed before the form-work. It can consist of ¼-inch mild steel rods at 6-inch centres. These should have been bent before any concrete is mixed, to overlap 6 inches on top of the mesh reinforcement on the floor, and to come within 3 inches of the top of the wall. These rods are tied with 16-gauge soft iron wire to the floor mesh. Four rows of horizontal rods should then be tied to the verticals, the first about 3 inches above what will be the finished level of the floor slab, and above this three rows 6 to 9 inches apart. These horizontal rods can be bent at right-angles to overlap each other at the corners, or, alternatively, they can be left straight, finishing at the ends of each side, in which case special bent angle-pieces (16 in all will be needed) can be prepared and tied at the corners to overlap with the horizontals. Concrete pools made in this way, either reinforced or not, should be waterproof and not require rendering with cement and sand.

It may be easier for the amateur to make the sides of the pool with brickwork. In this case the floor slab is made as described above, reinforced if considered necessary. The outer edges are roughened and a ½-inch-thick layer of mortar spread on them, also as above. The walls are then constructed of engineering bricks in

9-inch work, bedded in a mortar of 1 part cement, 3 parts of sand. The joints are raked back ⅜ inch to provide a key for rendering. This is carried out with two ⅜-inch coats of cement mortar, using a mixture of 1 part cement, 3 parts of sand.

When the pool is finished, the concrete must be seasoned before plants, fish or soil are introduced. This takes about a month, the

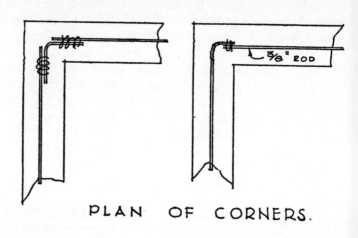

PLAN OF CORNERS.

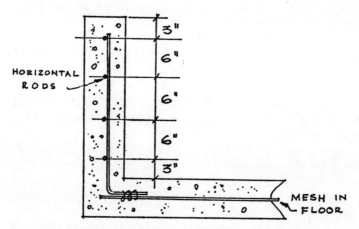

SECTION THROUGH WALL

DIAGRAM VII

Reinforcement for small pool

pool being emptied and refilled two or three times during that period and the walls and bottom well scrubbed. The process can be accelerated by treating the sides with sodium silicate, but it is advisable to test the pool water for small minnows or tadpoles before stocking with valuable fish.

The best time to put in water-lilies and other aquatics is in May. Fish and snails can follow two to three weeks later. It will be necessary to feed the fish for the first few weeks until the pool settles into balance.

CHAPTER XXII

Composts and Feeding

(1) The standard John Innes Potting Compost No. 3 consists of: 7 parts by volume of composted, partially sterilised medium loam, 3 parts by volume of peat, 2 parts by volume of coarse sand, to which is added John Innes Base Fertiliser at the rate of 15lb. per cubic yard and 3lb. chalk or 12oz. Base and 2¼oz. chalk per bushel. John Innes Base consists of 2 parts by weight of hoof and horn meal ⅛ inch grist (13% nitrogen), 2 parts by weight single superphosphate of lime (18% phosphoric acid), 1 part by weight of sulphate of potash (48% potash). The analysis of this mixture is: nitrogen 5·1%, soluble phosphoric acid 7·2%, potash 9·7%. The pH of the compost when mixed should be b tween 6·5 and 7. For calcifuges it should be between 5 and 5·5.

(2) For trees and shrubs which remain in their tubs for many years, 35% by bulk medium composted loam, 25% by bulk sphagnum moss peat, 25% by bulk coarse sand, 15% by bulk broken crocks or charcoal ⅛ inch. To this should be added John Innes Base at the rate of 15lb. per cubic yard—¾lb. per bushel. The pH of this mixture might naturally work out at between 5 and 5·5 and if so would be suitable for calcifuges. When needed for other plants calcium carbonate or magnesium limestone should be added to bring the pH up to between 6·5 and 7·0.

(3) The compost recommended by the Royal Horticultural Society's Gardens at Wisley for camellias—7 parts by bulk of turfy acid loam, 3 parts of granulated sedge peat, 2 parts of gritty lime-free sand. To each bushel is added 1½oz. of bone meal,

1½oz. of coarse hoof and horn meal. The pH of the final mixture should be between 5·0 and 5·5.

Loamless Composts

University of California Soil Mix C, 50% fine sand, 50% peat moss, with Fertiliser V (C) at the following rates per cubic yard:

2½lb. hoof and horn or blood meal
8oz. sulphate of potash
2½lb. single superphosphate
7½lb. Dolomite lime (magnesium limestone)
2½lb. calcium carbonate lime

University of California Soil Mix D, 75% peat moss, 25% fine sand, with Fertiliser mixture V (D) at the following rates per cubic yard:

2½lb. hoof and horn or blood meal
8oz. sulphate of potash
2lb. single superphosphate
5lb. Dolomite lime (magnesium limestone)
4lb. calcium carbonate lime

Both these University of California mixes should be planted within one week of preparation.

Fairfield, 75% peat, 25% sand, with fertiliser at the following rates per cubic yard of compost:

4lb. hoof and horn meal
6oz. potassium nitrate
1lb. sulphate of potash
3lb. single superphosphate
5lb. magnesium limestone
4lb. calcium carbonate

Liquid Feed

John Innes Liquid Feed is made up of 15 parts by weight of ammonium sulphate, 2¾ parts potassium nitrate and 2¼ parts mono-ammonium phosphate, dissolved at the rate of from ½ to 1 oz. per gallon of preferably soft water and used fresh. It can also be used dry, mixed with a carrier such as fine sand, in which case the rate of application is from ½ to 1 teaspoonful per 5-inch pot.

The private owner will probably not need as much as a cubic yard of material at a time. The following table is based on a 2-gallon bucket as the unit of measurement. A 2-gallon bucket holds a $\frac{1}{4}$ bushel, and to fit in with the John Innes proportions, the quantities are worked out to make 3 bushels of compost (12 bucketfuls).

Type of compost	Loam (buckets)	Peat (buckets)	Sand (buckets)	Fertiliser
John Innes No. 3	7	3	2	2½lb. John Innes Base
Fairfield		9	3	2½lb. Fairfield Fertiliser
U.C. Soil Mix C		6	6	2¼lb. U.C. V(C)
U.C. Soil Mix D		9	3	2lb. U.C. V(D)

Composted loam is produced when turves stacked in layers with strawy manure have been rotted down until the grass and most of the roots have decomposed. The *p*H should be about 6·3.

The John Innes Institute, Norwich, approve of moss peat, sedge peat and granulated peat, with particles grading evenly up to $\frac{3}{8}$ inches, a preponderance of $\frac{1}{8}$-inch particles and a minimum of dust. It is recommended that the *p*H should not be less than 3·5. The University of California recommend sphagnum moss peat finely ground.

The John Innes Institute recommend coarse sand with 60 to 70% of the particles between $\frac{1}{8}$ inch and $\frac{1}{16}$ inch in size. The University of California recommend find sand varying between $\frac{1}{50}$ inch and $\frac{1}{500}$ inch in size.

The following notes on quantities may be useful:

There are 21 bushels in a cubic yard
A 2-gallon bucket holds $\frac{1}{4}$ bushel
One bushel will fill 3½ 12in. pots
One bushel will fill 40 5in. pots
One bushel will fill a round tub 14in. × 16in.
2¼ bushels will fill a round tub 18in. × 20in.
6¼ bushels will fill 1 square tub 2ft. × 2ft. × 2ft.
21 bushels will fill 1 square tub 3ft. × 3ft. × 3ft.

But note that tubs and all containers should not be filled to the very top. From 2 to 4 inches should be left to allow for watering and for topdressings with fertilisers.

CHAPTER XXIII

Construction of Window Boxes

To make window boxes use soft wood or deal planed 1 inch thick, primed and painted three coats. The length can be determined by the width of the window, but 3 to 4 feet is the longest that can be handled. For a 6-foot-wide window, use two boxes each 3 feet long. The width of the box should not be less than 6 inches and preferably 10 or 11 inches, tapering if desired to 8 inches at the bottom. The depth inside should be from 7 to 8 inches. Screw the sides with brass screws to four corner posts 1 inch by 1 inch. Turn the box upside down and screw the bottom to the four sides with brass screws. Bore drainage holes in the bottom 1 inch in diameter at intervals of 12 inches, *i.e.* a box 3 feet long would have three 1-inch holes equally spaced along the centre line of the bottom. Softwood boxes should be painted with a priming coat, two undercoats and a finishing coat.

In the hotter parts of the United States and on south-facing aspects boxes are sometimes made with double walls. A $\frac{3}{4}$-inch board forms the main structural timber and an outer veneer of $\frac{3}{16}$-inch material provides for a $\frac{1}{2}$-inch space, which is filled with dry sphagnum moss. In America, too, a type of window box has been devised with a bottom sloping slightly towards the front, which is made with a strip of bent metal forming a gutter. A thin pipe can be connected to this to lead the water down the side of

159

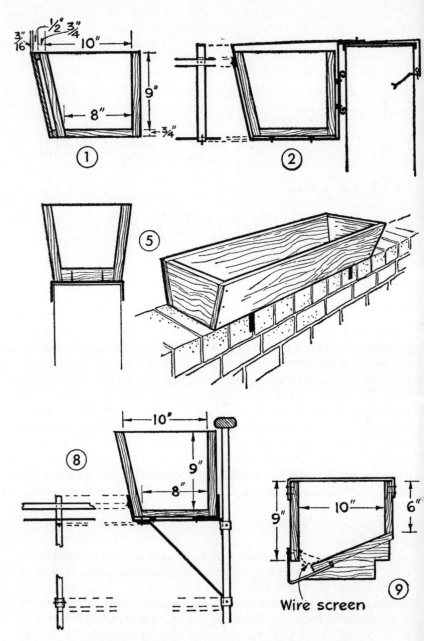

WINDOW BOXES: VARIOUS TYPES OF FIXING

1. Insulated window box   2. In front of stone wall

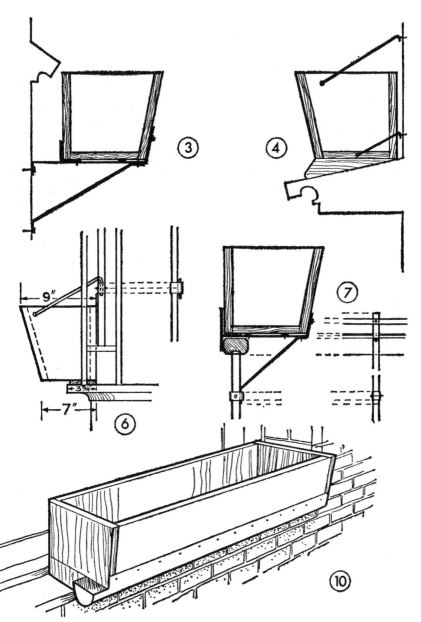

3. To house wall below narrow sill
4. On slanting sill
5. On top of wall
6. In front of balcony railing
7. On top of balcony railing
8. In front of balcony railing
9. Box with slanting bottom and wire screen
10. Box with gutter to prevent dripping

the house, so preventing drips from falling on to the pavement.

The box must be firmly secured to the window sill. This can be done by screwing a strip of metal 2 inches by $\frac{1}{4}$ inch to the box and bending the other end against the window frame and screwing it. In some cases it may be necessary to have wrought-iron brackets specially made. On sloping window sills wedge-chocks of wood must be made. Where the box is resting on the window sill thin fillets of wood should be screwed to the bottom along the width at either end to allow space for the water to escape when it has run out of the holes.

PART THREE—THE PLANTS

CHAPTER XXIV

Notes on Plants

Plants will be given a good start if the ground is first double dug, and some well-rotted cow manure worked into the bottom below what will be the level of the roots at the time of planting. Lavender, rosemary and other plants which naturally grow in thin, poor soils are better without the cow manure.

For trees a tree pit should be excavated 2 feet 6 inches square and at least 2 feet deep. On retentive soils it will be necessary to provide for drainage with a layer of coarse material in the bottom. In really retentive clay soils an agricultural tile drain will be needed leading away from the tree pit to a lower level to prevent the tree pit becoming a sump. The pit should be refilled with topsoil. It may be necessary to bring in some extra material for this purpose. Cow manure should be put in again at a level a little below that of the roots of the newly planted tree. The stake should be fixed before the tree is planted, driven well down to hard ground below the tree pit.

When the plant is put into position a liberal dusting of a mixture of fine peat, bone meal and hoof and horn meal over the roots and the surrounding soil will assist the initial establishment.

All plants benefit greatly from a top mulch of bulky organic material such as very well-decayed, crumbling animal manure, dried and crumbling spent hops, or coarse peat, to which bone meal and hoof and horn meal have been added. A mulch must be put on when the soil is wet and the ground warm, usually in October or late April. It is harmful to apply a mulch to cold or dry soil. To do so will simply mulch in and perpetuate these unfavourable conditions. Winter-planted trees or shrubs should therefore not be mulched until the following April. After planting, plants should be firmed in with the heel. The process can be repeated a month later and after frost.

Time of planting. Many plants can safely be planted in open weather at any time between November and the end of March. In practice this is what generally happens, because it is impossible for nurseries to send out the best part of a whole year's production in one or two selected months. None the less, there are optimum times for planting different plants and it will be useful to have these in mind for cases where it may be possible to make arrangements with a nursery far enough ahead.

Evergreens are best planted when the soil is warm, in October or April. October planting may be successful if a mild winter follows and if protection is given against drying winds, but I prefer to plant evergreens in April. At this time the soil is beginning to warm up, the drying east winds of March may be over, and there is a prospect of warm showers. But whenever evergreens are planted, it is absolutely essential to make sure that they never get dry at the roots in the first spring and summer after planting. There is nearly always a dangerous period of drought some time in every spring, no matter how wet and depressing the summer later turns out. In hot, dry weather it is useful to spray the foliage of evergreens and the bark and young foliage of deciduous trees with a syringe or spray attachment to a hose.

I prefer to get most of the deciduous trees into their positions in the second half of November, although there are certain exceptions to this. At this time the leaves will either have fallen or at least turned colour, and there will still be a little warmth left in the soil.

Many herbaceous plants are best planted in October, although a few, including achillea, may rot and die in a cold winter immediately after planting and are best put in in April.

In the notes that follow I have stated what I think are the best times for planting some plants. When no special time is proposed the general rule of November to the end of March can be taken to apply, subject to the general considerations of perfection just referred to. I have also shown in the list which plants are usually sent out in pots, which are tender at about the latitude of Kew, and which need a stake. I have included this because in my view a plant should have outstanding characteristics to be worth the trouble and ugly appearance of a stake.

Plant Notes. The compilation of the notes on plants was undertaken with the intention of giving detached factual descriptions of plants from recognised authorities, uncoloured by my own assessments; also to provide rather more information than is found in the usual nurseryman's catalogue, although of necessity much less than in, for instance, the Royal Horticultural Society's *Dictionary of Gardening*. The task proved larger than I had expected, but in spite of its many lacunae, I hope that it may be useful in making a choice of plants, and perhaps particularly to those interested in the sizes of leaves and flowers.

It will be obvious that the list of plants is both exclusive and capricious. It is exclusive because it is confined only to those which, in my opinion, can reasonably be brought within the influence of the house, and therefore omits many of the most beautiful garden plants and flowers which belong essentially to the farther, wilder garden—daffodils, honesty, sweet rocket and many trees and shrubs. It is capricious because it leaves out certain herbaceous plants which I never make use of—delphiniums, phlox, pyrethrums, and others which I actively dislike such as dahlias.

I am grateful to the Council of the Royal Horticultural Society for permission to draw so largely on the *Dictionary of Gardening*. I have also referred to other books included in the Bibliography printed at the end of this book. I am grateful to Mr Rowland Jackman for permission to make use of his *Planters' Handbook*, which I have used entirely as a source of the spread of trees and shrubs. I have also sometimes been guided by him in preference to other authorities when assessing the heights which certain plants are likely to reach in domestic surroundings. I am grateful to the Curator of the Royal Botanic Gardens, Kew, and to Mr Pearce for their assistance.

When the plants or flowers are illustrated in books included in the Bibliography, other than those which are primarily works of pictorial reference, I have indicated them as follows: (C) meaning a coloured illustration.

A.B.F.   *Annual and Biennial Flowers*, A. P. Balfour—Penguin
B.   *Trees and Shrubs Hardy in the British Isles*, W. J. Bean—John Murray

B.T.S.	*British Trees and Shrubs*, R. D. Meikle—Eyre & Spottiswoode
C.	*Camellias*, E. B. Anderson—Blandford
C.G.B.	*Collins Guide to Bulbs*, Patrick M. Synge—Collins
C.G.B.P.	*Collins Guide to Border Plants*, Frances Perry—Collins
G.F.	*Garden Flowers*, R. D. Meikle—Eyre & Spottiswoode
G.S.T.	*Garden Shrubs and Trees*, S. G. Harrison—Eyre & Spottiswoode
P.	*Pelargoniums*, Derek Clifford—Blandford
R.B.	*The Rose in Britain*, N. P. Harvey—Souvenir Press
R.H.S.D.	The Royal Horticultural Society's *Dictionary of Gardening*—The Clarendon Press in conjunction with the Royal Horticultural Society
S.G.G.P.	*Some Good Garden Plants*, Patrick M. Synge and James W. O. Platt—Royal Horticultural Society
T.T.C.	*Trees for Town and Country*, S. R. Badmin and B. Colvin—Lund Humphries
W.G.	*Water Gardens*—Frances Perry—Penguin

In addition to the books listed above, there are the following publications which are primarily works of pictorial reference. As nearly all species described in these notes are illustrated in one or other of these books, I have not included them in the keyed references against individual plants. These books are as follows:

Flowers in Colour, A. G. L. Hellyer—Collingridge

Herbaceous Garden Flora, F. K. Makins—Dent

Photo Album of Garden Plants, A. G. L. Hellyer and Christopher Lloyd—Collingridge

Garden Plants in Colour, A. G. L. Hellyer—Collingridge

The Encyclopaedia of Plant Portraits, A. G. L. Hellyer—Collingridge

The Identification of Trees and Shrubs, F. K. Makins—Dent

The Oxford Book of Garden Flowers, B. E. Nicholson, M. Wallis, E. B. Anderson, A. P. Balfour, M. Fish and V. Finnis—Oxford University Press

The Pocket Encyclopaedia of Roses, in colour, H. Edland—Blandford

Cymes, corymbs, panicles, racemes, spikes and umbels are inflorescences in which a number of flowers are grouped closely together. I have tried, not always successfully, to establish the overall size of these inflorescences, which from the point of view of scale is more important than the size of the individual flowers in each inflorescence.

A calcifuge is a plant which is intolerant of lime in the soil.

A SELECT LIST

Abutilon megapotamicum. Evergreen shrub.
   Height: 6ft. Leaves: 2 to 4in. Flowers: red and yellow, 1in.
   April–September. Pot grown. Needs a wall. Can be treated as
   a summer bedding plant or be used in window boxes.
Acacia, *see* **Robinia**
Acanthus mollis. Herbaceous perennial.
   Height: 3 to 4ft. Spread: 4ft. Leaves: 2ft. × 1ft, heart-shaped,
   many-lobed, with spiny bracts. Flowers: white or rose 2½in.
   in spikes 1½ft. long. July–August.
Achillea clypeolata. Herbaceous perennial.
   Height: 2½ft. Spread: 2ft. Leaves: finely cut, grey hairy.
   Flowers: lemon-yellow. July–September. Plant April.
African Marigold, *see* **Tagetes**
Agapanthus africanus. African lily. Evergreen perennial.
   Height: 2½ft. Spread: 2ft. Leaves: strap-shaped 4 to 10in. long,
   ⅛ to ½in. wide. Flowers: deep violet 1½ to 2in.; 30–60 in an
   umbel. Tender. Usually in tubs. Greenhouse in winter. Illus:
   A. mooreanus S.G.G.P. C.G.B.P.(C).
Agave americana. American Aloe. Succulent.
   Height: to 25ft. Spread: 12ft. Leaves: long, leathery 3 to 6ft. ×
   8in. Flowers: yellowish 2½ to 2¾in. in panicle. Plant dies after
   flowering. Tender. In tubs or pots. Greenhouse in winter.
Ageratum houstonianum. Half-hardy annual.
   Height: to 2ft. Flowers: blue. Tender. Grown in boxes or pots.
   Summer bedding. Plant out in June.
Ailanthus altissima (*A. glandulosa*). Tree of Heaven. Deciduous
   tree.
   Height: to 60ft. Leaves: 18 to 24 in panicle. Flowers: whitish-
   green in large terminal panicles. August. Illus.: T.T.C.

Ajuga reptans. Bugle. Herbaceous perennial.
> Height: 6 to 12in. widely spreading, carpeting. Leaves: 2 to 3in. (bronze-purple in var. *atropurpurea*). Flowers: blue (white in var. *alba*). May–July. Useful for shade and moist positions. Intrusive.

Alchemilla major (*A. mollis*). Lady's Mantle. Herbaceous perennial.
> Height: 1 to 1½ft., spreading, ground cover. Leaves: to 5in., softly hairy. Flowers: yellowish-green, minute, in branched panicles 3 to 4 in. June–July.

Almond, *see* **Prunus communis**

Aloe, *see* **Agave**

Aloysia, *see* **Lippia**

Alyssum, *see* **Lobularia**

Amaryllis belladonna. Belladonna lily. Bulbous plant.
> Height: 1 to 2ft. Leaves: strap shaped 12 to 20in. long, 1in. wide. Flowers: pink, fragrant, funnel-shaped 3½in. long, 1in. wide in umbels of 6 to 10 flowers., fragrant. August–October. Best against a warm wall. Plant bulbs in spring. Illus.: S.G.G.P. C.G.B.(C).

Anaphalis triplinervis. Herbaceous perennial.
> Height: 1½ft. Spread: 1ft. Leaves: 3 to 8in. long, ¾in. wide, white woolly. Flowers: white in a corymb. August. An everlasting flower.

Anchusa officinalis angustifolia. Biennial.
> Height: 12 to 15in. Spread: 12in. Flowers: intense mid-blue in terminal spikes. June–October. Plant April.

Anemone japonica alba. Japanese Anemone. Herbaceous perennial.
> Height: 4 to 5ft. Spread: 2ft. Flowers: white 2in. August–September.
> Sometimes pot grown.

Antirrhinum. Snapdragon. Herbaceous perennial. Treated as an annual.

A. nanum grandiflorum Majestic Avalanche.
> Height: 1½ft. Leaves: 1 to 3in. Flowers: white in close racemes. May–September. Pot or box grown. Summer bedding. Plant out in May.

Arbutus menziesii. Madrona. Evergreen tree.
> Height: 20 to 50ft. Spread: 20 to 30ft. Leaves: 2 to 6in. long; 1 to 3in. wide. Flowers: white, in terminal panicles 5 to 6in.

long. April–May. Pot grown. Tender. For the milder counties.
Plant April. Illus.: B.

A. unedo. Strawberry Tree. Evergreen tree.
Height: 15 to 25ft. Spread: 18 to 25ft. Leaves: 1¼ to 4in. long,
½ to 1½in. wide. Flowers: white or pinkish in drooping panicles.
October–December. Pot grown. Hardy in S. England and Ireland. Plant April. Illus.: B.T.S. T.T.C.

Artemisia lanata (*A. pedemontana*). 'Evergrey' shrub.
Height: 1 to 2in, prostrate, wide-spreading. Leaves: ⅛ to ¼in.,
silver, sharply aromatic. Pot grown. Plant April.

A. ludoviciana. Herbaceous perennial.
Height: 2 to 4ft. Spread: 2ft. Leaves: 1 to 3in. long; ½ to ¾in.
wide, white woolly. Flowers: ⅛in. in large compound panicles.
Autumn. Pot grown. Plant April. Illus.: S.G.G.P.

Asparagus sprengeri.
Height: 2 to 6ft. Leaves: 1 to 1½in. long; ₁₆in. wide. Pot
grown. Greenhouse plant used with summer bedding or in
window boxes.

Aubrieta deltoidea. Evergreen trailing perennial.
Height: to 6in. Leaves: ½in. Flowers: ¾in. April. Pot-grown.
Plant March–April. Aubrietas succeed best on lime soils.
  Barker's Double, deep silver-pink
  Church Knowle, silvery-blue
  Crimson Queen, carmine-crimson
  Dr Mules, deep violet-blue
  Gloriosa, satin-pink

Aucuba japonica. Evergreen shrub.
Height: to 15ft. Spread: 7 to 9ft. Leaves: 3 to 8in. long; 1½ to
3in. wide. Flowers: purple ½in. terminal panicles. March–
April. Insignificant. Fruit: scarlet berry ½in. Plant October or
April.

Azolla caroliniana. Fairy floating moss. Aquatic plant.

Bay, *see* **Laurus**

Beech, *see* **Fagus**

Begonia rex. Succulent herb.
Height: to 1ft. Leaves: 8 to 12in., dark green, variegated,
bronze. Pot grown. Greenhouse. Used for its foliage in summer
bedding or window boxes.

Belladonna Lily, *see* **Amaryllis**

Bergamot, *see* **Monarda**

Bergenia cordifolia (*Megasea cordifolia*). Herbaceous perennial.
Height: 12 to 20in. Spread: 2ft. Leaves: 1ft. round, turning beetroot colour after frost. Flowers: deep pink in cymes. February–April. Illus.: G.F.

Blechnum spicant. Hard Fern. Evergreen fern.
Height: 2ft. Plant April.

Box, *see* **Buxus**

Brugmansia, *see* **Datura**

Bugle, *see* **Ajuga**

Buxus sempervirens. Common Box. Evergreen shrub or tree.
Height: to 25ft. as tree. Spread: 15 to 30ft. as tree. Leaves: ½ to ¼in. Flowers: pale green in axillary clusters in April, insignificant. Plant April. As hedge, plants 1½ft. high, 15in. apart. As edging, plants 9 to 12in. high, 6in. apart. Illus.: B.T.S.

Callitriche autumnalis. Water Starwort. Aquatic plant.
A submerged oxygenating plant. Leaves eaten by fish. Put into pool in May.

Camellia japonica. Evergreen shrub.
Height: in tub probably to 6ft. Spread: probably to 3ft. (In open ground: height 30ft., spread 30ft.) Leaves: 3 to 3½in. long, 1¼in. wide. Flowers: 3 to 5in. March–May. Hardy, but flowers often damaged by frosts. Calcifuge. Pot grown. Usually in tubs. In open ground, plant April.

Althaeaflora. Crimson. Peony form, 4in. March–April. Illus.: C.
Elegans (Chandleri elegans). Rose-pink. Anemone form, 3½ in. March–April. Illus.: C.
Mathotiana. Deep red. Rose form, 4in. April.
Mathotiana alba. White. Formal double, 4½in. April. Illus.: C.
Nobilissima. White. Anemone form. 3 to 3½in. March.

C. × williamsii. Evergreen shrub.
Height: in open ground probably to 15ft. Leaves: about 1½ to 2¼in. Flowers: pink (vars. J. C. Williams, Donation), white (var. Francis Hanger), 3in. Pot grown. Plant April. Calcifuge.

Campanula isophylla. Prostrate perennial.
Leaves: 1½in. Flowers: lilac-blue, salver-shaped (white in var. *alba*) 1in. August. Tender. As summer bedding in window boxes or hanging baskets. Pot grown. Plant out in June.

C. lactiflora Loddon Anna. Herbaceous perennial.
Height: 4 to 5ft. Spread: 2ft. Leaves: 3in. Flowers: pale mauve,

1½in. in loose panicles 3½in. long. July–August. Needs staking.
Illus.: *C. lactiflora* S.G.G.P. *C. lactiflora* G.F. (C).

Catalpa bignonioides. Indian Bean. Deciduous tree.
Height: 30 to 35ft. Spread: 35 to 60ft. Leaves: 6 to 10in.,
heart-shaped. Smell said to be unpleasant when crushed.
Flowers: white, with yellow markings and purple spots, 1½in. in
erect panicles 8 to 10in. high. July. Pods: 8 to 15in. long; ⅜in.
wide, often persisting. Illus.: S.G.G.P. G.S.T.(C). T.T.C.

Catmint, *see* **Nepeta**

Ceanothus dentatus russellianus. Evergreen shrub.
On wall: height 20 to 25ft. Spread: 12 to 18ft. Leaves: ¼ to
1in. Flowers: light blue ½ to 1¼in. in panicles. May–June. Pot
grown. Tender. Requires a wall. Plant April.

Ceratostigma plumbaginoides. Herbaceous perennial.
Height: 1 to 1½ft. Leaves: ¾ to 2in. long. Flowers: purple-blue,
¾in. in terminal and axillary heads. July–October. Sometimes
pot grown. Illus.: G.F.(C).

C. willmottianum. Deciduous shrub.
Height: 2 to 4ft. Leaves: 1 to 2in. long; ½ to ¾in. wide. Flowers:
bright blue, white at base, 2½in. in clusters. August–October.
Pot grown. Plant April. Illus.: S.G.G.B.

Cercis siliquastrum. Judas Tree. Deciduous tree or shrub.
Height: 15 to 25ft. Spread: 12 to 15ft. Leaves: 2 to 3in. long,
2½ to 4in. broad. Flowers: bright purple-rose, ½ to ¾in. in
clusters of 3 to 4. May. Usually pot grown. Plant October or
April. Illus.: G.T.S.(C). S.G.G.P. T.T.C.

Chaenomeles speciosa (*C. lagenaria, Cydonia japonica*). Japanese
Quince. Japonica. Deciduous shrub.
Height: 3 to 12ft. Spread 3½ to 12ft. Leaves: 1½in. to 3½in.
Pot grown. Illus.: *C. japonica* G.S.T.

C.s. Hollandia. Height: 7 to 9ft.
Flowers: scarlet. February–April.

C.s. Minerva. Height: 5 to 7ft. Flowers: light vermilion.
February–April.

C. × *superba* Simonii.
Height: 3½ to 4ft. Spread: 3½ to 4ft. Flowers: dark crimson.
March–May. Illus.: S.G.G.P.

Chamaecyparis lawsoniana. Lawson's Cypress. Evergreen tree.
Height: to 100ft. Leaves: scale-like, bark reddish-brown.
Cones: ½in. Plant April. Illus.: T.T.C.

Cheiranthus × *allionii*. Siberian Wallflower. Herbaceous perennial. Treated as biennial.

Height: 1ft. Flowers: Orange or apricot. May. Sow seed in boxes under glass. May. Transplant June. Plant out 1ft. apart in October. Illus.: S.G.G.P.

C. cheiri. Wallflower. Herbaceous perennial. Treated as a biennial. Sow seed under glass in boxes in May. Plant out in summer. Transplant to final positions in October about 1ft. apart. Illus.: Giant mixed. A.B.F.

Blood Red. Height: 1½ft. Flowers: dark red. April–May.

Cloth of Gold. Height: 1½ft. Flowers: deep yellow. April–May.

Cranford Beauty. Height: 1½ft. Flowers: golden yellow. April–May.

Early-flowering Fire King. Height: 1½ft. Flowers: orange-scarlet. February–April.

Early-flowering Orange. Height: 2ft. Flowers: orange. February–April.

Early-flowering Primrose. Height: 2ft. Flowers: pale yellow. February–April.

Early-flowering Vulcan. Height: 2ft. Flowers: dark crimson. February–April.

Ellen Willmot. Height: 1½ft. Flowers: ruby-red. April–May.

Fire King. Height: 15in. Flowers: orange-scarlet. April–May.

Giant Brown. Height: 1½ft. Flowers: brown-red. April–May.

Harbinger. Height: 1½ft. Flowers: mahogany-brown. April–May.

Orange Bedder. Height: 1½ft. Flowers: orange-apricot. April–May.

Phoenix. Height: 1½ft. Flowers: chestnut-brown. February–April.

Primrose Monarch. Height: 1½ft. Flowers: pale yellow. April–May.

Scarlet Emperor. Height: 1½ft. Flowers scarlet. April–May.

Vulcan. Height: 9 to 12in. Flowers: dark crimson. April–May.

Yellow Phoenix. Height: 1½ft. Flowers: yellow. February–April.

Cherry, *see* **Prunus subhirtella autumnalis**
Cherry Laurel, *see* **Prunus laurocerasus**
Cherry Pie, *see* **Heliotropium**

Chimonanthus praecox (*C. fragrans*). Winter Sweet. Deciduous shrub.
Height: to 8ft. Spread: 10 to 12ft. (on wall). Leaves: 3 to 7in. long, 1in. wide. Flowers: outer petals greenish-yellow, inner petals brownish-purple, very strongly scented on bare branches. December–January. Pot grown. Plant April. Illus.: var. *luteus* G.S.T.

Choisya ternata. Mexican Orange Blossom. Evergreen shrub.
Height: 6 to 10ft. Spread: 8 to 10ft. Leaves: 1½ to 3in. Flowers: white, 1in. in corymbs 5 to 6in. Scented. April–May. Pot grown. Plant April. Illus.: G.S.T.

Christmas Rose, *see* **Helleborus niger**

Chrysanthemum frutescens. Marguerite. Shrubby perennial.
Height: to 3ft. Flowers: white or lemon-yellow, daisy-like with yellow disc, in many heads 2in. across. Summer. Tender. Usually treated as summer bedding plant. Plant out end May.

C. morifolium. Florist's chrysanthemum.
Height: 2 to 3ft. Leaves: 2 to 3in. Pot grown. Tender. Used in late summer and autumn for window boxes. Jante Wells, pompom. Bright yellow, spray. September.

Cinquefoil, *see* **Potentilla**

Cistus × corbariensis. Evergreen shrub.
Height: 1½ to 3ft. Spread: 6 to 9ft. Leaves: ¾ to 2in. long; ½ to 1in. wide. Flowers: white, yellow stain at base, 1½in. June. Pot grown. Plant April. Aromatic. One of the hardiest of the cistuses.

C. crispus. Evergreen shrub.
Height: 2 to 3ft. Spread: 3 to 4ft. Leaves: ¾ to 1½in. Flowers: purple-red, 1½ in. in terminal clusters. June. Pot grown. Not entirely hardy. Plant April. Aromatic.

C. × cyprius. Evergreen shrub.
Height: 6 to 8ft. Leaves: 2 to 4in. long; ½ to 1in. wide. Flowers: white with crimson blotch, 3in. in clusters of 3 to 6. June–July. Resinous. Aromatic. Pot grown. Plant April. Illus.: S.G.G.P.

C. ladaniferus. Evergreen shrub.
Height: 3 to 5ft. Spread: 4 to 5ft. Leaves: 2 to 4in. Flowers: white with crimson blotch, 3 to 4in. June–July. Leaves and stems resinously aromatic. Pot grown. Not entirely hardy. Plant April.

C. laurifolius. Evergreen shrub.

Height: 6 to 8ft. Spread: 7 to 9ft. Leaves: 1½ to 3in. long; ¾ to 1½in. wide. Flowers: white, 2½in. in clusters. June–August. Aromatic. Pot grown. Perhaps the hardiest of all the cistuses. Plant April.

C. × *lusitanicus.* Evergreen shrub.
Height: 1 to 2ft. Spread: 3 to 4ft. Leaves: 1 to 2½in. Flowers: white, crimson blotch, 2 to 2½in. June–July. Aromatic. Pot grown. Not entirely hardy. Plant April.

C. × *purpureus.* Evergreen shrub.
Height: 5 to 6ft. Spread: 7 to 8ft. Leaves: 1 to 2in. Resinous. Flowers: reddish with deeper red blotches, 2½ to 3in. June. Pot grown. Plant April. Illus.: S.G.G.P.

Citrus aurantium. Bigarade. Seville Orange. Evergreen tree.
Height: in tubs probably to 18ft. Leaves: 3 to 4in. Flowers: white, fragrant. July. Tender. Pot grown. Cultivated in tubs. Taken into greenhouse or orangery from mid-September to end May.

C. bergamia. Bergamot Orange. Evergreen tree.
Flowers: white, fragrant. Tender. Pot grown. Cultivated in tubs. Taken to greenhouse or orangery mid-September to end May.

C. nobilis. King Orange. Evergreen tree.
Flowers: white. Tender. Pot grown. Cultivated in tubs. Taken to greenhouse or orangery mid-September to end May.

C. n. deliciosa. Mandarin Orange. Evergreen tree.
Tender. Pot grown. Cultivated in tubs. Taken to greenhouse or orangery mid-September to end May.

C. sinensis. Sweet Orange. Evergreen tree.
Height in tubs probably 15 to 18ft. Flowers: white. Tender. Pot grown. Cultivated in tubs. Taken to greenhouse or orangery mid-September to end May.

Clary, *see* **Salvia**

Clematis armandii. Evergreen climber.
Height: 20 to 30ft. Leaves: 3 to 6in. long; 1 to 2½in. wide. Flowers: white, 2 to 2½in. April. Pot grown. Plant April. Illus.: S.G.G.P.
Apple Blossom. Leaves: bronzy-green. Flowers: pink-tinted.

C. × *jackmanii* Comtesse de Bouchard. Deciduous climber.
Flowers: pink, tinted mauve, 4 to 5in. June–October. Pot grown. Plant October or April.

C. × *lanuginosa* Henryi. Deciduous climber.

Height: 6 to 9ft. Leaves: to 5in. long, to 3in. wide. Flowers;
white 4 to 6in. June–July. Pot grown. Plant October or April.

C. × lanuginosa Mrs Cholmondeley. Deciduous climber.

Height: 6 to 9ft. Leaves: 5in. long; 3in. wide. Flowers: lavender-
blue, 4 to 6in. May–June and later. Pot grown. Plant October or
April.

C. montana rubens. Deciduous climber.

Height: 20 to 30ft. Leaves: 1½ to 4in. Flowers: pale pink, 2 to
2½in. May–June. Pot grown. Plant October or March. Illus.:
C. montana S.G.G.P.

C. × patens Lasurstern. Deciduous climber.

Height: to 12ft. Leaves: 2 to 5in. Flowers: lavender-blue. Cream
stamens, 4 to 6in. May and June, and in September. Pot grown.
Plant October or April.

C. × patens Nellie Moser. Deciduous climber.

Height: to 12ft. Leaves: 2 to 4in. Flowers: pale lilac with carmine
stripe, 4 to 6in. May and June and in September. Pot grown.
Plant October or April.

C. × viticella Ernest Markham. Deciduous climber.

Height: 8 to 12ft. Leaves: 4 to 5in. Flowers: petunia-red, about
2in. July–September. Pot grown. Plant October or April.

C. × viticella Ville de Lyon. Deciduous climber.

Height: 4 to 8ft. Leaves: 4 to 5in. Flowers: carmine-red, 2in.
July–October. Pot grown. Plant October or April.

Cobaea scandens. Climber.

Height: to 24ft. or more. Leaves: 4in. long; 1½ to 2in. wide.
Flowers: violet or white outside, green within, bell-shaped.
July–October. Tender. Pot grown. Plant in May. Treated as an
annual climber.

Coleus blumei. Herbaceous perennial.

Height: 12 to 18in. Leaves: 4in. or more, variegated, green,
bronze, yellow. Pot grown. Tender. Greenhouse for its foliage
and as summer bedding or in window boxes. Plant out in June.

Convallaria majalis. Lily-of-the-Valley. Rhizomatous perennial.

Height: 6 to 12in. Spread: 6in. spreading wider. Leaves: 4 to
7in. long. Flowers: white ½in., pendulous, in arching racemes,
strongly scented. May. Plant September–October. Illus.: G.F.

Corylus avellana. Hazel. Deciduous tree.

Height: 12 to 20ft. Leaves: 2 to 4in. Flowers: male catkins to
2½in. long. November–February. Nuts: ¾in. Illus.: B.T.S.

Cotinus coggygria. Smoke Tree. Wig Tree. Deciduous tree.
Height: 12 to16ft. Spread: 12 to 16ft. Leaves: 1½ to 3in., turning brilliant yellow in autumn. Flowers: pale grey-pink, small, in much branched feathery inflorescence. Illus.: S.G.G.P.

Cotoneaster conspicuus decorus. Evergreen shrub.
Height: to 3ft. Leaves: ¼ to ⅜in. Flowers: white, ½in. June. Red berries. Pot grown. Plant October or April. Illus. S.G.G.P.

C. dammeri (C. humifusus). Evergreen shrub. Prostrate, carpeting.
Leaves: 1in. long; ¼ to ⅝in. wide. Flowers: white ⅓ to ½in. June. Red berries. Pot grown. Plant October or April.

C. frigidus. Deciduous shrub.
Height: to 30ft. Leaves: 3 to 4in. Flowers: white, ½in. in clusters 2 to 3in. across. May. Red berries. Illus.: S.G.G.P.

C. salicifolius. Evergreen shrub or small tree.
Height: to 15ft. Spread: 8 to 10ft. Leaves: 1½ to 3in. long, ¼ to ¾in. wide. Flowers: white, ³⁄₁₆in. in corymbs 1½in. across. June. Red berries ¼in. Plant April. Illus.: G.S.T.

Cranesbill, *see* **Geranium**

Crataegus monogyna. Hawthorn. May. Deciduous tree.
Height: 20 to 30ft. Spread: 20 to 25ft. Leaves: 2in. deeply lobed. Flowers: white ½in. in clusters. June. Fruit: red ⅓in.

C. prunifolia. Deciduous tree.
Height: to 20ft. Spread: 20 to 25ft. Leaves: 1½ to 3½in. Turn crimson in autumn. Flowers: white ¾in. in rounded clusters 2¼ to 3in. across. June. Fruit: rich crimson ¾in.

Creeping Jenny, *see* **Lysimachia**

Crown Imperial, *see* **Fritillaria imperialis**

Cupressus macrocarpa. Monterey Cypress. Evergreen tree.
Height: to 70ft. Leaves: scale-like. Cones: 1 to 1½in. long, ¾ to 1in. wide. Tender. Plant May.

Cydonia, *see* **Chaenomeles**

Daphne mezereum Mezereon. Deciduous shrub.
Height: 3½ to 4½ft. Spread: 3½ to 4½ft. Leaves: 1½ to 3½in. long; ¼ to ¾in. wide, dull grey-green. Flowers: purple-red, ½in. very fragrant. February–March. Red berries ⅓in. Illus.: S.G.G.P. B.T.S.

Daturacornigera(D.knightii, Brugmansia knightii). Deciduous shrub.
Height: to 10ft. Flowers: white, funnel shaped, 5 to 6in. Tender. Pot grown. Cultivated in tubs taken to greenhouse mid-September to end May. Poisonous.

Day-Lily, *see* **Hemerocallis**

Deutzia × *elegantissima.* Deciduous shrub.

Height: 4½ to 5ft. Spread: 5 to 7ft. Leaves: 1½ to 4½in. Flowers: purple-rose ¾in., in corymbs 3in. across. May–June.

D. gracilis. Deciduous shrub.

Height: 3 to 4ft. Spread: 3 to 4ft. Leaves: 1 to 3in. Flowers: white ⅝ to ¾in. in panicles 1½ to 3in. long. June.

Dianthus plumarius. Garden Pink. Herbaceous perennial.

Height: 10in. Spread: 1 to 2ft. Leaves: grey. Flowers: clove-pink scented. June–July. Plant September or April.

Earl of Essex, rose-pink, fringed, double.

Inchmery, pale pink, double.

Paddington, pink, purple eye, double.

Mrs Sinkins, white, double.

White Ladies, white, double.

Elymus glaucus. Lyme grass. Perennial grass.

Height: to 3ft. Leaves: very short, blue-green.

Epimedium grandiflorum. Herbaceous perennial.

Height: 8 to 15in. Spread: 1ft. Leaves: 2 to 3in. Flowers: var. *niveum* white, var. *roseum* pink, var. *violaceum* pale violet, 1in. June. Sometimes pot grown. Plant April.

Euonymus radicans. Evergreen shrub. Procumbent.

Leaves: ½ to 1¼in. Flowers: greenish-white, ⅓in. in cymes up to 2in. Plant October or April.

Euphorbia wulfenii. Spurge. Evergreen shrub.

Height: to 4ft. Spread: to 6ft. Leaves: 5in., linear, close together, dark green. Flowers: apple green surrounded by yellow bracts in large dense terminal cymes. March–April. Pot grown. Poisonous. Plant October or April.

Fagus sylvatica. Common Beech. Deciduous tree.

Height: to 100ft. Spread: 70 to 90ft. Leaves: 2 to 3½in., turning russet brown. October–April. As hedge plant, plants 1½ to 2ft. high in double row. Rows 1½ft. apart. Plants 1½ft. apart in the rows. This means an overall calculation at the rate of 9in. apart, i.e. 4 plants per 3ft. run of hedge plus one to begin the line.

False Acacia, *see* **Robinia**

Fatsia japonica. Evergreen shrub.

Height: 8 to 15ft. Spread: 10 to 15ft. Leaves: 6 to 16in. deeply lobed. Flowers: milky white in umbels forming a branching

panicle 9 to 18in. long. October–November. Pot grown. Plant
April. Illus.: G.S.T.

Festuca ovina glauca. Perennial grass.
Height: 9in. Leaves: $\frac{1}{32}$in. wide, blue-green.

Ficus carica. Fig. Deciduous tree or shrub.
Height: 15 to 30ft. Leaves: 5 to 6in. deeply lobed. Pot grown.
Tender. Best on a wall. The variety Brunswick may be the
hardiest. Plant end March.

Fig, *see* **Ficus**

Firethorn, *see* **Pyracantha**

Fontinalis antipyretica. Willow Moss. Submerged aquatic. Mossy
foliage.
An oxygenating pool plant. Plant in pool in May.

Forget-me-not, *see* **Myosotis**

Forsythia × *intermedia.* Lynwood. Deciduous shrub.
Height: 8 to 12ft. Spread: 8 to 12ft. Leaves: to 3in. Flowers:
yellow $\frac{1}{2}$in. in clusters. March–April.

F. suspensa atrocaulis. Deciduous shrub.
More lax habit. Shoots and branches, purplish-black. Flowers:
lemon-yellow. March–April.

French Marigold, *see* **Tagetes patula**

Fritillaria imperialis. Crown Imperial. Bulbous plant.
Height: 3 to 4ft. Leaves: 5 to 6in. Flowers: yellow, bronze or
red, 2in. in a terminal umbel. Plant October. May need a stake.
Illus.: C.G.B.

Fuchsia magellanica riccartonii. Deciduous shrub.
Height: 4 to 8ft. Spread: 4 to 8ft. Leaves: 2in. Flowers: red
and purple, petals 1 to 2in. June–October. Pot grown. Plant
April. Illus. *magellanica* G.S.T.(C).

F. × *speciosa* (*F. hybrida*). Deciduous shrub.
Height: to 2ft. as bush plant, 2 to 2½ft. as short standard, 3 to
3½ ft. or more as standard. Leaves: to 4in. Flowers: to 3in. Pot
grown. Tender. Greenhouse or for balconies, window boxes or
summer bedding. Plant out May.
Keystone, tube and sepals, clear pink, corolla pearl-pink.
La Bianca, tube and sepals white suffused pink, corolla white.
Marin Glow, tube and sepals white, corolla fuchsia blue.
Marinka, crimson-scarlet, almost a self-colour.

Garrya elliptica. Evergreen shrub.
Height: 6 to 12ft. Spread: 8 to 12ft. Leaves: 1½ to 3in. Flowers:

Silver-grey catkins 6in. long. November–February. Pot grown. Plant October or April. Illus.: G.S.T. S.G.G.P.

Geranium, *see* **Pelargonium**

Geranium cinereum. Grey Cranesbill. Herbaceous perennial.
Height: 6in. Leaves: grey. Flowers: pale purple-pink with darker veining, 1½in. July–August.

G. endressii A. T. Johnson. Herbaceous perennial.
Height: 1½ft. Leaves: 3- to 5-lobed. Flowers: large, soft blue. Wargrave. Herbaceous perennial.
Height: 6 to 9in. Spread: 1ft. Leaves: lobed, grey. Flowers: light rose with darker veining. Summer.

G. grandiflorum. Lilac Cranesbill. Herbaceous perennial.
Height: 12 to 15in. Spread: 2ft. Leaves: 5-lobed. Flowers: blue veined with purple, purple eye. June–July. Illus.: C.G.B.P.(C).

G. pratense. Meadow Cranesbill. Herbaceous perennial.
Height: 1½ to 3ft. Spread: 2ft. Leaves 3 to 6in. Flowers: blue with red veins. 1in. June–September. Illus. var. *album* C.G.B.P.

Germander, *see* **Teucrium**

Gleditschia triacanthos. Honey Locust. Deciduous tree.
Height: probably 70ft. (140ft. in the wild). Leaves: 4 to 8in. pinnate. Flowers: green in racemes 2in. July. Illus.: T.T.C.

Gnaphalium, *see* **Helichrysum**

Grape, *see* **Vitis**

Grass, *see* **Elymus** *and* **Festuca**

Hard Fern, *see* **Blechnum**

Hartstongue Fern, *see* **Phyllitis**

Hawthorn, *see* **Crataegus**

Hazel, *see* **Corylus**

Hebe hulkeana (*Veronica hulkeana*). Evergreen shrub.
Height: 3ft. Leaves: 1 to 2in. long, ½ to 1½in. wide, dark shining green. Flowers: lavender or lilac in panicles 6 to 18in. May–June. Pot grown. Needs a wall. Plant April. Illus.: R.H.S.D.

Helianthemum nummularium Wisley Primrose. Evergreen sub-shrub.
Height: 1 to 1½ft. Spread: 2½ to 3½ft. Leaves: to 1¼in. silver. Flowers: bright lemon-yellow. June–September. Pot grown. Plant April.

H. rhodanthe carneum. Evergreen sub-shrub.
Height: 9 to 12in. Spread: 2 to 2½ft. Leaves: to 1¼in. silver. Flowers: soft pink, orange centre 1in. June–September. Pot grown. Plant April.

H. Supreme. Evergeen sub-shrub.
 Height: 9 to 12in. Spread: 2 to 2½ft. Leaves: to 1¼in. Flowers:
 dark crimson 1in. June–September. Pot grown. Plant April.
Helichrysum petiolatum (Gnaphalium lanatum). Everylasting flower.
 Sub-shrub.
 Height: to 2ft. Spread: to 2ft. Leaves: white, woolly. Flowers:
 cream-white in corymbs to 2in. across. July–September. Pot
 grown. Plant May.
Heliotrope, *see* **Heliotropium**
Heliotropium peruvianum. Heliotrope. Cherry Pie. Summer bedding
 plant.
 Height: 1½ to 2½ft. Spread: 12 to 18in. Flowers: lilac-violet
 variable ¼in. in terminal spikes. June–September. Pot grown.
 Tender. Summer bedding.
  Marguerite, dark blue.
  Princess Marina, purple-mauve.
  Vilmorin's Variety, deep purple.
Helleborus corsicus. Perennial herb with largely persisting evergreen
 leaves.
 Height: 2 to 3ft. Spread: 2ft. Leaves: 4 to 8in. long. Flowers:
 yellowish-green in large clusters 2in. March–April to August.
 Poisonous. Plant October. Illus.: C.G.B.P.
H. niger. Christmas Rose. Perennial herb with largely persisting
 evergreen leaves.
 Height: 1 to 2ft. Spread: 2ft. Leaves: 7 to 12in. in 7 to 8 seg-
 ments. Flowers: white, sometimes tinged rose, 2 to 3in. January–
 February. Plant October. Poisonous. Illus.: S.G.G.P. G.F.
H. orientalis. Lenten Rose. Perennial herb with largely persisting
 evergreen leaves.
 Height: 2ft. Spread: 1½ft. Leaves: to 16in. across with 5 to 11
 leaflets. Flowers: green to dark purple to 2½in. March–April.
 Plant October. Poisonous. Illus.: S.G.G.P.
Hemerocallis fulva. Day-lily. Herbaceous perennial.
 Height: 2½ft. Spread to 3ft. Leaves: erect 2ft. long, 1½in. wide.
 Flowers: orange-red with line of apricot in each petal, 4½in.
 July–August. Illus.: C.G.B.P.(C).
H. Hesperus. Day-lily. Herbaceous perennial.
 Height: 4ft. Spread: 3ft. Flowers: lemon-yellow. July–August.
Heucherella Bridget Bloom. Herbaceous perennial.
 Height: 1½ to 2ft. Spread: 12 to 18in. Flowers: brick-red-pink

½in. in narrow panicles. May–October. Plant April. Illus.:
C.G.B.F.(C).

Hibiscus syriacus. Deciduous shrub.
> Height: 6 to 8ft. Spread: 5 to 7ft. Leaves: 3-lobed, 2 to 4in.
> Flowers: 3in. bell-shaped. August–September.
>> Coeleste, single mauve.
>> Hamabo, single, pale pink to white with crimson centre.
>> Monstrosus, single white with dark purple centre.
>> Woodbridge, single rose-crimson with darker red blotches in
>> centre. Illus.: S.G.G.P.

Holly, *see* **Ilex**

Honey Locust, *see* **Gleditschia**

Honeysuckle, *see* **Lonicera**

Hosta fortunei. Plantain Lily. Funkia. Herbaceous perennial.
> Height: to 2ft. Spread: 2ft. Leaves: 5 to 8in. long, to 6in. wide,
> glaucous but less so than those of *H. sieboldiana,* Flowers: pale
> lilac, funnel shaped, 1½in. in racemes standing above foliage.
> July–September.

H. sieboldiana. Plantain Lily. Funkia. Herbaceous perennial.
> Height: 3ft. Spread: 2ft. Leaves: 10 to 14in. long; 6 to 10in.
> wide, glaucous, funnel-shaped. Flowers: whitish, tinged purple
> and green, 1 to 1½in. long in racemes 8 to 9in. standing above
> foliage. June.

H. undulata. Plantain Lily. Wavy-leafed Plantain. Herbaceous
perennial.
> Height: 2¼ft. Spread: 1½ft. Leaves: 6in. long; 3in. wide, green
> splashed with white. Flowers: pale lavender, funnel-shaped,
> 2in. in racemes standing above foliage. July–September.

Hottonia palustris. Water Violet. Perennial aquatic herb.
> Leaves: submerged. Flowers: lilac with yellow eye, fragrant.
> June. An oxygenating plant. Plant in May in loam in bottom of
> pool or in wire baskets or plastic crates.

Humea elegans. Biennial herb.
> Height: 5 to 6ft. Spread: 1½ to 2ft. Leaves: to 10in. long exhale
> a scent of incense. Flowers: coral-pink, minute, in long drooping
> panicles. July–October. Pot grown. Treat as summer bedding.
> Plant out in June. The foliage can cause dermatitis.

Hyacinthus orientalis. Florist's hyacinths. Scented.
>> Ostara, bright blue, with darker blue band. Early. Illus.:
>> C.G.B.(C).

City of Haarlem, primrose yellow. Late.
King of the Blues, indigo. Late.
Lady Derby, shell pink. Early.
L'Innocence, white. Early.
Queen of the Pinks, pink. Late.

Hydrangea macrophylla (*H. hortensis*). Deciduous shrub.
Height: 6 to 8ft. Spread: 7 to 9ft. (less in tubs). Leaves: 4 to
8in. Flowers: red, pink, white, purple, blue in corymbs 6 to
8in. July–September. Pot grown. Plant April. To produce blue
colour in flowers in alkaline soils, the plants must be treated
with aluminium sulphate.

H. petiolaris (*H. scandens*). Deciduous climber.
Height: to 50ft. Leaves: 2 to 4½in., heart shaped. Flowers:
white in corymbs 6 to 10in. June. Reddish peeling bark. Self-
clinging. Pot grown. Illus.: S.G.G.P. B.

Ilex aquifolium. English Holly. Evergreen tree.
Height: 40 to 50ft. Spread: 25 to 35ft. Leaves: 1 to 3in. long;
¾ to 2½in. wide, spiny, dark green. Flowers, small dull white.
May. Plant late April or early May and keep roots well watered
and foliage syringed all through first summer. Plant 2ft. apart
as hedge. Illus.: B.T.S. T.T.C.

I.a. camelliaefolia. Evergreen tree.
Height: 20 to 22ft. Spread: 15 to 18ft. Leaves: 5in. long; 2in.
wide, smooth. Flowers: small, dull white. Plant as for *I. aquifolium*. Illus.: S.G.G.P.

I.a. hodginsii. Evergreen tree.
Leaves: 3 to 4in. long; 2½in. wide. Plant as for *I. aquifolium*.

Indian Bean, *see* **Catalpa**
Ipomoea, *see* **Pharbitis**

Iris germanica. Common Iris. Herbaceous perennial, with rhizomatous rootstock.
Height: 2 to 3ft. Spread: 1 to 1½ft. Leaves: sword shaped 18in.
long; 1½in. wide. Flowers: 2½ to 3in., scented. June. Plant
August–September in full sun in calcareous soil. Leave tops of
rhizomes exposed above ground when planting.

Aline, azure blue.
Arabi Pasha, corn-flower blue.
Cliffs of Dover, creamy-white.
Jane Philipps, light blue.
Ola Kola, orange-yellow.

South Pacific, light blue.
Zantha, deep yellow.

I. pallida dalmatica. Herbaceous perennial.
Height: 3ft. Spread: 1 to 1½ft. Leaves: sword shaped 1½ft. long;
2in. wide, pale blue-green. Flowers: 3in., lavender-blue.
Scented. May–June.

I. unguicularis (*I. stylosa*). Herbaceous perennial.
Height: 15 to 24in. Spread: 12in. Leaves: 18 to 24in. long, ¼ to
½in. wide. Flowers: sky blue 3in., scented. November–March.
Plant in September in gritty soil in dry position exposed to full
sun. Illus. G.F.(C.).

Japonica, *see* **Chaenomeles**
Jasmine, *see* **Jasminum**

Jasminum nudiflorum. Winter Jasmine. Deciduous shrub.
Height: 12ft. on a wall. Leaves: ½ to 1½in. long. Flowers:
yellow ¾ to 1in. November–February. Pot grown. Plant October.
Illus.: S.G.G.P.

J. officinale. Common Jasmine. Semi-evergreen climber.
Height: to 30ft. Leaves: 2 to 2½in. Flowers: white ⅝in., strongly
scented. June–September. Pot grown. Plant April.

Jerusalem Sage, *see* **Phlomis**
Judas Tree, *see* **Cercis**

Laburnum alpinum. Scotch Laburnum. Deciduous tree.
Height: 30 to 35ft. Spread: 25 to 30ft. Leaves: 3-foliate. Leaflets:
1 to 3in.: Flowers: yellow in racemes 12in. long. June. Illus.:
L. vossii T.T.C.

Lamb's Tongue, *see* **Stachys**
Laurel, *see* **Prunus laurocerasus**

Laurus nobilis. Bay. Evergreen tree.
Height: in tubs to 7ft. Spread: to 4ft. Leaves: 1½ to 4in. long;
½ to 1½in. wide, dark glossy green, aromatic. Flowers: greenish-
yellow, small. Generally in tubs. Taken into shelter in winter.
Illus.: G.S.T.

Lavandula spica. Common or Mitcham Lavender. Evergreen shrub.
Height: 3 to 4ft. Spread: 3½ to 4½ft. Leaves: 1½ to 2in. long;
¼ in. wide, grey, aromatic. Flowers: grey-blue, ⅓ to 1in. in whorls,
fragrant. July–August. Plant April in lean soil.

Folgate Blue. Evergreen shrub.
Height: 1 to 1½ft. Spread: 1½ to 2ft. Flowers: soft lavender,
fragrant. June–July. Plant as for *L. spica*.

nana atropurpurea (Hidcote). Evergreen shrub.
> Height: 1 to 1½ ft. Spread: 1½ to 2ft. Flowers: deep purple blue, fragrant. June–July. Plant as for *L. spica.*
> Twickel Purple. Evergreen shrub.
> Height: 2 to 3ft. Spread: 2½ to 3ft. Flowers: purple, fragrant. July. Plant April in lean soil, as for *L. spica.*
> *vera.* The Dutch Lavender. Evergreen shrub.
> Height: 2 to 3ft. Spread: 4 to 6ft. Leaves: 1½ to 2in. long; $\frac{1}{12}$ to ¼in. wide, grey, aromatic. July–August. Plant as for *L. spica.*

Lavender, *see* **Lavandula**
Lavender Cotton, *see* **Santolina**
Lawson's Cypress, *see* **Chamaecyparis lawsoniana**
Lemon Verbena, *see* **Lippia**
Lenten Rose, *see* **Helleborus orientalis**
Lilac, *see* **Syringa**

Lilium auratum. Golden-rayed Lily of Japan. Bulbous plant.
> Height: to 8ft—less in pots. Leaves: 6 to 9in. long; ¾ to 1¼in. wide. Flowers: ivory-white with central band of yellow. Crimson spots. Open funnel-shaped. Strongly scented. August–September. Intolerant of lime. Needs a stake. Plant January–February. Illus.: C.G.B.(C).

L. candidum. Madonna Lily. Bulbous plant.
> Height: to 6ft. Spread: 12 to 18in. Leaves: 6 to 8in. long; ½ to 1in. wide. Flowers: white, trumpet-shaped, 2 to 3in., strongly scented. June. Plant August. Requires lime. Needs a stake. Illus.: C.G.B.(C). S.G.G.P.

L. regale. Regal lily. Bulbous plant.
> Height: 3 to 6ft. Spread: 2 to 3ft. Flowers: white inside, sulphur throat, rose-purple outside. Trumpet shaped, to 5in., strongly scented. July. Plant autumn–winter. Tolerant of lime. Needs a stake. Illus.: C.G.B.(C). S.G.G.P.

L. speciosum. Bulbous plant.
> Height: to 6ft. Leaves: 6 to 9in. long; 1 to 2in. wide. Flowers: white, suffused and spotted red, reflexed scented. September–October. Intolerant of lime. Plant January–February. May need a stake. Illus.: C.G.B.(C).
>> *L.s. album-novum.* Pure white with golden anthers, 3 to 4ft.
>> *L.s. magnificum.* Deep crimson spots and petals suffused with rose except for the tips, 5 to 6ft.

L.s. Melpomene. Dark crimson, heavily spotted purple, and margined white, 5 to 6ft.

L.s. rubrum. Deep pink, with crimson spots, 3 to 4ft.

Lily-of-the-Valley, *see* **Convallaria**

Lippia citriodora (*Aloysia citriodora*). Lemon Verbena. Deciduous shrub.
Height: 10 to 20ft. Leaves: 3 to 4in. long, ½ to 1in. wide. Lemon-scented. Flowers: pale purple, small, in slender downy panicles 3 to 5in. Pot grown. Tender. Plant May.

Lobelia erinus. Tender perennial.
Height: 4 to 12in. Largely trailing. Leaves: ¾in. Flowers: ¾in. Summer. Box- or pot-grown. Summer bedding. Plant out in May.
Cambridge Blue, light blue.
Crystal Palace, deep blue with dark foliage.
Mrs Clibran, deep blue, white eye.
Snowball, white.

Lobularia maritima. Sweet Alyssum. Annual.
Height: 6 to 9in. Leaves: 1 to 3in. Flowers: white, small, in corymbs, fragrant. May–September. Grown in boxes. Summer bedding. Plant out end May.

Locust Tree, *see* **Robinia**

London Pride, *see* **Saxifraga**

Lonicera japonica halliana. Honeysuckle. Evergreen climber.
Height: to 30ft. Leaves: 1½ to 3½in. long; ¾ to 1¾in. wide. Flowers: white, tinged purple, changing to yellow, 1¼ to 1½in., scented. July–October. Pot grown. Plant April.

L. periclymenum serotina. Late Dutch Honeysuckle. Deciduous climber.
Height: 10 to 20ft. Leaves: ½ to 2½in. long; 1 to 2in. wide. Flowers: reddish-purple, outside yellow, 2 to 2½in. in whorls. Scented. August–September. Pot grown. Plant April.

Lysimachia nummularia. Creeping Jenny. Herbaceous perennial.
Creeping; carpeting. Leaves: ½ to ¾in., golden in var. *aurea.* Flowers: bright yellow, ¾in.

Madonna Lily, *see* **Lilium candidum**

Madrona, *see* **Arbutus menziesii**

Magnolia denudata. Yulan. Deciduous tree.
Height: 25 to 40ft. Spread: 10 to 20ft. Leaves: 3 to 6in. long, 2½ to 3½in. wide. Flowers: white, bell-shaped, 5 to 6in. on bare

boughs. Scented. March–May. Plant October or April. Illus.: S.G.G.P. T.T.C.

M. grandiflora. Evergreen tree.
Height: 60 to 80ft. Leaves: 6 to 10in. long; 1 to 4in. wide; often felted brown on undersides. Flowers: white, cup-shaped, 8 to 10in., scented. July–September. Pot grown. Plant April.

M. sargentiana robusta. Deciduous tree or very large bush.
Height: perhaps to 50ft. Leaves: 4 to 8in. long, 2½ to 4½in. wide. Flowers: deep rose, cup-shaped but bending downward from the horizontal when fully open, 1ft. March–April. Plant April. Rare.

M. soulangiana. Deciduous tree.
Height: 20 to 30ft. Spread: 30 to 40ft. Leaves: 3 to 6in. long, 2½ to 3½in. wide. Flowers: white, stained purple at base, 5 to 6in. on bare boughs. Scented. April–May. Plant October or April. Illus.: S.G.G.P.

Mahonia aquifolium. Evergreen shrub.
Height: 2 to 4ft. Spread: 3 to 5ft. Leaves: 6 to 12in., pinnate. Leaflets: 3in. Flowers: yellow in erect racemes 2 to 3½in. February–April. Plant April.

M. japonica. Evergreen shrub (distributed as *M. bealii*).
Height: 5 to 7ft. Spread: 7 to 12ft. Leaves: 1ft., pinnate. Leaflets: 2 to 6in. Flowers: pale yellow in erect racemes 4 to 8in. Scented. February–March. Plant April.

Marigold, *see* **Tagetes**

Matthiola incana. Stock. Sub-shrubby biennial.
Height: 1 to 2ft. Leaves: 4in. Flowers: 1in. in terminal racemes (clove-scented). May–July. Tender. Summer bedding. Sow in March, under glass. Prick into boxes or pots April. Plant out May–June.

Beauty of Nice.
Height: 2ft. Flowers: in many colours in greenhouse. Sow in August under glass for winter flowering.
Brompton.
Height: 1 to 1½ft. Flowers: in many colours. April–July. Illus.: A.B.F.
East Lothian.
Height: 1ft. Flowers: in many colours. July–September.
Giant Perfection.
Height: 15 to 18in. branching habit. Flowers: in many colours. May–August. Illus.: A.B.F.

May, *see* **Crataegus**
Megasea, *see* **Bergenia**
Mexican Orange Flower, *see* **Choisya ternata**
Mezereon, *see* **Daphne**
Mock Orange, *see* **Philadelphus**
Monarda didyma Cambridge Scarlet. Bergamot. Herbaceous
perennial.
> Height: 2 to 3ft. Spread: 2ft. Leaves: to 8in., aromatic. Flowers:
> crimson-scarlet. June–September. Illus.: C.G.B.F.(C). S.G.G.P.
> G.F.

Monterey Cypress, *see* **Cupressus**
Morning Glory, *see* **Pharbitis**
Myosotis alpestris. Forget-me-not. Perennial herb.
> Height: to 2ft. Spread: 9 to 12in. Leaves: 3in. Flowers: blue
> with small yellow eye ⅛in. April–May. Spring bedding plant.
> Sow seed in boxes under glass in May. Transplant June. Plant
> out 9 to 12in. apart in October.
> > Blue Ball 6in., deep blue.
> > Royal Blue 1ft., deep blue.
> > Victoria 6in., clear blue, compact

Myriophyllum spicatum. Submerged aquatic.
> Finely cut leaves. An oxygenating pool plant. Plant in pool in
> May.

Myrtus communis. Myrtle. Evergreen shrub.
> Height: 10 to 12ft. Leaves: 1 to 2in. long; ⅛ to ¾in. wide,
> lustrous green, aromatic when bruised. Flowers: white, ¾in.,
> scented. July. Tender. Requires a wall. Pot grown. Plant April.

Nepeta faassenii (*N. mussinii*). Catmint. Herbaceous perennial.
> Height: 12in. Spread: 1 to 1½ft. Leaves: to 1½in., grey. Flowers:
> pale lavender, ½in. in whorls. May–Sept. Plant April. Illus.:
> C.G.B.P.(C). S.G.G.P.

Nerine bowdenii. Bulbous plant.
> Height: 1½ft. Leaves: 1ft. long; ½in. wide. Flowers: pale pink
> ½ to 3in. in umbels of 6 to 12 flowers. September. Plant August
> 6in. deep against a south-facing wall. C.G.B.

Nerium oleander. Oleander. Rose Bay. Evergreen shrub.
> Height: in tub probably to 6ft. Spread: in tub probably 4ft.
> Leaves: 4 to 6in. Flowers: white, yellow, red, purple, 3in. in
> terminal cymes about 8in. June–October. Tender. Usually in tubs.
> Taken to greenhouse mid-September to end May. Poisonous.

New Zealand Flax, *see* **Phormium tenax**

Nicotiana alata grandiflora (*N. affinis*). Tobacco Plant. Tender perennial.

Height: 2ft. Spread: 12 to 18in. Leaves: 6in. Flowers: white, 3 to 3½in., scented, June–September. Pot or box grown. Summer bedding. Plant in June. Illus.: A.B.F.

Variety Lime Green. Flowers: pale green, yellow.

Nut, *see* **Corylus**

Nymphaea. Water-lily. Water plant.

Plant in pool in May.

Froebelii, flowers: wine-crimson 3 to 4in. Scented. Depth: 1 to 1½ft.

Hermine, flowers: white, 2 to 3in. standing out of the water. Depth: 1 to 1½ft.

James Brydon, flowers: crimson 4 to 6in. Depth: 1½ to 2ft. Illus: W.G. S.G.G.P.

Laydekeri purpurata, flowers: bright red 1 to 2in. Depth: 6 to 12in.

Marliacea albida, flowers: white 4 to 6in. Depth: 1½ to 2ft.

Marliacea chromatella, flowers: yellow 4 to 6in. Depth: 1½ to 2ft. Illus. W.G.

odorata alba, flowers: white, scented, 3 to 4in. Depth: 1 to 1½ft.

odorata sulphurea, flowers: yellow 3 to 4in. Depth: 1 to 1½ft.

odorata turicensis, flowers: pink 3 to 4in. Depth: 1 to 1½ft.

Pink Opal, flowers: deep coral-pink 1 to 2in. Depth: 6 to 12in.

pygmaea alba, flowers: white 1in. Depth 4 to 12in.

pygmaea helvola, primrose yellow 1in. Depth: 4 to 12in.

Somptuosa, flowers: rose-pink 4 to 6in. Depth: 1 to 2ft.

Oleander, *see* **Nerium**

Orange, *see* **Citrus**

Origanum microphyllum. Sub-shrub.

Height: 1ft. Leaves: very aromatic. Flowers: pink, small. June. Tender. Pot grown. As summer bedding. Plant out in June.

Osmunda regalis. Royal Fern. Deciduous fern.

Height: to 6ft. Plant in April.

Osmarea × *burkwoodii.* Evergreen shrub.

Height: 9 to 12ft. Spread: 9 to 12ft. Leaves: 1½in. Flowers: ivory-white. April. Scented. Pot grown. Plant in April. Illus.: S.G.G.P.

Oxlip, *see* **Polyanthus**

Paeonia lactiflora Eva. Peony. Herbaceous perennial.
Height: 3ft. Flowers: pale crimson-lilac, single to semi-double.
Scented. May–June. Plant April.
Victoria. Herbaceous perennial.
Height: 3ft. Flowers: crimson, single. Scented. May–June.
Plant April.
Whitleyi major. Herbaceous perennial.
Height: 3ft. Leaves: 3 to 4in. Flowers: white, single, 3in.
Scented. May–June. Plant April.

P. lutea ludlowii. Tree Peony. Deciduous shrub.
Height: 6ft. Spread: 9 to 12ft. Flowers: yellow, single, 4½in.
May–June. Plant October or April. Illus.: *P. lutea* G.S.T.

P. suffruticosa Reine Elizabeth. Tree Peony. Deciduous shrub.
Height: 5 to 6ft. Flowers: crimson, double. Plant October or
April.

P. suffruticosa Yano Okima. Tree peony.
Flowers: white, semi-double. Plant October or April.

Pansy, *see* **Viola × wittrockiana**

Parthenocissus henryana. Self-clinging deciduous climber.
Leaves: 1½ to 5in. Fruit: dark blue. Pot grown. Plant April.

Passiflora caerulea. Passion Flower. Deciduous climber.
Leaves: 4 to 7in., palmately 5- to 7-lobed. Flowers: blue centre,
cream-white sepals 3 to 4in. June–September. Pot grown. Not
entirely hardy. Plant April.

Passion Flower, *see* **Passiflora**

Pearlwort, *see* **Sagina procumbens**

Pelargonium capitatum. Sub-shrub.
Height: 3ft. Leaves: 1 to 3in., aromatic. Flowers: pink with
purple veining, small. Summer. Pot grown. Tender. Greenhouse
plant. Can be used with summer bedding. Plant out in June.
Illus.: P.
Clorinda. Scented-leaved Geranium.
Leaves: aromatic. Flowers: large, cerise. June–September. Pot
grown. Greenhouse or summer bedding. Plant out in June.

P. crispum variegatum. Sub-shrub.
Height: 2 to 3ft. Leaves: fan-shaped ½ to 1½in., edged with pale
yellow, aromatic. Flowers: mauve. Summer. Pot grown. Tender.
Greenhouse plant. Can be used with summer bedding. Plant out
in June.

P. denticulatum. Pheasant's foot. Sub-shrub.
Height: 3ft. Leaves: 1½ to 3in. deeply cut to mid rib, aromatic.
Flowers: lilac, about ½in. Summer. Pot grown. Tender. Green-
house plant. Can be used with summer bedding. Plant out in
June. Illus.: P.

P. × *domesticum.* Regal. Show. Fancy Pelargonium. Martha
Washington. Sub-shrub.
Height: to 1½ft. Leaves: 2 to 4in. Flowers: large. Pot grown.
Tender. Greenhouse plant used for summer, bedding in sheltered
positions.

Carisbrooke (Ballerina), pale pink with dark maroon feather-
ing on upper petals. Illus.: P.(C).
Duchess of Teck, white, frilled.
Evelyn Cole, rose-pink. Upper petals crimson edged with
pink, frilled.
Lord Bute (Purple Robe). Purple-black with red picotee edge.
Rose of Devon. Pale rose-lilac, darker feathering on upper
petals.

P. × *fragrans.* Nutmeg-scented Geranium. Sub-shrub.
Height: 1ft. Leaves: 1in. heart-shaped, slightly glaucous, aromatic. Flowers: white, with red veins on upper petals, small.
Summer. Pot grown. Tender. Greenhouse plant. Can be used
with summer bedding. Plant out in June.

P. peltatum. Ivy-leaved Geranium. Sub-shrub.
Height: to 3ft., spreading. Leaves: 2 to 3in. Flowers: 1in. in
5- to 7-flowered umbels. June–September. Pot grown. Summer
bedding plant. Plant out in June.

Abel Carrière, flowers: orchid purple, double.
Audrey Clifton, flowers: cerise-crimson.
Galilee, flowers: pink, double.
L'Élégante, leaves: ivy-green with mauve-lilac margin.
Flowers: white, single, feathered brown-purple. Illus.: P.
La France, flowers: mauve-pink, double. Illus.: P.(C).
Madame Crousse, flowers: mauve-pink, double.
Mrs W. A. R. Clifton, flowers: Orient red, double.

P. tomentosum. Sub-shrub.
Height: to 3ft. Leaves: to 4in., aromatic. Flowers: white, about
½in. Summer. Pot grown. Tender. Greenhouse plant. Can be
used with summer bedding. Plant out in June. Illus.: P.

P. zonale. Zonal Geranium. Horseshoe Geranium. Sub-shrub.

Height: to 15in. Leaves: 3 to 5in. Flowers: in umbels 2 to 3in.
Pot grown. Greenhouse or summer bedding. Plant out in June.

    A. M. Mayne, fuchsia-purple, double.

    Caroline Schmidt, flowers: cerise, double. Leaves: green, edged cream.

    Chelsea Gem, flowers: shell-pink, double. Leaves: green, edged white.

    Decorator, jasper-red, semi-double. Illus.: P.

    Doris Moore, cherry, single.

    Double Henry Jacoby, crimson, double. Illus.: P.(C).

    Gustav Emich, signal-red, double. Illus.: P.(C).

    Hermine, white, double.

    Irene, light crimson, semi-double.

    King of Denmark, salmon, double.

    Maxim Kovalevski, orange, single.

    Millfield Rival, fuchsine-pink, single, white eye. Illus.: P.(C).

    Mr Henry Cox, fancy leaf pelargonium. Leaves: gold, purple, red, cream. Flowers: pink. Pot grown. Plant out in June. Illus.: leaves P.(C).

    Mrs Lawrence, pale carmine (shorter).

    Paul Crampel, scarlet, single.

    Pink Bouquet (Irene strain), pale lilac-pink, semi-double.

    Queen of the Whites, white, single.

    Red Black Vesuvius, flowers: scarlet, small. Leaves: dark green with black zone.

    Toyon (Irene strain), scarlet single.

    Trulls Hatch (Irene strain), salmon-pink, semi-double.

    Verona, leaves: pale gold. Flowers: lilac-pink. Illus.: leaf P.(C).

Peony, *see* **Paeonia**

Petunia. Herb or sub-shrub.

Height: 10 to 18in. Leaves: ¾ to 2in. Flowers: 2 to 4in., trumpet-shaped, sometimes fragrant. June–September. Pot and box grown. Tender. Summer bedding. Plant out in June.

    Candy Apple, vivid scarlet.

    Gipsy Ballerina, crimson-scarlet.

    Glacier, white.

    Grandiflora Capri, blue-violet.

    Inimitable, maroon and white striped.

    Psyche, mauve, veined pale blue.

Red Ensign, crimson-scarlet.

Rose of Heaven, light pink. Illus.: A.B.F.

Sutton's Blue Bedder, medium blue.

Pharbitis tricolor (*Ipomoea rubro-caerulea*). Morning Glory. Annual climber.

Leaves: bean-shaped. Flowers: opening china blue. June–September. Tender. Pot grown. Summer climber. Plant out in June.

Philadelphus × *lemoinei* Manteau d'Hermine. Mock Orange. Syringa. Deciduous shrub.

Height: 3½ to 4ft. Spread: 5 to 6ft. Leaves: 1 to 2½in. Flowers: white, 1in. Scented. June.

P. microphyllus. Mock Orange. Syringa. Deciduous shrub.

Height: 4 to 5ft. Spread: 5 to 7ft. Leaves: ½ to ¾in. long; ¼ to ⅓in. wide. Flowers: white 1in. Scented. June.

P. Sybille. Mock Orange. Syringa. Deciduous shrub.

Height: 2½ to 3½ft. Spread: 4 to 5ft., arching habit. Flowers: white, purple centres. Scented. June. Illus.: S.G.G.P.

Phillyrea decora. Evergreen shrub.

Height: 5 to 8ft. Spread: 7 to 10ft. Leaves: 2 to 5in. long; ½ to 1¾in. wide. Flowers: white ¼in. in axillary clusters. Scented. April–May. Plant October or April.

Phlomis fruticosa. Jerusalem Sage. Evergreen shrub.

Height: 2 to 4ft. Spread: 3 to 4ft. Leaves: to 4in., wrinkled, grey-green above, grey underside. Flowers: yellow, 1in. in whorls 3in. June. Pot grown. Plant April. Illus.: S.G.G.P.

Phormium tenax. New Zealand Flax. Evergreen herb.

Height: 6 to 8ft. Spread: 8 to 12ft. Leaves: sword-shaped 6 to 8ft. long; 4 to 5in. wide. Flowers: dull red 2 to 2½in. Summer. Tender. Plant in April.

Phyllitis scolopendrium. Hartstongue Fern. Evergreen.

Height: 2ft.

Plant April.

Pink, *see* **Dianthus**

Plantain Lily, *see* **Hosta**

Polyanthus (*Primula acaulis* × *P. veris*). Oxlip. Herbaceous perennial. Height: 9 to 12in. Spread: 12in. Leaves: 4 to 5in. long; 1½in. wide. Flowers: mixed colours. March–April. Spring bedding. Sow seeds February–March under glass. Prick out and harden in cold frame: plant in nursery bed June. Transplant to flowering position in September.

Pomegranate, *see* **Punica**

Potentilla arbuscula. Deciduous shrub.
Height: 4ft. Spread: 2 to 3ft. Leaves: 1 to 1½in. Flowers: buttercup-yellow, ½in. June-October. Plant April. Sometimes pot grown.

P. nana argentea (*P. beesii*). Deciduous shrub.
Height: 1 to 1½ft. Spread: 2 to 3ft. Leaves: grey. Flowers: buttercup-yellow. August–October. Pot grown. Plant April.

Prunus communis (*P. amygdalus*). Common Almond. Deciduous tree.
Height: 20 to 25ft. Spread: 20 to 25ft. Leaves: 3 to 6in. Flowers: pale pink, single, 1½ to 3in. March. Illus.: T.T.C.

P. c. Pollardii (*P. amygdalo-persica* Pollardii). Deciduous tree.
Height: 20 to 25ft. Spread: 20 to 25ft. Leaves: 3 to 6in. Flowers: deep pink, double or semi-double, 2 to 2½in.

P. laurocerasus. Common or Cherry Laurel. Evergreen shrub.
Height: 15 to 20ft. Spread: 15 to 20ft. Leaves: 3 to 6in. Flowers: white, ⅓in. in racemes 2 to 5in. April. Plant in October or April, as hedge, 2ft. apart.

P. lusitanica. Portugal laurel. Evergreen shrub.
Height: 10 to 15ft. Spread: 15 to 20ft. Leaves: 2½ to 5in. long; 1½ to 2in. wide. Flowers: white ½ to 1½in. across in racemes 6 to 10in. long. June. Fruit: ⅓in. dark purple. Plant April.

P. subhirtella autumnalis. Winter Cherry. Deciduous tree.
Height: 20 to 25ft. Spread: 25 to 30ft. Leaves: 1½ to 3in. Flowers: white, semi-double, ¾in. in clusters. November–February. Illus.: S.G.G.P.

Punica granatum. Pomegranate. Deciduous tree.
Height: in tubs probably 7 to 8ft. Leaves: 1 to 3in. long; ⅓ to 1in. wide. Flowers: scarlet-red, 1 to 1½in. June–September. Tender. Usually in tubs. Taken to greenhouse October–May. Will survive in southern England on south walls.

Pyracantha atalantioides. (*P. gibbsii*) Firethorn. Evergreen shrub.
Height: 15 to 18ft. Leaves: 1½ to 3½in. long; ¾ to 1¾in. wide. Flowers: white, ⅓in. June. Red berries. Pot grown. Plant October or April.

P. rogersiana. Firethorn. Evergreen shrub.
Height: 15 to 18ft. Leaves: ½ to 1½in. long; ¾ to 1¾in. wide. Flowers: white, ⅓in. June. Reddish-orange berries, var. *flava* yellow berries. Pot grown. Plant October or April. Illus.: var. *aurantiaca* S.G.G.P.

Quince, *see* **Chaenomeles**

Regal lily, *see* **Lilium regale**

Rhododendron. Hardy hybrid. Evergreen shrub.
Height: in tub probably 6 to 8ft. Spread: 4 to 6ft. Leaves: 6in. Flowers: in large trusses. May. Calcifuge.
Cynthia, rose-crimson.
Doncaster, crimson-scarlet.
Pink Pearl, rose-pink, fading lighter.

R. arboreum. Evergreen tree.
Height: 30 to 40ft. Spread: 20 to 40ft. Leaves: 4 to 8in. long; 1 to 2in. wide. Flowers: blood-red 1½ to 2in. in compact heads 4 to 8in. across. March–April. Tender. Plant in April. Illus.: B.

Rhus cotinus, *see* **Cotinus coggygria**

R. typhina. Stag's-horn Sumach. Deciduous tree.
Height: 10 to 15ft. Spread: 12 to 16ft. Leaves: 1 to 2ft., pinnate, turning scarlet in autumn. Flowers: greenish in panicles 4 to 8in. July–August.

Robinia pseudoacacia. Locust Tree. False Acacia. Deciduous tree.
Height: up to 70ft. Spread: 25 to 30ft. Leaves: pinnate 6 to 12in. Leaflets: 1 to 2in. Flowers: white in racemes 4 to 7in. June. Illus.: T.T.C., var. *decaisneana* G.T.S.

Romneya trichocalyx. Herbaceous perennial.
Height: 5 to 7ft. Leaves: 3 to 5in., glaucous. Flowers: white with yellow stamens, poppy-like, 3 to 5in. July–October. Pot grown. Plant April.

Rosa × *anemonoides* (*R. sinica* Anemone), 1896. Evergreen climbing rose.
Leaves: 1½ to ¾in. Flowers: pale pink, blotched darker pink, 2 to 3in. April. Pot grown. Tender. Needs a wall.

R. banksiae, 1824. Banksian Rose. Evergreen climbing rose.
Height: to 20ft. Leaves: 2½in. Flowers: yellow, single or double, 1in. in many flowered umbels. Slightly scented. May–June. Pot grown. Tender. Needs a wall.

R. × *bracteata* Mermaid, 1918. Deciduous climber.
Height: to 30ft. Leaflets: 5 to 9, ¾ to 1½in., shining. Flowers: sulphur-yellow, single, 5in. June–October. Pot grown. Hardy. Succeeds on north walls. Plant October or April. Illus.: S.G.G.P.

Apricot Silk, 1964. Hybrid tea rose. Flowers: apricot, scented. June–October.

Emily Gray, 1916. Wichuraiana rambler rose.

Leaves: almost evergreen. Flowers: copper-yellow. June.

Ena Harkness, 1946. Hybrid tea rose. Deciduous shrub.
Height: 2½ft. Flowers: crimson, double. June–September.

Ena Harkness, Climbing, 1954. Climbing hybrid tea rose.
Deciduous climber.   Flowers: crimson. June–September.

Fragrant Cloud, 1963. Hybrid tea rose.
Flowers: coral red, strongly scented. June–October.

Gloire de Dijon, 1853. Climbing tea rose. Deciduous climber.
Flowers: buff-yellow, double, flat shape. Scented. May–September.

Gold Gleam, 1966. Hybrid floribunda rose.
Flowers: canary yellow, slightly scented. June–October.

Iceberg, 1958. Floribunda rose. Deciduous shrub.
Height: 3ft. Flowers: greenish-white, buds flushed pink. June–October.

Lady Hillingdon, 1917. Climbing tea rose. Deciduous climber.
Flowers: apricot, double. Scented. June–September.

Madame Alfred Carrière, 1879. Climbing noisette rose.
Flowers: white, tinted blush, double. Scented. Summer and autumn.

Madame Pierre Oger, 1879. Bourbon rose.
Height: 6ft. Flowers: pale to deep pink, cup shaped. June and sporadically to September.

Message, 1955. Hybrid tea rose.
Flowers: white, shaded green at base, scented. June–October.

Old Pink Moss, 1727. *R. centifolia muscosa.*
Height: to 6ft. Flowers: rose pink, mossed, strongly scented. End June–mid-July.

Ophelia, climbing, 1920. Climbing hybrid tea rose. Deciduous climber.
Flowers: mother-of-pearl, small. Scented. June–September.

Pernille Poulsen, 1965. Hybrid floribunda rose.
Flowers: coral salmon, slightly scented. June–October.

Pink Parfait, 1962. Hybrid floribunda.
Flowers: apricot-rose. June–October.

Plentiful, 1960. Hybrid floribunda rose.
Flowers: cup shaped, pink, scented. June–October.

Queen of Denmark, 1826. Hybrid *R. alba.*
Height: 5ft. Flowers: pink, full, with crinkled centres, strongly scented. End June–mid July.

Red Dandy, 1960. Floribunda rose. Deciduous shrub.
Height: 3ft. Flowers: crimson, double. June–October.
sinica anemone, *see* R. × anemonoides
Souvenir de la Malmaison, 1842. Bourbon rose.
Height: to 10ft. Flowers: full, quartered, pale pink, deepening
towards centre, strongly scented. June and sporadically to Sep-
tember.
Super Star, 1960. Hybrid tea rose. Deciduous shrub.
Height: 4ft. Flowers: flame-scarlet, semi-double. June–October.
Zéphirine Drouhin, 1868. Hybrid Bourbon rose. Deciduous shrub.
Height: to 12ft., thornless. Flowers: cerise, double. Scented.
May–June and September.

Rosemary, *see* **Rosmarinus**
Rosmarinus lavandulaceus (*R. officinalis prostratus*). Spanish Rose-
mary. Evergreen shrub.
　　Height: 1½ to 2ft. Spread: 4 to 5ft. Leaves: linear to 2in. long;
　　1/16 to ⅛in., aromatic. Flowers: lavender blue, ½ to ¾in., fragrant.
　　April–May. Tender. Pot grown. Plant April.
Rosmarinus officinalis. Rosemary. Evergreen shrub.
　　Height: to 6ft. Spread: 6 to 7ft. Leaves: linear to 2in. long;
　　1/16 to ⅛in. wide, aromatic. Flowers: pale violet ½ to ¾in. in axils
　　of previous year's shoots. Fragrant. May. Pot grown. Plant in
　　April.
R.o. Corsican Blue. Rosemary. Evergreen shrub.
　　Height: 3½ to 4ft. Spread: 6 to 8ft. Leaves: linear to 2in. long;
　　1/16 to ⅛in. wide, aromatic. Flowers: porcelain blue ½ to ¾in.
　　Fragrant. April–June. Tender. Pot grown. Plant April.

Royal Fern, *see* **Osmunda regalis**
Rue, *see* **Ruta**
Ruta graveolens. Jackman's Blue. Evergreen shrub.
　　Height: 2½ to 3½ft. Spread: 3 to 4ft. Leaves: 2 to 3in., pinnate,
　　opalescent blue. Flowers: dull yellow, ¾in. in terminal corymbs.
　　June–September. Pot grown. Plant April.
Sagina procumbens. Pearlwort. Perennial herb.
　　Creeping. Leaves: linear ⅛ to ⅜in. Flowers: white, very small,
　　solitary. May–August.
Salvia ambigens (*S. caerulea*). Sub-shrub.
　　Height: to 5ft. Leaves: 2 to 5in. Flowers: violet-blue, 1½ to 2in.
　　in racemes to 6in. September–October. Half-hardy. Plant April.
　　Pot grown. Illus.: R.H.S.D.

S. grahamii. Evergreen shrub.
Height: to 4ft. Leaves: 1in., blackcurrant scented. Flowers: deep crimson turning purple, 1in. in racemes to 1ft. July–October. Pot grown. Tender. Needs a wall. Plant May.

S. officinalis hispanica (*S. lavandulifolia*). Evergreen shrub.
Height: 2 to 2½ft. Spread: 3 to 4ft. Leaves: 2 to 4in., aromatic. Flowers: pale blue in racemes to 4in. June. Plant April.

S. o. purpurascens. Purple Sage. Evergreen shrub.
Height: 2½ to 3ft. Spread: 4 to 5ft. Leaves: 1 to 1½in., reddish-purple. Flowers: purple, blue and white, ¾in. in racemes. June. Pot grown. Plant April.

S. patens. Gentian Sage. Perennial herb.
Height: to 2½ft. Spread: 1½ft. Flowers: deep blue, 2in. August–September. Pot grown. Half-hardy. Treat as summer bedding plant. Plant May.

S. sclarea turkestanica. Clary. Biennial herb.
Height: 3 to 3½ft. Spread: 2ft. Leaves: 8 to 9in., pungent. Flowers: white, tinged pink; rosy-white bracts, 1in., in panicles. August. Needs a stake. Illus.: C.G.B.P.(C).

S. × *superba.* (*S. virgata nemorosa*) Herbaceous perennial.
Height: 2 to 3ft. Spread: 2ft. Leaves: to 3in. Flowers: blue-purple in spikes to 8in., brownish-purple bracts. July–August. Illus.: C.G.B.P.(C).

Santolina chamaecyparissus (*S. incana*). Lavender Cotton. Evergreen shrub.
Height: 1½ to 2ft. Spread: 2½ to 3½ft. Leaves: 1 to 1½in. long; ⅛in. wide, very crowded, white felted. Flowers: yellow, ½ to ¾in. July–August. Pot grown. Plant April.

Saxifraga umbrosa. London Pride. Herbaceous perennial.
Height: to 1ft. Spread: 1ft. Leaves: to 2in., reddish beneath. Flowers: white and pink with red spots, ¼in. in loose panicles. May–July.

Senecio cineraria (*S. maritima*). Sub-shrub.
Height: 1 to 2ft. Leaves: deeply pinnately lobed 2 to 6in. long, ½ to 4in. wide, white woolly. Flowers: creamy-yellow to ½in. in cymes. Summer. Pot grown. Tender. Plant out in May.

S. laxifolius. Evergreen shrub.
Height: to 4ft. Spread: 4 to 6ft. Leaves: 1½ to 2½in. long; ¾ to 1¼in. wide, grey. Flowers: lemon-yellow 1in. in panicles 5 to 8in. long. Summer. Pot grown. Plant April. Illus.: R.H.S.D.

Skimmia japonica fragrans. Evergreen shrub.
Height: 3 to 5ft. Spread: 5 to 7ft. Leaves: 3 to 4in. Flowers: white in panicles 2 to 3in. Spring. Red berries. Calcifuge. Plant April.

Smoke Tree, *see* **Cotinus coggygria**

Snapdragon, *see* **Antirrhinum**

Sorbus aria lutescens. Whitebeam. Deciduous tree.
Height: 30 to 40ft. Spread: 30 to 40ft. Leaves: 2 to 4½in., green above, silver undersides. Flowers: white, ⅓in. in clusters 3 to 4in. across. May. Illus.: *S. aria* T.T.C. B.T.S.

Spurge, *see* **Euphorbia**

Stachys lanata. Lamb's Tongue. Herbaceous perennial.
Height: 1 to 1½ft. Leaves: silver-grey, woolly. Flowers: pale purple, small, in ascending spikes. June–August. Plant April.

Stag's-horn Sumach, *see* **Rhus typhina**

Stocks, *see* **Matthiola**

Strawberry Tree, *see* **Arbutus unedo**

Sweet Alyssum, *see* **Lobularia**

Syringa, *see* **Philadelphus**

Syringa vulgaris. Lilac. Deciduous tree or shrub.
Height: 15 to 18ft. Leaves: 2 to 6in. Flowers: in panicles 6 to 8in. Scented. May.
Charles Joly, deep reddish-purple, double.
Katherine Havemeyer, lobelia-violet, suffused purple-lilac, semi-double or double.
Madame Lemoine, white, double.

Tagetes erecta. African Marigold. Annual.
Height: to 4ft. Leaves: pinnate, 6in., pungent. Flowers: yellow-orange to 4in. June–October. Grown in pots or boxes. Tender. Summer bedding. Plant out in June.
Hawaii to 3ft.
Spun Gold, 9 to 12in.

T. patula. French Marigold. Annual.
Height: to 1½ft. Leaves: to ¾in. Flowers: yellow, 2in. June–October. Tender. Box or pot grown. Summer bedding. Plant June.
Lemon King, 8 to 9in., pale yellow.
Naughty Marietta, Height: 1ft., Flowers: gold and maroon.
Orange Glow, 8 to 9in., orange.

Taxus baccata. English Yew. Evergreen tree.
Height: 40 to 60ft. Spread: 40 to 60ft. Leaves: ½ to 1½in., narrow, spirally arranged. Flowers: small, yellow. February.

Seeds dark green in red fleshy axil. Poisonous. Plant April. As
hedge plants 3ft. high, 20in. apart. Prune April.

Teucrium fruticans. Tree Germander. Evergreen shrub.
    Height: 2 to 5ft. Leaves: to 1½in., grey. Flowers: blue, ¾in. in
terminal racemes. Summer. Tender. Pot grown. Plant April.

Thorn, *see* **Crataegus**

Thuja plicata (*T. lobbii*). Western Red Cedar. Coniferous. Evergreen
tree.
    Height: to 100ft. or more. Leaves: about ¼in. closely pressed to
shoots. Resinous. Cones: ⅓ to ½in. Plant April.

Thyme, *see* **Thymus**

Thymus serpyllum. Thyme. Evergreen sub-shrub.
    Prostrate, mat-forming. Leaves: ¼ to ⅜in. long; ¹⁄₁₆in. wide,
aromatic. Flowers: purplish, ¼in. in whorls ⅜ to ¾in. June–
September. Pot grown. Plant April.

Tillaea recurva. Submerged aquatic.
    An oxygenating pool plant. Plant in pool in May.

Tobacco Plant, *see* **Nicotiana**

Tree Germander, *see* **Teucrium**

Tree of Heaven, *see* **Ailanthus**

Tulip. Bulbous plant.
    Leaves: basal and stem to 6in. Plant November
    Early Single, flowering about end of April.
        Bellona, yellow, 15in.
        Couleur Cardinal, crimson, 13in.
        Diana, white, 12in.
        Prince of Austria, red-orange, scented, 15in.
        Van der Neer, purple, 12in.
    Early Double, flowering about end of April.
        Orange Nassau, orange-red, 11in.
        Scarlet Cardinal, scarlet, 11in.
        Schoonord, white, 12in.
        Vurbaak, scarlet, flushed orange, 12 in.
    Darwin hybrids, flowering early May.
        Golden Springtime, golden yellow, 26in.
        Holland's Glory, scarlet, 22in.
    Bizarre, flowering in May.
        Absalon, yellow, flamed and feathered mahogany. May, 2ft.
        Insulinde, yellow, bronze, purple, mahogany. May, 2ft.

Bybloem, flowering in May.

   May Blossom, creamy-white, veined bluish-purple. May, 1½ft.
Lily-flowered, flowering in May.

   White Triumphator, white. May, 2½ft.

Tulipa eichleri;
   Height: 1ft. Flowers: scarlet inside, pinkish-buff outside, 4 to
5ft. End April. Plant November. Illus.: C.G.B.

T. fosteriana Princeps;
   Vermilion-scarlet, large flowers, 16in. Mid-April.

T. greigii;
   Height: 1ft. Leaves: mottled mauvish-purple. Flowers: scarlet.
Plant November.

T. ingens;
   Height: 1ft. Flowers: scarlet-crimson. Mid-April. Plant
November.

Verbascum bombyciferum (*V.* Broussa). Biennial.
   Height: 4 to 6ft. Spread: 2ft. Leaves: white, woolly. Flowers:
pale yellow. June–July. Pot grown. Plant April.

Verbena rigida (*V. venosa*). Herbaceous perennial. Usually treated
as summer bedding.
   Height: to 2ft. Leaves: 2 to 3in. Flowers: mauve-purple in
dense spikes 1 to 3in. Summer. Pot or box grown. For summer
bedding plant out in May.

Veronica hulkeana, *see* **Hebe hulkeana**

Viburnum × *burkwoodii*. Evergreen shrub.
   Height: to 10ft. Spread: 9 to 12ft. Leaves: 1½ to 4in.
   Flowers: pinkish, becoming white, in clusters 2½ to 3½in.
March–May.

V. davidii. Evergreen shrub.
   Height: 2 to 3ft. Spread: 4 to 5ft. Leaves: 3 to 5in. Flowers:
dull white in flat corymbs 2 to 3in. June. Fruit: shiny blue, ¼in.
Plant April.

V. juddii. Deciduous shrub.
   Height: 4 to 8ft. Spread: 6 to 8ft. Flowers: white, tinged pink,
in clusters 2¼ to 3¼in. April–May.

V. tinus. Laurustinus. Evergreen shrub.
   Height: 7 to 10ft. Spread: 8 to 10ft. Leaves: 1½ to 4in. long;
¾ to 1¾in. wide. Flowers: white, pink in bud, ¼in. in terminal
clusters 2 to 4in. across. Sometimes pot grown. Plant April.

V. tomentosum Lanarth Variety. Deciduous shrub.

Height: 9 to 12ft. Spread: 10 to 15ft. Leaves: 2 to 4in. Flowers: white in flat clusters 3 to 4in. May.

Vinca minor. Periwinkle. Evergreen shrub.

Prostrate, ground cover. Leaves: 1 to 1½in. Flowers: pale blue-mauve, 1in. April–May. Pot grown. Plant April. Good in shade.

Viola × williamsii. Viola. Perennial herb.

Height: 3 to 8in. Spread: 6in.

Chantreyland, apricot-yellow.

Lady Tennyson, white with small yellow eye.

Maggie Mott, pale lavender-blue.

Pickering Blue, bright purplish-blue.

Sutton's Large Flowered Campanula Blue, sky-blue, small yellow eye.

V. × wittrockiana. Garden Pansy. Annual or short lived perennial.

Height: 4 to 9in.

Winter flowering.

Celestial Queen, sky-blue.

Ice King, white with dark eye.

March Beauty, mid-blue.

Orion, buttercup-yellow.

Winter Sun, golden-yellow with dark eye.

Summer flowering.

Clear Crystals, white, red, yellow, orange, light blue, dark blue, all without faces.

Coronation Gold, Flowers: golden-yellow.

Felix strain. Mixed colours, black, whiskered markings from centre.

Swiss Giant, yellow, dark maroon face.

Ullswater, violet-blue, dark purple face.

Vitis coignetiae Deciduous climber.

Height: 60 to 90ft. Leaves: to 12in., turning crimson in autumn. Fruit: ½in., black with purple bloom. Autumn. Pot grown. Plant April.

V. henryana, *see* **Parthenocissus henryana**

V. vinifera. Grape Vine. Deciduous climber.

Height: to 50ft. Leaves: 3 to 6in. Pot grown. Plant April.

Golden Chasselas (Royal Muscadine), golden-yellow grapes.

Madeleine Royale, white grapes.

Pirovano 14, black grapes.

Wallflower, *see* **Cheiranthus**
Water Lily, *see* **Nymphaea**
Water Violet, *see* **Hottonia palustris**
Western Red Cedar, *see* **Thuja plicata**
Whitebeam, *see* **Sorbus**
Wig Tree, *see* **Cotinus coggygria**
Winter Cherry, *see* **Prunus**
Winter Jasmine, *see* **Jasminum**
Winter Sweet, *see* **Chimonanthus**

Wisteria floribunda 'Macrobotrys' (*multijuga*) Deciduous climber.
 Height: to 30ft. Leaves: 10 to 15in., pinnate. Flowers: ¾in., pale
 violet or lavender in racemes. Scented. June. Pot grown. Plant
 April.
W. sinensis. Deciduous climber.
 Height: to 100ft. Leaves: 10 to 12in., pinnate. Flowers: bluish-
 violet, 1in. in racemes 1ft. Scented. May. Pot grown. Plant
 April.

Yew, *see* **Taxus baccata**
Yucca gloriosa. Evergreen shrub.
 Height: to 8ft. Leaves: 2 to 2½ft. long; 2in. wide, sword-shaped
 with stiff point. Flowers: creamy-white, tinged red or purple
 outside, 4in. in erect panicles 3 to 6ft. high. Scented at night.
 Generally September. Pot grown. Plant April.
Yulan, *see* **Magnolia denudata**

BRITISH STANDARDS IN
NURSERY AND HORTICULTURAL PRACTICE

Gardeners, in common with others at the 'receiving end' of production and distribution, will find the British Standards a reliable guide to normal acceptable quality. In their own words the British Standards Institution's main function is to 'draw up voluntary standards and codes of practice by agreement among all the interests concerned—manufacturing, using, professional and distributive—and to promote their adoption'.

The Institution, which dates from 1901, is financed by subscriptions from firms, trade associations, local authorities, professional institutions and other interested bodies, by a Government grant and by sale of its publications. It produced the first standards for horticulture, including landscape work, in 1965.

Among those standards which may be of direct interest to gardeners with terraces are:

BS 3936, Nursery Stock. Part 1, Trees and Shrubs, which after giving definitions of different types and shapes of trees and shrubs provides a table which includes normal retail sizes at which trees and shrubs are usually obtainable. To take three examples, Magnolia soulangiana 1½–3ft., Lilacs 2–4ft., Viburnum tinus (Laurustinus) 1–1½ft. It is often possible to find larger plants than the sizes given if the purchaser has the time and the knowledge where to look for them, or has a tame consultant whose business it is to know where he can put his hands on above-average specimens, but to an average gardener, advance knowledge that these are the usual sizes may prevent disappointment when the plants arrive.

BS 3936, Nursery Stock. Part 2, Roses, from which a purchaser can learn that good plants should have a minimum of two shoots arising directly from the union or one shoot which branches not more than 2½in. above the union, that there should be a minimum of three major roots, and that root growth shall arise within 2½in. of the base of the union.

BS 3936, Nursery Stock. Part 7, Bedding plants grown in boxes or trays, in which, after stating that the plants should be true to name, have been pricked out, and are growing in a weed-free, disease-free, pest-free compost, reference is made to the maximum desirable number of different plants in each box offered for sale. The most valuable part of this British Standard is the stipulation that plants grown in boxes or trays shall not be offered for sale before certain dates, depending on the region. For instance, Petunias should not be offered for sale before early May in the London area, mid-May in Birmingham, and late May in Aberdeen. Therefore a retailer who displays boxes of Petunias for sale in London in mid-April is not complying with this British Standard, and a purchaser should recognise this and also that by buying them at that time for planting in the open ground he is incurring a risk of losing them all through a late frost.

BS 3936, Nursery Stock. Part 9, Bulbs, Corms, and Tubers, which chiefly gives information on minimum sizes of different bulbs.

BS 3969, Turf, which gives a list of common botanical names of desirable and undesirable grasses, of perennial weeds, soil conditions, dimensions of turves, etc, but no descriptions or drawings to enable the grasses or weeds to be identified.

BS 4156, Peat, giving the desiderata for pH, moisture content, ash, particle size and yield.

BS 3975, Glossary for Landscape Work, Part 4, Plant Description, and BS 3975, Glossary for Landscape Work, Part 5, Horticultural, arboricultural and forestry practice, will give the private gardener a working knowledge of the technical terms of the nurseryman and the jargon of the landscape contractor, and reveal to him the meaning of such words as bulb, calcicole, calcifuge, corm, fasciation, fastigiate, feathered, panning, pleaching, rhizome, stratification, tuber, vernalisation.

There are three other British Standards largely concerned with skilled operations, but a knowledge of the recommendations made in the Standards will assist the owner of a garden to keep a knowledgeable eye on work in progress.

BS 4428, Recommendations for General Landscape Operations

excluding hard surfaces, dealing with the practical operations of, for instance, spreading top soil, drainage, seeding, turfing and planting.

BS 3998, Recommendations for tree work, which gives useful information on pruning and training, and the good cautionary advice 'when it is known that the death of a tree has been caused by the honey fungus, *Armillaria mellea*, it is essential that the stump and roots should be removed and burned'. It also gives precise instructions for feeding trees of mature size. This is most important and too often neglected. Proper fertilising of old trees will preserve their vigour and shape past maturity, and it will also encourage rapid growth of younger trees.

BS 4043, Recommendations for transplanting semi-mature trees. This gives information on the whole process, from the preparation by root pruning, which must be done at a sufficient interval before extraction to allow for development of a new fibrous root system, methods of extraction, loading and transporting, to replanting and securing.

A full list of British Standards is available from the BSI Sales Office, 101–113 Pentonville Road, London, N.1.

METRICATION

In 1965 the Government, through the Board of Trade, announced that it was impressed by the case put to it by industry and would encourage a change to the metric system of weights and measures. It expressed the hope that within ten years (i.e. by 1975) the greater part of the country's industry will have effected the change. This change is already progressively taking place in industry, but as its effects are unlikely to have made a significant impact on general horticultural practice sufficiently early to warrant the use of metric units throughout the text of this book, I have for the convenience of readers set out below precise metric conversions for most of the dimensions, weights, volumes and power referred to. In practice manufacturers will seldom apply precise metric conversions but will adopt rounded-off metric sizes. For instance, a paving slab 3ft × 2ft will no longer be made at that size and offered as 914·4mm × 609·6mm, but instead manufactured at the new rounded-off size of 900mm × 600mm.

In order to harmonise measuring practices, the Système International d'Unités (SI) is coming into international use. Under this system there are six base units, of which in this book we are concerned with four, metre (m), kilogramme (kg), second (s), kelvin (K). (The others are ampère (a) and candela (cd).)

The general recommendation for the use of International System (SI) units is that prefixes representing 10 raised to a power which is a multiple of 3 are particularly preferred. This is to avoid the danger of confusion that might arise where two different multiples closely related in value are used in the same context. This means that for most technological purposes the use of the millimetre is preferred to the use of the centimetre.

The base unit for length is the metre (m). The recommended multiple is the kilometre (km) or 10^3m, and a recommended sub-multiple the millimetre or 10^{-3}m.

For area the base unit is the square metre (m^2), the multiple the square kilometre (km^2) and a recommended sub-multiple the square millimetre (mm^2).

For volume the base unit is the cubic metre. A sub-multiple is the cubic millimetre but the litre may also be used.

For mass the base unit is the kilogramme; a preferred sub-multiple is the gramme.

The unit of power derived from base units is the watt (W).

METRIC CONVERSION TABLES

In all the tables below metric equivalents are stated to four significant figures.

LENGTH
CONVERSION FACTORS

Metric	Inches	Feet	Yard
1mm	0·039	0·003	—
1cm	0·393	0·032	0·011
1m	39·37	3·280	1·093

Inches	mm	cm	m	Feet	mm	cm	m
1/8	3·175	0·317		1	304·8	30·48	0·305
1/4	6·350	0·635		2	609·6	60·96	0·610
3/8	9·525	0·952		3	914·4	91·44	0·914
1/2	12·70	1·270		4	1219	121·9	1·219
5/8	15·87	1·587		5			1·524
3/4	19·05	1·905		6			1·829
7/8	22·22	2·222		7			2·134
1	25·40	2·540		8			2·438
2	50·80	5·080		9			2·743
3	76·20	7·620		10			3·048
4	101·6	10·16		11			3·353
5	127·0	12·70		12			3·658
6	152·4	15·24		13			3·962
7	177·8	17·78		14			4·267
8	203·2	20·32		15			4·572
9	228·6	22·86		16			4·877
10	254·0	25·40	0·254	17			5·182
11	279·4	27·94	0·279	18			5·486
12	304·8	30·48	0·305	19			5·791
18	457·2	45·72	0·457	20			6·096
				30			9·144
				40			12·19
				50			15·24

AREA
CONVERSION FACTORS

Metric	Sq inches	Sq feet	Sq yards
1mm²	—	—	—
1cm²	0·155	0·001	—
1m²	1550	10·76	1·196

Sq inches	mm²	cm²	m²
1	645·2	6·452	
2	1290	12·90	
3	1936	19·36	
4	2581	25·81	
5	3226	32·26	
6	3871	38·71	
7	4516	45·16	
8	5161	51·61	
9	5806	58·06	
10	6452	64·52	
11	7097	70·97	
12	7742	77·42	0·007
18	—	116·1	0·012
144	—	929·0	0·093

(1 sq foot)

1 sq yard (1296 sq ins)	0·836 square metres or m²

1 acre (4840 sq yds)	4046·86 square metres or m²
	0·4047 hectares
	0·0040 square kilometres or km²

VOLUME
CONVERSION FACTORS

Metric	Pints	Galls
1 millilitre	0·0017	0·0002
1 litre	1·7598	0·220
1 cubic metre	1759·8	219·9

Imperial	Millilitres	Litres	cm³	m³
½ pint	284·0	0·284	284·1	
1 pint	568·0	0·568	568·3	
1 quart	1136	1·136	1136	
½ gallon	2273	2·273	2273	
1 gallon	4546	4·546	4546	
1 bushel		36·37		0·036
1 cubic foot		28·32		0·283
1 cubic yard		764·5		0·764

Mass
Conversion Factors

Metric	Oz	Lbs
1 Gramme	0·035	0·0022
1 Kilogramme	35·26	2·205

Imperial	g	kg
1 ounce	28·34	0·028
1 lb	453·6	0·454
7 lbs	3175	3·175
14 lbs	—	6·350
28 lbs	—	12·70
56 lbs	—	25·40
1 cwt	—	50·80
1 ton	—	1016

VOLUME—RATE OF FLOW

Gallons per minute	Litres per second	Litres per minute	Litres per hour	m^3 per hour	Gallons per hour
1	0·075	4·55	272·7	0·273	60
2	0·151	9·09	545·5	0·545	120
3	0·227	13·64	818·3	0·818	180
4	0·303	18·18	1091	1·091	240
5	0·378	22·73	1363	1·363	300
6	0·454	27·27	1636	1·636	360
7	0·530	31·82	1909	1·909	420
8	0·606	36·37	2182	2·182	480
9	0·681	40·91	2454	2·454	540
10	0·759	45·46	2727	2·727	600
11	0·833	50·00	3000	3·000	660
12	0·909	54·55	3273	3·273	720
13	0·985	59·10	3545	3·545	780
14	1·060	63·64	3818	3·818	840
15	1·135	68·10	4091	4·091	900
16	1·212	72·74	4364	4·364	960
17	1·288	77·28	4636	4·636	1020
18	1·363	81·83	4909	4·909	1080
19	1·438	86·38	5182	5·182	1140
20	1·515	90·92	5455	5·455	1200

POWER
CONVERSION FACTOR
(1 watt = 0·00134 horsepower)

Horsepower	Watts
$\frac{1}{32}$	23·30
$\frac{1}{16}$	46·60
$\frac{1}{8}$	93·91
$\frac{1}{4}$	186·4
$\frac{1}{2}$	372·8
$\frac{3}{4}$	559·2
1	745·7
2	1491
3	2237
4	2982
5	3728

TEMPERATURE

°F	°C
0	−17·78
4	−15·56
8	−13·33
12	−11·11
16	− 8·89
20	− 6·67
24	− 4·44
28	− 2·22
32	0·00
36	2·22
40	4·44
44	6·67
48	8·89
52	11·11
56	13·33
60	15·56
64	17·78
68	20·00
72	22·22
76	24·44
80	26·67
84	28·89
88	31·11
92	33·33
100	37·78
212	100·00

The following metric sizes have been agreed to by the industries concerned.

Paving. Pre-cast paving flags will be available in two thicknesses, 50mm and 63mm, in the following sizes:

Type A.   600 × 450mm
Type B.   600 × 600mm
Type C.   600 × 750mm
Type D.   600 × 900mm

At the time of going to press manufacturers have not announced metric dimensions for slabs for terraces and gardens.

Bricks. The Imperial Standard format of 9in × 4½in × 3in for the brick when laid in position with its mortar joint will be expressed as 225mm × 112·5mm × 75mm. The average mortar joint of ⅜in will be expressed as 10mm and the brick itself, previously described as 8⅝in × 4½in × 2⅝in, will have the metric dimensions of 215mm × 102·5mm × 65mm.

Horticulture. At the time of writing no firm decision has been reached on metric approximations, but it is probable that heights of plants may be expressed in 'rounded-off' centimetres. Thus 6ft (15·24cm) may become 15·0cm. Rates of sowing grass seed may be:

$$1\text{oz per square yard} = 35\text{g per metre}^2$$
$$1\tfrac{1}{2}\text{oz per square yard} = 50\text{g per metre}^2$$
$$2\text{oz per square yard} = 70\text{g per metre}^2$$

BOOKS WHICH MAY BE CONSULTED

Anderson, E. B.—*Camellias*—Blandford

Baker, Kenneth F.—*The U.C. System for Producing Healthy Container-Grown Plants*—University of California, Division of Agricultural Sciences

Balfour, A. P.—*Annual and Biennial Flowers*—Penguin Books and R.H.S.

Bean, W. J.—*Trees and Shrubs Hardy in the British Isles*—John Murray

Beazley, Elisabeth—*Design and Detail of the Space Between Buildings*—Architectural Press

Church, Thomas D.—*Gardens are for People*—Reinhold Publishing Corporation, New York

Clifford, Derek—*Pelargoniums*—Blandford

Crane, H. H.—*Pansies and Violas*—Collingridge

Crowe, Sylvia—*Garden Design*—Country Life

Edland, H.—*The Pocket Encyclopaedia of Roses*—Blandford

Evison, J. R. B.—*Gardening for Display*—Collingridge

Genders, Roy—*Bedding Plants*—John Gifford

Hampton, F. A.—*The Scent of Flowers and Leaves*—Dulau

Harrison, S. G.—*Garden Shrubs and Trees*—Eyre & Spottiswoode

Harvey, N. P.—*The Rose in Britain*—Souvenir Press

Hellyer, A. G. L.—*Flowers in Colour*—Collingridge
Photo Album of Garden Plants (with Christopher Lloyd)—Collingridge
Garden Plants in Colour—Collingridge
The Encyclopaedia of Plant Portraits—Collingridge

Hervey, George F., and Jack Hems—*The Book of the Garden Pond*—Stanley Paul

Hurtwood, Lady Allen of, and Susan Jellicoe—*The New Small Garden*—The Architectural Press

Huxley, A. J.—*Garden Terms Simplified*—Collingridge
Hyams, Edward—*Vineyards in England*—Faber & Faber
Lawrence, W. J. C., and J. Newell—*Seed and Potting Composts*—
George Allen & Unwin
Macself, A. J.—*Ferns for Garden and Greenhouse*—Collingridge
Makins, F. K.—*Herbaceous Garden Flora*—Dent
The Identification of Trees and Shrubs—Dent
Masson, Georgina—*Italian Gardens*—Thames & Hudson
McKay, W. B.—*Building Construction*—Longmans
Meikle, R. D.—*Garden Flowers*—Eyre & Spottiswoode
Nicholson, B. E., M. Wallis, E. B. Anderson, A. P. Balfour,
M. Fish, and V. Finnis—*The Oxford Book of Garden Flowers*—
Oxford University Press
Page, Russell—*The Education of a Gardener*—Collins
Perry, Frances—*Collins Guide to Border Plants*—Collins
Water Gardens—Penguin
Rhode, Eleanor Sinclair—*The Garden Book of Sir Thomas Hanmer,
Bart.*—Gerald Howe (The Bodley Head)
Robinson, W.—*The English Flower Garden*—John Murray
Roper, Lanning—*Successful Town Gardening*—Country Life
Royal Horticultural Society: edited Fred J. Chittenden—*Dictionary
of Gardening*—The Clarendon Press
edited Patrick M. Synge and James W. L. Platt—*Some Good
Garden Plants*—The Royal Horticultural Society
Sitwell, Sir George—*On the Making of Gardens*—Gerald Duck-
worth
Sordo, Enrique, and Wim Swaan—*Moorish Spain*—Elek Books
Stevens, Roger—*The Land of the Great Sophy*—Methuen
Sunset Magazine—*Sunset Garden and Patio Building Book*—Lane
Book Company, Menlo Park, California
Landscaping for Western Living—Lane Book Company, Menlo
Park, California
Gardening in Containers—Lane Book Company, Menlo Park,
California
Synge, Patrick M.—*Collins Guide to Bulbs*—Collins
Teuscher, Henry—*Window Box Gardening*—The Macmillan
Company, New York
Thomas, Graham Stuart—*Shrub Roses of To-day*—Phoenix
House
Old Shrub Roses—Phoenix House

Villiers-Stuart, C. M.—*Gardens of the Great Mughals*—Black
  Spanish Gardens—Batsford
Woodward, Marcus—*Gerard's Herball*—Gerald Howe (The
  Bodley Head)
Yorke, F. R. S., and Penelope Whiting—*Specification*—The
  Architectural Press

Books published since 1965:
Fairbrother, Nan—*Men and Gardens*—The Hogarth Press
Fish, Margery—*Cottage Garden Flowers*—David & Charles
  Gardening on Clay and Lime—David & Charles
  Ground Cover Plants—David & Charles
  We Made a Garden—David & Charles
Hay, Roy, and Synge, Patrick M.—*The Dictionary of Garden
  Plants in Colour*—Michael Joseph
Jellicoe, Susan and Geoffrey—*Modern Private Gardens*—Abelard-
  Schuman

PROFESSIONAL INSTITUTES
AND TRADE ASSOCIATIONS

Assistance and more information on matters discussed in this book can be obtained from the following professional bodies and institutions:

Garden Design
The Secretary,
The Institute of Landscape Architects,
12 Carlton House Terrace,
London, S.W.1.

Italy
The Director,
The Italian Institute of Culture,
39 Belgrave Square,
London, S.W.1.

Spain
The Director,
The Spanish Institute,
102 Eaton Square,
London, S.W.1.

Gardens (General)
The Royal Horticultural Society,
Vincent Square,
Westminster,
London, S.W.1.

British Standards
British Standards Institution,
2 Park Street,
London, W1Y 4AA.

John Innes	John Innes Institute, Colney Lane, Norwich, NOR 7OF.
Trade Associations	The General Secretary, The Horticultural Trades Association, Roman Wall House, 3rd Floor, No. 1 Crutched Friars, London, E.C.3.
	The Secretary-General, The Association of European Landscape and Sports Ground Contractors, Landsforeningen af Danske Anlaegsgartnere, Ndr. Fasanvej 133, 2000 Copenhagen F., Denmark.
	The Secretary, The Joint Council of Landscape Industries, 140 Bensham Lane, Thornton Heath, Surrey. CR4 7YU.
	The Secretary, The Cement and Concrete Association, 52 Grosvenor Gardens, London, S.W.1.
Gravel	The Secretary, The Sand and Gravel Association of Great Britain, 48 Park Street, London, W1Y 4HE.
Precast Concrete	The Secretary, The British Precast Concrete Federation, 9 Catherine Place, London, S.W.1.

Stone	The Secretary, The British Stone Federation, Alderman House, 37 Soho Square, London, W.1.
Slate	The Secretary, English Slate Quarries Association, 11–12 West Smithfield, London, E.C.1.
	The Secretary, The North Wales Slate Quarries Association, 267 High Street, Bangor, North Wales.
Marble	The Secretary, The Marble and Granite Association, Sardinia House, 52 Lincoln's Inn Fields, London, W.C.2.
Bricks	The Secretary, The Brick Development Association Limited, 3–5 Bedford Row, London, W.C.1.
	The Secretary, The National Federation of Clay Industries, Drayton House, 30 Gordon Street, London, W.C.1.
Quarry Tiles	The Secretary, The Floor Quarry Association, Federation House, Stoke-on-Trent, ST4 2RU.

INDEX

Abbreviations: d = line-drawing, p = photograph facing page given

Abutilon megapotamicum, 121, 170
Acanthus mollis, 87, 170
Achillea clypeolata, 80, 83, 87, 170
  planting, 166
Adgate, Dave, 107
African marigold, *see Tagetes erecta*
Agapanthus, 95, 108p
  africanus (*A. umbellatus*), 100, 170
Agave americana (American Aloe), 100, 103, 170
Ageratum houstonianum, 170
Ailanthus altissima (*A. glandulosa*), 86, 170
Ajuga reptans, 36p, 171
Alchemilla major (*A. mollis*), 89, 171
algae, 52
Allen, W. Godfrey, M.A., F.S.A., F.R.I.B.A.,:
  design, 108p
Almond, *see Prunus communis*
Aloysia, *see Lippia*
Alyssum maritimum (*Lobularia maritima*), 73, 188
Amaryllis belladonna, 67, 171
American aloe, *see Agave americana*
Anaphalis triplinervis, 83, 171
Anchusa officinalis angustifolia, 82–83, 171
Anemone japonica, 90
  alba, 80, 171
Antirrhinum nanum grandiflorum Majestic Avalanche, 171
aquatic plants, 51–53
Arbutus, 88
  menziesii, 92, 171
  unedo, 92, 52p, 172
Artemisia lanata (*A. pedemontana*), 78, 172
  ludoviciana, 172

Asparagus fern, 121
Asparagus sprengeri, 172
atrium, 19
Aubrieta, 119
  deltoidea, 172
Aucuba, 119
  japonica, 172
awning, 35
Azolla caroliniana, 172

baffle screen, 34
balcony, 18
balustrade, 29
Banksian Rose, *see Rosa banksiae*
barbecue, 29
barrier between terrace and garden, 29
Bay, *see Laurus nobilis*
Bean, W. J.: *Trees & Shrubs Hardy in the British Isles*, 64, 99
Beech, *see Fagus*
beer cask: as plant container, 112-13
Begonia rex, 121, 172
  tuberous-rooted, 122
Belladonna lily, *see Amaryllis belladonna*
bench, 29p
  space required, 26
Bergenia cordifolia, 88, 173
bird bath, 29
Blechnum spicant, 90, 173
books containing illustrations, 167–8
Box, *see Buxus*
brick: for paving, 45–46, 29p
  laying, 133
  types, 45–46
British Standards, 206

Brookes, John
  design, 35
Brown, Capability, 25
Brugmansia, *see Datura*
Bugle, *see Ajuga*
butterflies, 36–37
Buxus (Box), 88
  sempervirens, 173
  in window box, 119

Caerhays Castle, 93
calcium carbonate, 126
California, University of: soil mixes, 157,
  158
Callitriche autumnalis, 52, 173
Camellia, 87, 88
  classification, 97
  compost, 126, 156–7
  japonica: in tubs, 96–97, 173
    Althaeaflora, 97, 173
    Elegans, 97, 173
    Mathotiana, 97, 173
    alba, 97, 173
    Nobilissima, 97, 173
  protecting, 97
  watering, 96
  x *williamsii*, 173
    Donation, 173
    Francis Hanger, 173
    J. C. Williams, 173
Campanula isophylla, 121, 173
  lactiflora Loddon Anna, 76, 173–4
cask: as plant container, 112–13
Catalpa bignonioides, 86–87, 174
Catmint, *see Nepeta*
Ceanothus dentatus russellianus, 75, 174
Cedar, *see Cedrus*
Cedrus, 29p
ceramic pots, 112
Ceratostigma plumbaginoides, 88, 174
  willmottianum, 174
Cercis siliquastrum, 92, 174
Chaenomeles, 87
  speciosa, 174
    Hollandia, 78, 174
    Knaphill Scarlet, 80
    Minerva, 78, 174
  x *superba* Simonii, 82, 174
chair, 29–30, 36p
  space required, 26
chalet fence, 33–34
Chamaecyparis lawsoniana (Lawson's
  Cypress), 32, 119, 174

Cheiranthus × *allionii*, 68, 175
  cheiri, 175
    Blood Red, 67, 175
    Cloth of Gold, 68. 175
    Cranford Beauty, 68, 175
    Ellen Willmott, 67–68, 175
    Fire King, 68, 175
    Giant Brown, 68, 175
    Harbinger, 68, 175
    Orange Bedder, 68, 175
    Persian Carpet, 68
    Phoenix, 68, 175
    Primrose Monarch, 68, 175
    Scarlet Emperor, 68, 175
    Vulcan, 68, 175
    Yellow Phoenix, 68, 175
Cherry laurel, *see Prunus laurocerasus*
Cherry Pie, *see Heliotropium*
Chimonanthus praecox, 65, 176
'Choisya ternata*, 65, 176
Christmas Rose, *see Helleborus niger*
Chrysanthemum frutescens, 68, 176
  Jante Wells, 118–19
  morifolium, 176
Church, Thomas D.: designs, 53p, 77p,
  77p
Cineraria, 118
Cinquefoil, *see Potentilla*
Cistus × *corbariensis*, 66, 176
  crispus, 75, 176
  × *cyprius*, 66, 176
  ladaniferus, 66, 176
  laurifolius, 66, 176–7
  × *lusitanicus*, 75, 177
  × *purpureus*, 177
Citrus aurantium, 101, 177
  bergamia, 101, 177
  in France, 125–6
  nobilis, 101, 177
    deliciosa, 101, 177
  sinensis, 101, 102, 177
  in tubs, 101–2
Clary, *see Salvia sclarea*
clay pots, 111, 116p
Clematis armandii, 63, 177
    Apple Blossom, 63–64, 177
  × *jackmanii* Comtesse de Bouchard,
    177
  × *lanuginosa* Henryi, 64, 177–8
    Mrs Cholmondeley, 178
  montana rubens, 63, 178
  × *patens* Lasurstern, 64, 178
    Nellie Moser, 178

in tubs, 110
× *viticella* Ernest Markham, 178
Ville de Lyon, 64, 178
climbers: on east-facing wall, 79
on house, 61–64
in tubs, 110
on west-facing wall, 75
Cobaea scandens, 36p, 178
in tubs, 110
cobbles, 45, 52p
laying, 133
Coleus, 121
blumei, 178
colour schemes, 57–58, 70–71, 103–4, 105
compost: for tubs, 123–6, 156–8
quantities, 158
composted loam, 158
concrete, 39, 52p
laying, 130
for pool, 152, 153
precast, 39–40
types and sizes, 131
reinforcing, 153, 154d
concrete paving, 29p, 52p, 76p, 108p
laying, 130–1
types and sizes made, 131
concrete tubs, 112
Convallaria, 90
majalis, 178
coping for pool, 51
Corbin, Robert J.: design, 109p
Corylus (Hazel), 93
avellana, 178
Cotinus coggygria, 92, 179
Cotoneaster conspicuus decorus, 88, 179
dammeri (*C. humifusus*), 88, 179
frigidus, 88, 179
salicifolius, 88, 179
courtyard, 20
Cranesbill, *see Geranium*
Crataegus monogyna, 179
prunifolia, 179
crazy paving, 42
Creeping Jenny, *see Lysimachia nummularia*
Crowe, Sylvia, P.P.I.L.A.: designs, 29p, 37p, 76p
Crown Imperial, *see Fritillaria imperialis*
Cupressocyparis × leylandii, 33
curves in design, 76p
Cydonia, flowering, *see Chaënomeles*

Daphne mezereum, 88, 179
Datura cornigera (*D. knightii*), 100, 102–3, 179
Day-lily, *see Hemerocallis*
Deutzia × elegantissima, 88, 180
gracilis, 88, 180
Dianthus plumarius, 180
Earl of Essex, 83, 180
Inchmery, 83, 180
Mrs Sinkins, 83, 180
Paddington, 83, 180
White Ladies, 83, 180
Ditchley Park Orangery, 52p
Dolomite lime, 126
Dreissena polymorpha, 53

East-facing bed, 79–80
Elymus glaucus, 180
Epimedium grandiflorum, 89, 180
Rose Queen, 89
violaceum, 89, 180
Euonymus radicans, 87, 180
Euphorbia wulfenii, 80, 180
evergreens: planting, 166

Fagus (Beech), as hedge, 32
sylvatica, 180
Fairfield loamless compost, 124–5, 157, 158
False Acacia, *see Robinia*
Fatsia, 87, 88
japonica, 80, 180–1
fence: as wind filter, 33–34
ferns, 90
fertiliser, 157
Festuca ovina glauca, 181
Ficus carica, 75, 181
Brunswick, 75, 181
Fig, *see Ficus*
Figleaf Palm, *see Fatsia japonica*
Firethorn, *see Pyracantha*
fish, 51, 53
breeding, 52
number for pool, 53
flint paving, 108p
foliage, 57
colour schemes, 57
contrasts, 29p
in window box, 121
Fontinalis antipyretica, 53, 181
Forget-me-not, *see Myosotis*

Forsythia, 89
  × *intermedia* Lynwood, 87, 181
  suspensa atrocaulis, 181
fountain, 29, 50–51, 93p
  jet, 54
  pumps for, 137–42
  in Spain, 54, 93p
  in stocked pool, 54
fountain basin, 54–55, 93p
French marigold, *see Tagetes patula*
Fritillaria imperialis, 90, 181
Fuchisa Keystone, 122, 181
  La Bianca, 122, 181
  magellanica riccartonii, 88–89, 181
  Marin Glow, 122, 181
  Marinka, 181
  in window box, 122
furniture, garden, 29–30
  space required, 26

Garrya elliptica, 181–2
Geranium cinereum, 83, 182
  endressii A. T. Johnson, 82, 182
    Wargrave, 82, 182
  grandiflorum, 182
    alpinum, 83
  pratense, 80, 183
Geraniums, *see Pelargonium*
Gerard, John: quotation, 90
Germander, *see Teucrium*
Gleditschia triacanthos, 86, 182
Granada: fountains of Generalife, 54, 93p
granite setts, 44–45
  laying, 132–3
grape, *see Vitis*
grass seed, 134
gravel, 38–39
  laying, 129–30
Gruffydd, J. St Bodfan, F.I.L.A.: design, 76p

hanging basket, 114–15
Hard fern, *see Blechnum spicant*
Hart's-tongue fern, *see Phyllitis scolopendrium*
Hawthorn, *see Crataegus*
Hazel, *see Corylus*
Hebe hulkeana, 77, 182
hedge: types, 32–33
  as wind filter, 31

Helianthemum, 83
  nummularium Wisley Primrose, 82, 182
  rhodanthe carneum, 82, 182
  Supreme, 82, 183
Helichrysum petiolatum, 108, 120, 183
Heliotropium, 84
  peruvianum, 183
    Marguerite, 71, 183
    Princess Marina, 71–72, 183
    Vilmorin's Variety, 183
Helleborus corsicus, 89, 183
  niger, 89, 183
    altifolius, 89
  orientalis, 89, 183
Hemerocallis, 87
  fulva, 183
  Hesperus, 80, 183
herbaceous plants: in shade, 89–90
  for towns, 87–88
Heucherella Bridget Bloom, 183–4
Hibiscus, 87
  syriacus, 184
    Coeleste, 98, 184
    Hamabo, 98, 184
    Monstrosus, 98, 184
    Woodbridge, 98, 184
  in tubs, 98
hoggin, 38
Holland: gardens, 29p, 37p
Holly, *see Ilex*
Honey Locust, *see Gleditschia*
Honeysuckle, *see Lonicera*
Honolulu: lanai, 18
Hosta,
  fortunei, 89, 184
  sieboldiana, 89, 184
  undulata, 89, 184
Hottonia palustris, 52, 184
house: bed against, 61–74
  bed opposite, 81–83
  unity with outdoors, 28, 28p
Humea elegans, 73–74, 184
Hyacinthus, 84
  orientalis, 184–5
    City of Haarlem, 69, 105, 185
    King of the Blues, 105, 185
    Lady Derby, 69, 105, 185
    L'Innocence, 69, 105, 185
    Ostara, 69, 105, 184
    Queen of the Pinks, 105, 185
  in tubs, 105
Hydrangea Blue Wave, 89
  colour, 89, 185

macrophylla (*H. hortensis*), 89, 185
petiolaris (*H. scandens*), 79, 185

Ilex (Holly), 87, 88
aquifolium, 185
camelliaefolia, 32, 185
hodginsii, 32, 185
as hedge, 32
India: gardens, 28, 35–36
Indian Bean, *see Catalpa bignonioides*
Ipomoea rubro-caerulea, 110, 195
Iris, 87
germanica Aline, 80, 185
Arabi Pasha, 80, 185
Cliffs of Dover, 80, 185
Jane Philipps, 80, 185
Ola Kola, 80, 185
South Pacific, 186
Zantha, 186
pallida dalmatica, 83, 186
unguicularis (*I. stylosa*), 67, 186
island bed, 83–84
Italy: Renaissance gardens, 28

Jacobsen, Arne: design, 108p
Japanese Anemone, *see Anemone hupe-hensis*
Japonica, *see Chaenomeles*
jardinière, 111–12, 117p
Jasmine, *see Jasminum*
Jasminum, in tubs, 110
nudiflorum, 186
officinale, 186
Jellicoe, G. A., C.B.E., F.R.I.B.A., M.T.P.I., P.P.I.L.A.: designs, 26–27, 28p, 52p
Jerusalem sage, *see Phlomis fruticosa*
John Innes Base Fertiliser, 156
John Innes composts, 123–4
potting No. 3, 156, 158
John Innes Liquid Feed, 157
Judas Tree, *see Cercis siliquastrum*

Knightshayes Court, 29p

Laburnum, 88
alpinum, 86, 186
Lady's Mantle, *see Alchemilla*
Lamb's Tongue, *see Stachys lanata*
lanai, 18, 77p
landscape: blending with, 28
'borrowing from', 28
landscape architecture, 28, 28p

Laurus nobilis (Bay), 186
in tubs, 98–100
Laurustinus, *see Viburnum tinus*
Lavandula (Lavender), 65–66, 165
spica (*L. officinalis*), 75, 186
Folgate Blue, 75, 186
nana atropurpurea (Hidcote), 66, 75, 187
Twickel Purple, 75, 187
vera (Dutch), 64p, 66, 187
Lavender, *see Lavandula*
Lavender cotton, *see Santolina*
lawn: drainage, 47, 135–6
edging, 47, 135d, 136
foundations, 135
seeding, 48, 134
for terrace, 47–49
turfing, 47–48, 134–5
weeds in, 48–49
Lawson's Cypress, *see Chamaecyparis lawsoniana*
Lemon Verbena, *see Lippia citriodora*
Le Nôtre, André, 26
Lenten Rose, *see Helleborus orientalis*
Lilac, *see Syringa*
Lilium auratum, 109, 110, 187
candidum, 77, 110, 187
regale, 77, 187
speciosum, 109–10, 187
album-novum, 109, 187
magnificum, 109–10, 187
Melpomene, 188
rubrum, 110, 188
in tubs, 109–10
Lily-of-the-valley, *see Convallaria*
limestone: for paving, 40
Lippia citriodora (Lemon Verbena), 32, 64–65, 188
protecting, 65
in tubs, 100
loam: composted, 158
sterilisation, 124
loamless compost, 124–5, 157, 158
Lobelia erinus, 188
Lobularia maritima, 73, 188
loggia, 18
London Pride, *see Saxifraga umbrosa*
Lonicera japonica halliana, 188
periclymenum serotina, 188
louvred screen, 33
Lovejoy, Derek, M.A. (Harvard), Dip. T.P., A.R.I.B.A., M.T.P.I., F.I.L.A.: designs, 28, 28p

Lysimachia nummularia, 188
   aurea, 88, 188

Madonna lily, *see Lilium candidum*
Madrona, *see Arbutus menziesii*
magnesium limestone, 126
Magnolia, 88
   denudata, 86, 93, 188–9
   grandiflora, 61–62, 189
      Exmouth, 62
      Goliath, 62
   sargentiana robusta, 93, 189
   soulangiana, 86, 93, 189
Mahonia, 88
   aquifolium, 189
   japonica, 189
marble: laying, 132
   for paving, 42–43, 37p
   surfaces, 43–44
   types, 43
Marigold, *see Tagetes*
Matthiola (Stock), 70, 84
   incana, 189
      Beauty in Nice, 189
      Brompton, 71, 189
      East Lothian, 71, 189
      Giant Perfection, 70, 71, 189
May, *see Crataegus*
Megasea, *see Bergenia*
Mereworth Castle, 102
metrication, 209
Mexican Orange Flower, *see Choisya ternata*
Mezereon, *see Daphne mezereum*
Mock Orange, *see Philadelphus*
Moghul gardens, 35
Monarda didyma Cambridge Scarlet, 83, 190
Monterey Cypress, *see Cupressus macrocarpa*
moths, 36–37
mulching, 165–6
mussel, 53
Myosotis alpestris, 190
   Blue Ball, 68, 190
   Royal Blue, 68, 190
   in window box, 122
Myriophyllum spicatum, 53, 190
Myrtle, *see Myrtus*
Myrtus communis, 77, 88, 190

Nepeta faassenii (*N. mussinii*), 83, 190

Nerine bowdenii, 67, 190
Nerium oleander (Oleander), 100, 103, 190
Newman, L. Hugh, 36
New Zealand Flax, *see Phormium tenax*
Nicotiana alata grandiflora, 70, 191
   Lime Green, 70, 191
   Norham Gardens, 76p
Nymphaea: depth for, 51–52
   Froebelii, 52, 191
   Hermine, 51, 191
   James Brydon, 51, 191
   Laydekeri purpurata, 52, 191
   Marliacea albida, 51, 191
      chromatella, 51, 191
   odorata alba, 52, 191
      sulphurea, 52, 191
      turicensis, 52, 191
   Pink Opal, 52, 191
   planting, 52
   pygmaea alba, 52, 191
      helvola, 52, 191
   Somptuosa, 51, 191

Oak, *see Quercus*
Oleander, *see Nerium oleander*
Orange, *see Citrus*
orangery, the, 101, 102
Origanum microphyllum, 73, 191
Osmarea × *burkwoodii*, 88, 191
Osmunda regalis, 90, 191
Oxford: Norham Gardens, 76p
Oxford, University of: University College, 44, 29p, 37p
Oxlip, *see Polyanthus*
oxygenating plants, 52–53

Paeonia lactiflora, 192
      Eva, 77, 192
      Victoria, 77, 192
      Whitleyi major, 77, 192
   lutea ludlowii, 77, 192
   suffruticosa, 192
      Reine Elizabeth, 77, 192
      Yano Okima, 77, 192
Page, Russell, O.B.E., F.I.L.A., designs, 72, 36p
   Education of a Gardener, 26, 27
Pansy, *see Viola* × *wittrockiana*
parapet wall, 29
Parthenocissus henryana, 64, 192
Pasley, A. du Gard, A.I.L.A., 35
   designs, 76p, 93p
Passiflora, 64
   caerulea, 192

Passion Flower, *see Passiflora*
patio, 19–20
paving: laying, 129–33
  types, 38–46
pavior, 46
pebble mosaic, 45
Pelargonium (Geranium) A. M. Mayne,
  106, 120, 194
  Abel Carrière, 193
  Audrey Clifton, 108, 193
  capitatum, 73, 192
  Carisbrooke, 193
  Caroline Schmidt, 120, 194
  Chelsea Gem, 120, 194
  Clorinda, 108, 192
  crispum variegatum, 108, 192
  denticulatum, 73, 193
  Doris Moore, 106, 194
  Double Henry Jacoby, 106, 119, 194
  Duchess of Teck, 193
  Evelyn Cole, 193
  × *fragrans*, 73, 193
  Galilee, 108, 120, 193
  Genie, 107
  Gustav Emich, 106, 119, 194
  Hermine, 106, 194
  Irene, 107, 120, 194
  ivy-leaved, 108, 119, 120
  King of Denmark, 106, 119, 120, 194
  La France, 108, 193
  L'Élégante, 108, 120, 193
  Lord Bute, 193
  Madame Crousse, 120, 193
  Maxim Kovalevski, 106, 194
  Mr Henry Cox, 120, 194
  Mrs Lawrence, 119–20, 194
  Mrs W. A. R. Clifton, 193
  Paul Crampel, 106, 108, 119, 120, 194
  Pink Bouquet, 107, 194
  pots for, 107
  Queen of Whites, 106, 194
  Red Black Vesuvius, 107, 194
  regal, 193
  Rose of Devon, 193
  scented-leaved, 73
  tomentosum, 73, 108, 193
  Toyon, 107, 194
  Trulls Hatch, 107, 194
  in tubs, 95, 106–8
  Verona, 83, 194
  in window box, 117, 119–20, 121
    feeding, 117–18
  zonal, 106–8, 119–20, 193–4

Peony, *see Paeonia*
Periwinkle, *see Vinca*
Persia: gardens, 19
Peskett, Eric: design, 93p
Petunia Alderman, 109
  Candy Apple, 121, 194
  Capri, 109, 121, 194
  Gipsy Ballerina, 109, 194
  Glacier, 121, 194
  Grandiflora hybrids, 109
  Inimitable, 194
  Psyche, 194
  Red Ensign, 109, 195
  Rose of Heaven, 109, 195
  Sutton's Blue Bedder, 195
  in tubs, 95, 108–9
  in window box, 117, 120–1
Pharbitis tricolor, 110, 195
Philadelphus, 89
  × *lemoini* Manteau d'Hermine, 195
  microphyllus, 87, 195
  Sybille, 87, 195
Phillyrea decora, 87, 195
Phlomis fruticosa, 82, 36p, 195
Phormium tenax, 95, 195
*p*H test, 126
Phyllitis scolopendrium, 90, 195
Pink, *see Dianthus*
Plantain Lily, *see Hosta*
plant containers, 111–14, 108p
  116p, 117p, 133p
planting times, 166
plants: choosing, 59–60
  feeding, 165
  list of, 170–205
  mulching, 165–6
Polyanthus (*Primula acaulis* × *P. veris*),
  69, 195
Pomegranate, *see Punica granatum*
Pompeii: gardens, 28
pool: cleaning, 54
  construction, 152–5
  depth, 51
  emptying, 146–8, 147d, 148d, 149d
  fish for, 53
  for fountain, 54–55
  overflow, 146–8, 147d, 148d, 149d
  plants for, 51–53
  reinforcing, 153, 154d
  shape, 50
Portugal laurel, *see Prunus lusitanicus*
Potentilla, 89
  arbuscula, 80, 196

nana argentea (*P. beesii*), 82, 83, 196
pots, *see* tubs and pots
Prunus communis (*P. amygdalus*, Almond), 88, 91, 196
  Pollardii, 86, 196
  laurocerasus, 196
  lusitanica, 196
  in tubs, 95
  subhirtella autumnalis, 91, 196
pump: chamber for, 148–51, 150d
  output, 140–2
  types, 137–42
    comparison, 144–5
pump, submersible, 143–4
  motors for, 143–4
pump, surface: non-self priming, 137–42, 138d, 139d
  motors for, 142
  self priming, 142–3
  motors for, 143–4
Punica granatum: in tubs, 100, 196
Pusey House, 26, 28p, 108p, 91, 121
Pyracantha, 87
  atalantioides (*P. gibbsii*), 79, 196
  rogersiana, 79, 196

quarry tile, 46, 93p
  laying, 133
Quercus (Oak), 91
Quince, *see Chaenomeles*, 174

Ramshorn snail, 53
redwood: as terrace floor, 53p
Regal lily, *see Lilium regale*
Rhododendron, 197
  arboreum, 197
  compost for, 126
  in tubs, 95–96
Rhus, 87
  cotinus (*Cotinus coggygria*), 92, 179
  typhina, 91–92, 197
Robinia (False Acacia), 91
  pseudoacacia, 86, 197
Rome: gardens, 28
Romneya trichocalyx, 78, 197
Rosa × *anemonoides* (*R. sinica* Anemone), 32, 62, 197
  Apricot Silk, 197
  banksiae (Banksian Rose), 32, 62, 197
  × *bracteata* Mermaid, 63, 80, 197
  Emily Gray, 63, 197–8
  Ena Harkness, 63, 198
  Fragrant Cloud, 198

Gloire de Dijon, 63, 198
Gold Gleam, 198
Iceberg, 76, 198
Lady Hillingdon, 63, 198
Madame Alfred Carrière, 62, 80, 198
Madame Pierre Oger, 198
Message, 198
Old Pink Moss, 199
Ophelia, 63, 198
Pernille Poulsen, 199
Pink Parfait, 199
Plentiful, 199
Queen of Denmark, 199
Red Dandy, 76, 198
sinica anemone, 62
Souvenir de la Malmaison, 199
Zéphirine Drouhin, 63, 199
Rose Bay, *see Nerium oleander*
Rosemary, *see Rosmarinus*
Rosmarinus, 65, 165
  lavandulaceus (*R. officinalis prostratus*), 199
  officinalis, 75, 199
    Corsican Blue, 199
Royal Fern, *see Osmunda regalis*
Rue, *see Ruta*
Ruta graveolens Jackman's Blue, 82, 83, 199
Ruys, Mien: design, 29p, 37p, 108p

Sagina procumbens, 199
Salvia ambigens, 77–78, 199
  grahamii, 66, 200
  officinalis hispanica (*S. lavandulifolia*), 66, 83, 200
  o. purpurascens, 82, 200
  patens, 68, 200
  sclarea turkestanica, 76, 200
  × *superba* (*S. virgata nemorosa*), 80, 87, 200
sandstone: for paving, 40–41
Santolina chamaecyparissus (*S. incana*), 200
Saxifraga umbrosa, 87, 200
scale, 25–27
  in plants, 56–57
scent: bed for, near house, 61–74
screen against wind, 31–35
screen wall, 34–35, 76p
sculpture, 29
Senecio cineraria (*S. maritima*), 107–8, 120, 200
  laxifolius, 81–82, 200

Seville: fountain, 54, 93p
shade, 77p
    provision for, 35
shady positions: herbaceous plants for, 89–90
    shrubs for, 88–89
    trees for, 88, 81p
shrubs: compost, 124–5, 156
    against east-facing wall, 79–80
    against house, 64–66
    opposite house, 81–82
    mulching, 166
    for pots, 95–97, 102–3
    in shade, 88–89
    for towns, 87
    against west-facing wall, 75–77, 78
site for terrace, 28–29
Sitwell, Sir George: *On the Making of Gardens*, 28
Skimmia japonica fragrans, 87, 88, 200
slate: laying, 132
    for paving, 44
Smoke Plant, *see Cotinus coggygria*
snail, 53
Snapdragon, *see Antirrhinum*
soil: in town gardens, 85
Sorbus, 88
    aria lutescens, 86, 201
Latin America, 28
Spain: fountains, 54, 93p
    gardens, 19–20, 28
Spurge, *see Euphorbia*
Stachys lanata, 83, 201
staddle stones, 29
Stag's horn Sumach, *see Rhus typhina*
Stocks, *see Matthiola*
Stoke Court, 93
stone: artificial, 112
    for paving, 40–41
        laying, 131–2
        patterns, 41–42
stone containers, 112
Strawberry Tree, *see Arbutus unedo*
Stuart, Mrs C. M. Villiers-: *Gardens of the Great Mughals*, 35–36
    Spanish Gardens, 19
Sumach, *see Rhus*
sun: protection from, 35, 53p, 77p
Sweet Alyssum, *see Lobularia maritima*
Synge, Patrick M.: *Collins Guide to Bulbs*, 67
Syringa, 87
    Charles Joly, 98, 201

Katherine Havemeyer, 98, 201
    Madame Lemoine, 98, 201
    in tubs, 97–98
    vulgaris, 201

table, 29–30, 36p
    space required, 26
Tagetes erecta (African Marigold), 201
    Hawaii, 109, 121, 201
    Spun Gold, 109, 121, 201
        in window box, 118, 121
    feeding, 118, 125
    patula (French Marigold), 201
        Lemon King, 109, 201
        Naughty Marietta, 201
        Orange Glow, 109, 201
        in window box, 117, 118, 121
Taxus baccata (Yew), 201–2
    on edge of terrace, 93, 29p
    as hedge, 32
    in town, 86
terrace: definition, 20–21
    laying, 129–33
terracotta containers, 94–95, 111–12, 116p, 117p
Teucrium fruticans, 77, 202
Teuscher, Henry: *Window Box Gardening*, 104–5, 121, 160–1
Thuja plicata (*T. lobbii*), 32, 202
Thyme, *see Thymus*
Thymus serpyllum, 67, 202
Tillaea recurva, 53, 202
Tobacco plant, *see Nicotiana*
town garden: plants for, 85–88
    preparing soil, 85
    trees in, 85–87
Tree Germander, *see Teucrium fruitcans*
Tree of Heaven, *see Ailanthus altissima*
trees: at edge of terrace, 93
    compost for, 124–5, 156
    mulching, 166
    overhanging garden, 85
    planting, 165
    in shade, 88
    on terrace, 91–92
    for town garden, 86–87
    in tubs, 94, 97–102
        moving, 113
        renewing compost, 113–14, 125–6
    tubs for, 94, 113
trellis: as wind filter, 33
Trengwainton, 93
tubs and pots: climbers for, 110

compost for, 123–6, 156–8
  renewing, 113–14, 125–6
drainage, 123
flowers for, 104–10
moving, 113
ornamented, 94–95
plant qualities required for, 105–6
shrubs for, 95–97, 102–3
trees for, 97–102
types, 111–14
  108p, 116p, 117p
Tulip, see Tulipa
Tulipa, 84
  Bizarre Absalon, 122, 202
    Insulinde, 202
  Bybloem May Blossom, 122, 202
  Darwin hybrid, 84
    Golden Springtime, 84, 202
    Holland's Glory, 84, 202
  Early Double, 104, 119
    Orange Nassau, 104, 105, 202
    Scarlet Cardinal, 104, 202
    Schoonord, 105, 202
    Vuurbaak, 104, 202
  Early Single, 104, 119
    Bellona, 105, 202
    Couleur Cardinal, 104, 202
    Diana, 104, 202
    Prince of Austria, 104, 202
    Van der Neer, 104, 105, 202
  eichleri, 105, 203
  fosteriana Princeps, 104, 203
  greigii, 105, 203
  ingens, 105, 203
  Lily-flowered White Triumphator, 122, 202
  in tubs, 104–5
  in window box, 119

U.C. soil mix, 157, 158
United States of America: gardens, 28, 77p
  shade in, 35, 53p, 77p
unity of design, 25, 26, 28p
University of California soil mixes, 157, 158
urn, 114
  plants for, 108

verandah, 18
Verbascum bombyciferum (V. Broussa), 77, 203

Verbena rigida (V. venosa), 203
Veronica: shrubby species, see Hebe
Versailles caisse, 114
Viburnum × burkwoodii, 80, 87, 203
  davidii, 82, 83, 203
  juddii, 78, 87, 89, 203
  tinus (Laurustinus), 86, 203
  tomentosum, 87
    Lanarth Variety, 78, 89, 203
Victoria Memorial flower beds, 119
Villiers-Stuart, Mrs C. M.: Gardens of the Great Mughals, 35–36
  Spanish Gardens, 19
Vinca minor, 88, 203–4
Vine: climbing on frame, 64, 96p
  see also Parthenocissus and Vitis
Viola × williamsii (Viola), 84
  Chantreyland, 72, 204
  Lady Tennyson, 72, 204
  Maggie Mott, 72, 204
  Pickering Blue, 72, 204
  Sutton's Large Flowered Campanula Blue, 72, 204
× wittrockiana (Pansy), 204
  Celestial Queen, 69, 204
  Clear Crystals, 204
  Coronation Gold, 72
  Felix Strain, 72, 204
  Ice King, 69, 204
  March Beauty, 69, 204
  Orion, 69, 204
  Swiss Giant, 72, 204
  Ullswater, 72, 204
  Winter Sun, 69, 204
Violas, miniature, 72
  winter-flowering, 68–69
Vitis coignetiae, 64, 204
  outdoor: for wine, 64
  vinifera, 204
    Golden Chasselas (Royal Muscadine), 64, 204
    Madeleine Royale, 64, 204
    Pirovano, 14, 64, 204

Wakefield, G. R.: Camellias for Every Garden, 96
wall: as parapet, 29
  plants against:
    facing east, 80
    facing south, 64–66
    facing west, 75–76, 77

plants on, 32
   facing east, 79
   facing south, 61–64
   facing west, 75
   as wind break, 31–32, 34–35
Wallflower, *see Cherianthus*
Water-lily, *see Nymphaea*
Water Violet, *see Hottonia palustris*
west-facing bed, 75–78
   shrubs for, 75–77, 78
Western Red Cedar, *see Thuja plicata*
Wexham Springs, Buckinghamshire, 26–27
Whitebeam, *see Sorbus*
Wig Tree, *see Cotinus coggygria*
Wilder, Thornton, 43
wind, protection from, 31–35
window box, 116
   construction, 159–62
   drainage, 117
   fertiliser for, 117
   fixing, 160d, 161d

flower qualities required for, 118
   painting, 116
   plants for, 117–22
   types, 159, 160d, 161d
Winter Cherry, *see Prunus subhirtella autumnalis*
Winter Jasmine, *see Jasminum*
Winter Sweet, *see Chimonanthus*
Wisteria 'Macrobatrys' (*multijuga*), 62, 205
   sinensis, 62, 205
Worldwide Butterflies, 36

Yew, *see Taxus*
York stone, 32, 40–41, 44
   jointing, 41
   patterns, 41–42
   from pavements, 41
Yucca, 87
   gloriosa, 78, 96
   in tubs, 95
Yulan, *see Magnolia denudata*